European Workshop

THE IMPROVEMENT OF THE BUILT ENVIRONMENT AND SOCIAL INTEGRATION IN CITIES

Selected Papers and Conclusions

Berlin 9-11 October 1991

EF/92/04/EN

European Workshop

THE IMPROVEMENT OF THE BUILT ENVIRONMENT AND SOCIAL INTEGRATION IN CITIES

Selected Papers and Conclusions

Berlin 9-11 October 1991

European Foundation
for the Improvement of Living and Working Conditions

Cataloguing data can be found at the end of this publication.

Luxembourg: Office for Official Publications of the
European Communities, 1992

ISBN 92-826-3944-4

© Copyright: The European Foundation for the
Improvement of Living and Working Conditions,
1992. For rights of translation or reproduction,
application should be made to the Director,
European Foundation for the Improvement of
Living and Working Conditions, Loughlinstown
House, Shankill, Co. Dublin, Ireland.

Printed in Ireland

EUROPEAN WORKSHOP ON THE IMPROVEMENT OF THE BUILT ENVIRONMENT AND SOCIAL INTEGRATION IN CITIES

organised by

THE EUROPEAN FOUNDATION FOR THE IMPROVEMENT OF LIVING AND WORKING CONDITIONS

in collaboration with

THE SENATE OF BERLIN

SELECTED PAPERS AND CONCLUSIONS

EDITED
by
JACQUELINE MILLER
and
VOULA MEGA

1992

CONTENTS

INTRODUCTION
by
Jacqueline Miller, Free University of Brussels
and
Voula Mega, European Foundation for the Improvement of Living and Working Conditions

1

PROGRAMME OF THE WORKSHOP

7

Opening Address
by
Sandro Giulianelli, Cabinet of Mr Carlo Ripa di Meana, Commission of the European Communities

13

Welcoming Address
by
Clive Purkiss, Director, European Foundation for the Improvement of Living and Working Conditions

17

PAPER INTRODUCING THE WORKSHOP
Social Justice, Postmodernism and the City
by
David Harvey, School of Geography, University of Oxford

21

PAPER BY THE SENATE OF BERLIN
Berlin: Social and Environmental Reconstruction in a Unifying Region
by
Edith Brickwell

41

SELECTED PAPERS AND CONCLUSIONS OF THE WORKING GROUP ON TRANSPORTATION, ENVIRONMENT AND SOCIAL INTEGRATION IN CITIES ... 47

COMPOSITION OF THE WORKING GROUP ... 49

PAPERS

Transport, Environment and Social Integration in Cities
by
Laurie Pickup, Transport and Travel Research, Oxford ... 51

Transport Policy and Social Integration in Cities
by
Chris Jensen-Butler, University of Aarhus ... 73

Commuting in the Metropolitan Area of Lisbon: Effects on the Quality of Life and on the Environment
by
Lia Vasconcelos and **J.D. Geirinhas**, New University of Lisbon ... 91

ABSTRACTS OF THE PAPERS ... 110
by
Antje Flade[*], Institut Wohnen und Umwelt, Darmstadt
Klaus Schlabbach[*], Town Planning Authority, Darmstadt

CONCLUSIONS, RECOMMENDATIONS ... 113
by
Margaret Grieco, University of Oxford

VIII

SELECTED PAPERS AND CONCLUSIONS OF
THE WORKING GROUP
ON
PREVENTING AND FIGHTING CRIME/DELINQUENCY AND THE URBAN ENVIRONMENT   117

COMPOSITION OF THE WORKING GROUP   119

PAPERS

Crime Prevention Facing the 1990's: Another View   121
by
Sandra Walklate, University of Salford

Preventing and Fighting Crime/Delinquency and the   137
Urban Environment
by
Peter Lumsden, Committee on Crime, Irish Parliament

ABSTRACTS OF THE PAPERS   145
by
Clelia Boesi*, Region of Lombardy, Milan
Vincent-Pierre Comiti, Ministry of Social Affairs, Paris
Lindsay MacFarlane*, OECD, Paris
Lina Marsoni*, Municipality of Milan
Chara Paraskevopoulou*, Hellenic Agency for Local
Development and Local Government, Athens

CONCLUSIONS, RECOMMENDATIONS   151
by
Sandra Walklate, University of Salford

SELECTED PAPERS AND CONCLUSIONS OF THE WORKING GROUP ON SOCIAL HOUSING AND QUALITY OF THE URBAN ENVIRONMENT — 153

COMPOSITION OF THE WORKING GROUP — 155

PAPERS

Social Housing and the Quality of the Urban Environment
by
Uwe Wullkopf, Institut Wohnen und Umwelt, Darmstadt — 157

Reconceptualising Housing Quality
by
Philip Potter, Klaus Novy Institut e.V., Cologne — 165

Housing Solutions/Environmental Problems
by
Thomas Maloutas, National Centre of Social Research, Athens — 177

ABSTRACTS OF THE PAPERS — 188
by
John Bell[*], Community Development Foundation, London
Francine Boudru[*], FEANTSA, Brussels
Paul Burton[*], School for Advanced Urban Studies, University of Bristol
Claude Leroy[*], A.I.Q.V., Paris
John Lomax[*], Bank of England, London
Voula Mega[*], European Foundation, Dublin
John O'Connell[*], Dublin Travellers Education and Development Group

CONCLUSIONS, RECOMMENDATIONS — 196
by
Marie Ganier-Raymond, IFS, Berlin

SELECTED PAPERS AND CONCLUSIONS OF THE WORKING GROUP ON SOCIAL INTEGRATION AND CREATION OF NEW URBAN ACTIVITIES   201

COMPOSITION OF THE WORKING GROUP   203

PAPERS

Social Integration and New Urban Activities   205
by
Paul Lawless, School of Urban and Regional Studies, Sheffield City Polytechnic

Social Integration and Creation of New Urban Activities   221
by
Alan Sinclair, The Wise Group, Glasgow

Urban Forestry   229
by
Margaret Sweeney, SICA Innovation Consultants, Dublin

ABSTRACTS OF THE PAPERS   240
by
Bob Catterall, London 2000, UK
Brigitte Gaiffe, ELISE/AEIDL, Brussels
Tony Gibson, Neighbourhood Initiatives Foundation, UK
Geneviève Lecamp, OECD, Paris
Pierre-Yves Maugen[*], Ministry of Research and Technology, Paris
Pascale Mistiaen[*], DEFIS - ASBL, Brussels
William Roe, CEI Consultants, Edinburgh
Yelena Shomina, USSR Academy of Sciences
Richard Welsh[*], National Association for Urban Studies, UK

CONCLUSIONS, RECOMMENDATIONS   254
by
Philippe Morin, RACINE, Paris

SELECTED PAPERS AND CONCLUSIONS OF
THE WORKING GROUP
ON
THE CO-EXISTENCE OF URBAN FUNCTIONS AS A MEANS TO ENSURING
ENVIRONMENTAL PROTECTION AND SOCIAL INTEGRATION   259

COMPOSITION OF THE WORKING GROUP   261

PAPERS

Living Spaces in the Europe of Twelve Urban Cultures   263
in Mutation
by
Yannis Tsiomis, School of Architecture, Paris - La Villette

Integration and Partnership in the Revitalisation of   269
Urban Areas
by
Nuno Portas, University of Oporto

From De-urbanisation to Re-urbanisation? Spatial   277
Challenges for a Contemporary Urban Culture
by
André Loeckx, Catholic University of Leuven

ABSTRACTS OF THE PAPERS   291
by
Tjeerd Deelstra*, International Institute for the
Urban Environment, Delft
Panayiotis Getimis*, Pantion University of Social
and Political Science, Athens
Ekhart Hahn, Wissenschaftszentrum Berlin
Richard V. Knight*, Urbinno Network, London
Alexander S. Matrosov*, Moscow City Government

CONCLUSIONS, RECOMMENDATIONS   298
by
Sten Engelstoft, University of Copenhagen

ANNEX   303

List of Participants

INTRODUCTION

by

Jacqueline Miller, Free University of Brussels
and
Voula Mega, Research Manager, European Foundation
for the Improvement of Living and Working Conditions

This workshop is the second in a series of three workshops included in the Foundations's work programme on protection and improvement of the urban environment 1990-1992. The key issues on which these workshops focus are the result of discussions, in a working group in 1989, composed of representatives of the various directorates of the Commission, the governments, international organisations, trade unions, employers' associations as well as independent experts.

This working group took account, in particular, of the discussions at the Foundation's Round Table on the Role of the Social Partners in improving the environment and of research work already undertaken by the Foundation, by the European Commission, by certain international organisations and by universities and research centres.

The work already completed by the Foundation had provided a sound basis for debates on urban social environmental policies. Five years before the workshop, the Foundation had already produced a report on 'Living Conditions in Urban Europe', summarising the impact of social and economic changes on the structure of cities and the quality of life, examining trends in demography, labour markets, housing provision and drawing particular attention to the process of marginalisation which are creating and reinforcing social inequalities within cities.

Social integration in relation to the improvement of the urban environment was in fact one of the three key issues suggested for one of the workshops, to be hosted by European Cities. The Senate of Berlin was a dynamic collaborator and host. Dr Edith Brickwell from the Senate, together with Mr Jørn Pedersen and Mrs Wendy O'Conghaile from the Foundation and the editors, worked closely in order to prepare the workshop. We established first the priority themes and sub-themes and then we looked for the participants to make a special contribution. In fact, almost all participants were key persons: they delivered papers, they acted as chairmen and rapporteurs and participated fruitfully in the discussions. The quantity and quality of papers presented being high, it was very difficult for us to choose the limited number of papers we could include in this publication. In fact, it would be impossible to include more than three papers per working group and our task was limited in choosing the most representative papers, the ones which covered most of the suggested themes and provoked much of the, sometimes controversial, discussion. We are aware that papers of very high quality are not included. However, all abstracts and the papers corresponding to abstracts followed by an asterisk may be obtained in full upon request.

As the themes initially suggested are concerned, we had to look into five major units (as many as the working groups) covering the most important issues of the workshop's subject. The units are totally interpenetrable, and the themes of each one have a specific common denominator, related to the improvement of the urban environment. The first common denominator is the creation of an adequate transportation environment to achieve social integration, the second the creation of an environment promoting prevention and fighting crime and delinquency, the third one the creation of a social housing environment, and the fourth the creation of a new economic environment. Last but not least, the fifth unit was brought about by the Commission's concerns on urban environment. The mix of land uses and functions, after decades of rigid zoning, is a concept to be highlighted.

Major themes and issues go transversally into all thematic units, on which each working group based its work. Considerations integrated design comprehensive policies for vulnerable groups of the urban society, environmental awareness, synergy of the bodies involved, solidarity and partnership.

All themes and sub-themes suggested by the Foundation are following. They provided just a framework for discussions, a framework which was highly enlarged and deepened by all participants.

THEMES BY WORKING GROUP

I. TRANSPORTATION, ENVIRONMENT AND SOCIAL INTEGRATION IN CITIES

I.A   Access to public/private transport and mobility for 'vulnerable' social groups (old, handicapped, young, poor, marginal, ethnic minorities, groups in transition). Deprivation of transport and social exclusion.
Cost, time, frequency, comfort and general effectiveness of public urban transport for each fragile population.

I.B   Commuting for the disadvantaged and the urban environment.
The social landscape of 'home-workplace' travel and the surrounding built environment.

I.C   'Home-shopping' travel and 'home-services, facilities' for different social groups. The environmental components.

I.D   Special transport infrastructure (e.g. access to the underground) and special transport services (e.g. minibus) by private-public companies: Partnerships, innovative action. Forms of social integration achieved.

I.E   Specific social demand for transport services and planning leading to social integration. The user's point of view.

I.F   Industrial transport design for less-polluted urban environment and greater social benefit. The resulting social cost. The local authorities' point of view.

I.G   Industrial transport design for healthier environment and management schemes for social effectiveness. The employers' (car industry and transport companies) point of view.

I.H   Planning the transport environment (mass transit media, footpaths, cycle paths) for social cohesion. Estimates for the cost to improve the urban environment through transport and the effectiveness of the social integration achieved.

II.   PREVENTING AND FIGHTING CRIME/DELINQUENCY AND THE URBAN ENVIRONMENT

II.A   Crime as the result of lack of social integration in cities. The spatial distribution of crime. Crime types in inner-, outer-cities, special areas. Socio-economic and environmental characteristics of these areas.

II.B   Interrelationships between disqualification, exclusion, crime and environmental degradation. Quality of the built and physical environment and safety in cities.

II.C   Urban crime typology (from deviant behaviour and delinquency to racism) and social groups involved in crime (unemployed, poor, young, migrants, ...) and groups affected by crime (elderly, ...). Environmental quality distribution.

II.D   Innovative action to combat, limit and prevent crime, reported at international level (Council of Europe). Environmental components of this action.

II.E   Innovative action by bodies in charge of crime prevention (police, youth centres, ...), improving the urban environment to prevent crime.

II.F   Local innovative action and environmental solutions. Grass-roots and neighbourhood schemes improving the local environment to prevent crime. The dynamics of local mobilisation.

II.G   Positive discrimination and emancipation of vulnerable groups. Social urban development and delinquency prevention.

II.H   Education and training for environmental awareness and crime prevention. Public participation to reverse the downward spiral of decline.

III.   SOCIAL HOUSING AND QUALITY OF THE URBAN ENVIRONMENT

III.A   Mass housing and pressures on the environment in urban fringes, run-down city centres and fragile urban zones. The development of the need for social housing and the need for a better environment.

III.B Location, design and comfort. Private and public health. Quality of the air, water and land. Noise levels. Energy and waste management. Green spaces. Quality of the surrounding environment.

III.C Aesthetics and functionality. Special facilities for elderly, handicapped, children. Amenities and social services. Access to transport and activities.

III.D The multisectoral partnership approach in urban regeneration through housing. Synergies between the central government, the local community, the public, private and non-profit sectors.

III.E Internationally innovative action to improve social housing environment (OECD reports).

III.F State and local authority initiatives to improve social housing environment and facilitate social integration. Special action for migrants and highly mobile groups. Ethnic integration.

III.G Real estate market, land prices and housing development. Financing owner-occupied and rental housing.

III.H Local movements involved in environmental action for the social integration of the population living in social houses (including association of the users).

IV. SOCIAL INTEGRATION AND CREATION OF NEW URBAN ACTIVITIES

IV.A The involvement of the disadvantaged in creative urban activities and the concern for the quality of the urban environment. New skills and access to new jobs.

IV.B Involving the local population in environmental protection and urban renewal. The environmental market of neighbourhoods in crisis. Employment opportunities (in control of pollution and noise, cleanliness of the town) and voluntary schemes (energy saving, collection and recycling of waste, building rehabilitation and the greening of vacant land).

IV.C Revitalisation through integrated socio-economic approaches. The international experience. Local partnerships and transnational networks.

IV.D Joint private-public initiatives for economic regeneration and social integration in environmentally sensitive urban zones.

IV.E The social economy sector in its relationship to the environment and training schemes for the integration of the deprived.

IV.F New models of training and new financial instruments for social integration. Creation of educational, social and cultural services improving the environment and facilitating social integration in cities.

IV.G Social mastering of new information technologies and creation of urban environmental activities for the disadvantaged.

IV.H The urban environment as a common denominator of the co-ordination and synergy between business, training and research opportunities, local action for adjusting sectoral interventions for the most destitute groups.

V. THE CO-EXISTENCE OF URBAN FUNCTIONS AS A MEANS TO ENSURING ENVIRONMENTAL PROTECTION AND SOCIAL INTEGRATION

V.A The separation of urban functions - by modern city planning - as generator of social segregation and duality (city of two speeds).

V.B The appropriate mix of urban functions. The scale of the co-existence (building, complex, street, neighbourhood, area, ...) and environmental and social advantages and problems.

V.C Relationships between co-existence of functions and co-existence of social groups. Scale of co-existence and degree of integration. The environmental factor.

V.D Innovative action and good practice in integrating functions and people in urban zones in difficulty. Projects and partnerships.

V.E Co-existence of urban uses as a means to promote cross-sectoral approach, revitalisation and environmental and social improvement.

V.F The environmental design for the integration of functions and social groups in cities. The new emerging urban identity and ideology.

V.G Reinforcing the social fabric by mixing the urban functions and improving the overall environment. The processes of renewal and conservation, choice, diversity and potential for improvement.

V.H Creating a new urban culture based on the cultural dialectics between social groups and respecting the environment as the basic resource for every activity (the environmental culture?).

V.I Managing urban change and social equity for a sustainable urban environment.

V.J The gender approach for environmental protection and social integration in cities.

The co-editors would like to thank Philip Potter, Klaus Novy Institut for revising the papers presented by non-English native speakers and Sally Pilkington for proof-reading and copy-editing the document.

EUROPEAN WORKSHOP

ON

THE IMPROVEMENT OF THE BUILT ENVIRONMENT AND SOCIAL INTEGRATION IN CITIES

Berlin, 9-11 October 1991

PROGRAMME

WEDNESDAY 9 October

08.30-09.45   Registration of participants

10.00-11.15   **OPENING PLENARY SESSION**

   Chairperson: Jørn PEDERSEN, European Foundation for the Improvement of Living and Working Conditions

   Welcome and opening of the Workshop by

   - Wolfgang BRANONER, Secretary of State for Urban Development and Environmental Protection
   - Andreas TROGE, Vice-President, Federal Environmental Agency
   - Georges GLYNOS, Representative of the Cabinet of Ms Vasso PAPANDREOU, Commission of the European Communities
   - Sandro GIULIANELLI, Representative of the Cabinet of Mr Carlo RIPA DI MEANA, Commission of the European Communities
   - Clive PURKISS, Director, European Foundation for the Improvement of Living and Working Conditions
   - Enrique RETUERTO, Deputy Director, CEDEFOP

11.15-11.45   Coffee/tea break

11.45-12.45   **FIRST PLENARY SESSION**
   Chairperson: Eric VERBORGH, Deputy Director, European Foundation for the Improvement of Living and Working Conditions

   Presentation of the background paper to the workshop by David HARVEY, School of Geography, University of Oxford

   Discussion

13.00-14.30   Lunch

14.30-16.30 **SECOND PLENARY SESSION**
Chairperson: Wendy O'CONGHAILE, European Foundation for the Improvement of Living and Working Conditions

Presentation of the main theme papers introducing the working groups

Working Group 1: 'Transportation, Environment and Social Integration in Cities', introduced by Laurie PICKUP, Travel and Transport Research, Oxford

Working Group 2: 'Preventing and Fighting Crime/Delinquency and the Urban Environment', introduced by Lina MARSONI, Municipality of Milan

Working Group 3: 'Social Housing and Quality of the Urban Environment', introduced by Uwe WULLKOPF, Institut Wohnen und Umwelt, Darmstadt

Working Group 4: 'Social Integration and Creation of New Urban Activities', introduced by Paul LAWLESS, Sheffield City Polytechnic

Working Group 5: 'The Co-existence of Urban Functions as a Means to Ensuring Environmental Protection and Social Integration', introduced by Yannis TSIOMIS, Ecole d'Architecture de Paris - La Villette

16.30-17.00 Coffee/tea break

17.00-17.30 Video Presentation

19.30-22.00 Reception and dinner offered by the Senate of Berlin

THURSDAY 10 October

09.00-13.00 WORKING GROUPS - Organisation of the work, presentation of issue papers, innovative experiments and case studies

Working Group 1 : Chairperson: Enrique CALDERÓN, Universidad Politécnica, Madrid

Working Group 2 : Chairperson: Mairín QUILL, TD, Committee on Crime, Dail Eireann, Dublin

Working Group 3 : Chairperson: Olgierd Roman DZIEKÓNSKI, Deputy Mayor of Warsaw

          Working Group 4 :   **Chairperson:** John REID, University College Dublin

          Working Group 5 :   **Chairperson:** René SCHOONBRODT, Directorate-General XI, Commission of the European Communities

[11.00-11.30   Coffee/tea break]

13.00-14.30   Lunch

14.30-18.00   **WORKING GROUPS - discussion; preparation of reports and recommendations**

[16.00-16.30   Coffee/tea break]

18.00   Drink offered by the Director of CEDEFOP

FRIDAY 11 October

9.00-11.00   **THIRD PLENARY SESSION**
Chairperson: Edith BRICKWELL, Senate of Berlin

          Presentation of reports and recommendations from working groups

          Working Group 1 :   Report by Margaret GRIECO, University of Oxford

          Working Group 2 :   Report by Sandra WALKLATE, University of Salford

          Working Group 3 :   Report by Marie GANIER-RAYMOND, IFS, Berlin

          Working Group 4 :   Report by Philippe MORIN, RACINE, Réseau d'Appui et de Capitalisation des Innovations Européennes, Paris

          Working Group 5 :   Report by Sten ENGELSTOFT, University of Copenhagen/Commission of the European Communities, DG XII

          Discussion

11.00-11.30   Coffee/tea break

11.30-13.00   **CONCLUDING PLENARY SESSION**
Chairperson: Voula MEGA, European Foundation for the Improvement of Living and Working Conditions

Recent developments in Berlin : Edith BRICKWELL, Senate of Berlin

Addressing the workshop:

- Eugène MULLER, Economic and Social Committee
- Cees POST, European Investment Bank
- René SCHOONBRODT, Directorate-General XI, Commission of the European Communities
- Stephen FOX, Directorate-General XVI, Commission of the European Communities
- Olgierd Roman DZIEKÓNSKI, Deputy Mayor of Warsaw

General report of the workshop by Jacqueline MILLER, Free University of Brussels

Discussion on conclusions and suggestions emerging from the workshop

Closure of the workshop by Jørn PEDERSEN

13.00-14.30   Lunch

14.30   Optional tour of Berlin visiting, notably, areas with urban revitalisation projects and areas experiencing particular problems, both in the eastern and western part of the city (Kreuzberg, Friedrichshain, Scheunenviertel, Prenzlauer Berg, Marzahn)

Venue:

>CEDEFOP
>(European Centre for the Development
>of Vocational Training)
>Jean Monnet House
>Bundesallee 22
>D-1000 Berlin 15
>
>Tel: 30-88.41.20/88.412
>Fax: 30-88.41.22.22

Organising Committee:

European Foundation:	Jørn PEDERSEN
	Wendy O'CONGHAILE
	Voula MEGA
	Bríd NOLAN (Promotion)
	Ann McDONALD (Conference Officer)
Senate of Berlin:	Edith BRICKWELL
General Rapporteur:	Jacqueline MILLER
	Free University of Brussels

Conference Secretariat:

European Foundation:	Hanne HANSEN
Senate of Berlin:	Gabrièle SCHUGK
	Hergen SCHWARZER

OPENING ADDRESS

by

Sandro Giulianelli
Cabinet of Mr Carlo Ripa di Meana
Commission of the European Communities

Introduction

The title of this workshop: 'The improvement of the built environment and social integration in cities' is particularly interesting because of the activities launched by the Commission of the European Communities through its Green Paper on the Urban Environment. For this reason, on behalf of Mr Ripa di Meana, the member of the Commission of the European Communities responsible for the environment, I would like to emphasise that we shall take account of the outcome of the discussions and debates held at this workshop in our future work in Brussels. In the Green Paper we tried to get away from the idea of an environment limited to certain specific aspects like air quality, water quality, noise levels, etc. and to think of the urban environment as an integrated whole, in other words a complex system where economic, social and cultural factors interact.

The Green Paper contains an **idea of what a city is**; an idea which, over and above the specific differences, I feel holds true from Athens to Copenhagen; an idea which, in substance, aims to re-establish the basic meaning of the city and the reason for its being. Latin has two words, 'URBS' and 'CIVITAS', to indicate the two meanings, the physical and the social aspects of a city. In modern day society the qualities of 'CIVITAS', i.e. social harmony, interpersonal exchange, variety of life, etc. are, with a few exceptions, dying out. The outlying districts, densely built-up and impersonal, certainly lack such qualities. I am thinking in particular of the semi-illicit 'borgate' on the outskirts of Rome, of the ring of tumbledown tower blocks around Barcelona and of the amorphous mass of buildings on the periphery of Athens.

In these cases the outskirts mean places of exclusion and remoteness, not only from the decision-making centres, but also from places of culture and social exchange and variety, which are the privilege of a distant urban centre. This is the idea of the 'two-speed city' that Michel Cantal-Dupart talks about in connection with Paris: on the one hand, the Paris within the 'périphérique' ring road, i.e. the city of power and prestige, the Paris we know and love and the Paris we talk about; on the other, the 'banlieue', which is shut out of cultural life, denied the opportunities offered by the other Paris and cut off from any idea of 'centrality'.

Starting from this situation of environmental breakdown, we have retraced our steps in an attempt to find the origin of the problems, that is to say, the structure of urban areas, calling into question what in the vast majority of cases is the underlying functional model. The abstract model at the heart of the town planning projects which have governed the development of our cities, the 'ville radieuse' of Le Corbusier in the 1930s, has proved to be disastrous with its claim to reproduce all the phenomena which go to make up a city, with a given set of functions organised along the lines of functional separation and satisfaction of a predetermined number of needs. This model does not work. On the contrary, it has generated vast, faceless suburbs, business districts teeming by day but empty and sinister at night, run-down historical centres and the growing need for mobility, with the consequent damage to the environment caused by private traffic.

With the adoption of the Green Paper by the European Parliament at its session in September, the administrative process as such came to an end. We now have to go ahead with a number of priority measures.

The first of these measures is to set up an **international working group** of experts to analyse the current situation in the twelve Member States and to use this information to determine how the environmental viewpoint can be incorporated into town planning processes. At the same time it will be advising the Commission on the specific topics contained in the Green Paper.

The second measure is to launch an **exchange programme** to allow the cities of Europe to share their experiences, either by encouraging the establishment of networks or by funding exchanges of technical staff and experts. During our round of consultations we realised that cities are often not sufficiently aware of what is being achieved by cities elsewhere in terms of projects and experience which could be applied to other similar cases.

The third measure is to launch **pilot projects** designed to find new experimental solutions which could be applied to specific environmental problems.

We therefore launched five case studies:

Genoa, where we are considering the possibility of restoring part of the old city centre.

Copenhagen, where we are studying the restoration of a peripheral residential quarter built in the 1930s.

Blois, a small French town where we are considering a global approach to the urban environment.

Hamburg, where we are studying the green areas of the city.

Madrid, where we are deciding how to improve Villaverde, a severely depressed suburb.

These projects are still in their initial stages but we expect to have preliminary guidelines for action within one year.

Obviously, any attempt to make real changes to a city will be extremely expensive. It is important therefore to make this a joint effort, mobilising both public and private resources.

In our own case, the Directorate-General for the Environment of the Commission of the European Communities has developed a new financial instrument - LIFE - currently being studied by the Council of Ministers which this year makes provision for some ECU 30 million. It is our intention to earmark a considerable proportion of this Fund for the urban environment and, in particular, for the launching of pilot projects which, besides being examples of possible new methods of intervention, could have important repercussions in terms of the more traditional legislative activities of the Community.

I can also report that we are working on a study into the recovery of abandoned industrial areas and social housing, which will also contain a number of practical proposals drawing on ECSC funds.

I would like to make it quite clear that the institutions of the Community are not in any way trying to take over from local and national authorities.

For this reason, we do not see any point in legislative changes to involve the Commission directly in town and country planning and development processes. However, we do feel the Commission can play a guiding role by making recommendations and by extending the scope of the existing environmental impact directive to incorporate assessment of the impact of town planning and development policies on urban areas.

All our action on the urban environment is based on a number of general principles contained in the Green Paper. I would like to make these principles clear by summarising them into a number of points which might serve as food for thought and discussion and ultimately provide inspiration for the revitalisation of the cities of Europe.

Firstly: encourage mixed use of urban areas, with co-existence of a wide variety of social groups and activities.

This objective will not only maintain the character of our cities but will integrate residential areas with manufacturing areas, thus reducing the need for travel and daily commuting, with obvious benefits for the environment.

Secondly: maintain and enhance the identity of the city, by re-establishing the important links between places and their history.

This means respecting the individual character of each city, not only in the old city centre but also in the surrounding area, and avoiding measures which do not take account of the importance of history and natural features. In other words, we should fight against the 'international style' which is destroying our cities and filling them with those anonymous buildings devoid of any imagination or cultural identity which are the same in Paris and Berlin, London and Madrid.

In restoring old city centres, it is also important not to forget the rights of the original inhabitants.

Thirdly: channel the development and growth of cities into disused city areas (e.g. abandoned industrial areas, former military premises, and disused infrastructure) rather than taking over more land on the periphery.

It is generally true to say that the days of urban sprawl, which saw the cities take over large areas of land on their peripheries, are over.

It is now important to work towards making urban areas more habitable by sewing together the torn fabric and taking advantage of unused areas to provide the city with better infrastructure more in keeping with the needs of its population. The halt in population growth should facilitate this process, although the extent of immigration from the Third World and from Eastern Europe remains an unknown factor.

Fourthly: reduce the impact of private transport on urban areas.

The damage caused by urban traffic is so obvious that I do not need to dwell on it. What we need is carefully co-ordinated planning combined with transport policies designed to make public transport competitive compared with private cars, investigating specific measures which will vary from case to case, but with the common aim of freeing old city centres from the traffic congestion caused by private cars.

Fifthly: maintain the quality of open spaces and green areas.

Planners have been losing sight of the need to provide the open spaces which have been a feature of the history of European cities. The clear result is not only that urban quality is impaired but also that citizens cease to identify with the city in which they live.

There are a number of examples of great interest in this connection in various cities of Europe, often connected with the planning of roads and pedestrian areas. Sometimes, just one simple object carefully located can conjure up the very image of the city. I am thinking for example of the bollards which are a typical feature of Amsterdam, the famous 'Maurice' advertising columns in Paris, and the red telephone boxes in London (which unfortunately have virtually all disappeared).

Sixthly: incorporate into urban management policies rules on energy saving and the intelligent use of resources.

It is important to rationalise the use of energy for transport, industry and domestic purposes while at the same time recovering and recycling urban waste. Cities must get into the habit of solving their own problems and limiting their impact on the surrounding environment.

Seventhly: ensure that city dwellers are involved in decisions on the organisation of the city and the management of environmental problems.

This aim can be achieved by establishing procedures which will allow citizens to participate directly in decisions affecting their environment, encouraging them to set up voluntary working parties and providing easy access to facts and figures.

These seven principles will constitute the guidelines for our work in Brussels and the basis for measures on the urban environment. Cities are an integral part of environment policy, and this major cultural project is designed to protect and restore their architectural, social and human heritage, a heritage of which Europe can be justly proud.

WELCOMING ADDRESS

by

**Clive Purkiss
Director
European Foundation
for the Improvement of Living and Working Conditions**

On behalf of the Foundation may I join my welcome to you all to that of the other speakers and thank each one of you for coming together here in Berlin to share your experience.

I must immediately say how very grateful we are for the co-operation and generosity of the Senate of Berlin in co-organising and hosting this workshop. Indeed I would like to take this opportunity to thank the Senate, and especially the Senate Administration for Urban Environmental Protection, for all the help and co-operation which it has given the Foundation over the last 3 to 4 years. A special compliment is due to Dr Brickwell and Mrs Schugk of the Senate Administration for all their efforts to ensure the success of this workshop.

This is the third time in as many months that I have been here in CEDEFOP: that is itself a clear sign of the close and fruitful co-operation that our sister organisations have enjoyed since our twin birth in 1975. Once more Mr Retuerto, we are indebted to you and CEDEFOP for making your facilities available to the Foundation.

We are delighted that with us today are Mr Glynos of the Cabinet of Mrs Vasso Papandreou and Mr Giulianelli of the Cabinet of Mr Ripa di Meana. Their presence reinforces once more the links which have been built over the years between the Commission and the Foundation. They have presented to us an excellent context in which to see our work. Mr Giulianelli last December attended the first of this series of workshops, that dealt with Cities and the Global Environment, and was held in The Hague. He is a key person behind Commissioner Ripa di Meana's initiative to start a Community Urban Environmental Programme, which is being taken forward by the Urban Environment Unit of the Commission's Directorate-General XI. We are very pleased too, therefore, to have with us here Mr René Schoonbrodt as the representative of DG XI.

The Foundation's programme on the urban environment, in the years 1990-1992, is being built around three workshops. It follows from recommendations made by a working group of representatives of Governments, the Commission of the EC, the social partners, international organisations and independent experts. As I have already mentioned, the first of these meetings dealt with Cities and the Global Environment. The proceedings of that meeting will be printed and sent to all of you. The third of our workshops on Land Use Management and Environmental Improvement is scheduled for early May 1992. This is being organised in co-operation with the Municipality of Lisbon and the Portuguese Ministry of the Environment. I am very happy that

Mr Rui Godinho, the Vice-President of the Municipality of Lisbon, is with us today and that the Portuguese Ministry of the Environment is also represented by Mrs Christina de Jésus Garrett.

The Hague and Lisbon workshops are almost purely environmental in their content, but this Berlin workshop aims at linking the environmental, social and economic issues in urban areas and at examining them in a coherent and integrated framework. This is an approach which the Foundation applies to much of its work. It reflects, at the same time, our activities since 1985, on social and economic issues in urban areas, including, for instance, living conditions in general, housing and young people in transition to adult life and the problems they face, as well as our extended environment programme 1989-1992.

It is not by accident that we meet in Berlin today. Already during the discussions in the Foundation's Working Groups, in which Dr Edith Brickwell of the Senate Administration was the German representative, it became quite evident that Berlin would be the ideal setting for this workshop. At that time, the wall had not yet disappeared, but the political situation had changed, and, because of its location - a city linking Eastern and Western Europe - and because of its urban, its cultural and its cosmopolitan traditions, yet a city pointing towards a new era, Berlin was clearly an ideal venue for a meeting like this. A meeting which will be looking into some of the most crucial problems facing a large number of cities in both Eastern and Western Europe. I hope that you will be able to take the opportunity whilst here to find out for yourselves how the challenges are being faced. I am sure you will all join me in congratulating the Senate in the establishment of the European Academy of the Urban Environment yesterday. We all wish it well in its tasks.

This workshop is about people - ordinary people - in towns and cities throughout Europe - about their desires and how they might be better met. As Mr Glynos has said, our society is becoming still more complex and this is reflected in our cities. The response to various problems has often been piecemeal and the result of isolated decisions. But these are unlikely to lead to viable solutions. On the contrary the development of our urban areas has to be dealt with in a wide policy context, crossing society as a whole and in a forward looking perspective, if we are to ensure that decisions are not to become obsolete a few years after they have been taken. Of course it is going to require innovative thinking as well as the kind of integrated approach to which I referred a moment ago. We have got to learn to handle the complex situations in our cities. As Mr Giulianelli has said it will require bringing together a combination of environmental, social, economic, transport and many other solutions. And we will need to ensure that the decisions taken are integrated into a regional, national and, indeed, a European framework. And they must reflect long-term solutions. Without such an approach, we are likely to repeat the mistakes of the past, and we will fail in our effort to create a better and more liveable urban environment. The presentations and discussions at this workshop will, I am sure, bring forward and develop new ideas and point to innovative solutions regarding the way in which we will have to handle our urban problems in the future. I therefore see the workshop as having potential for making a major contribution to further policy-oriented discussion and decision-making on urban issues at various levels. I am grateful to you for being here to exchange ideas, to give your own special insights into the problems we face and, above all, I am sure, help us achieve a practical and useful outcome from our work.

PAPER INTRODUCING THE WORKSHOP

SOCIAL JUSTICE, POSTMODERNISM AND THE CITY

by

David Harvey
Halford Mackinder Professor of Geography
University of Oxford

The title of this essay is a collage of two book titles of mine written nearly twenty years apart, **Social Justice and the City** and **The Condition of Postmodernity**. I here want to consider the relations between them in part as a way to reflect on the intellectual and political journey many have travelled these last two decades in their attempts to grapple with urban issues but also to examine how we now might think about urban problems and how by virtue of such thinking we can better position ourselves with respect to solutions. The question of **positionality** is, I shall argue, fundamental to all debates about how to create infrastructures and urban environments for living and working in the twenty-first century.

1. Justice and the Postmodern Condition

I begin with a report by John Kifner in the **International Herald Tribune** (August 1st, 1989) concerning the hotly contested space of Tompkins Square Park in New York City - a space which has been repeatedly fought over, often violently, since the 'police riot' of August 1988. The neighbourhood mix around the park was the primary focus of Kifner's attention. Not only were there nearly 300 homeless people, but there were also:

'Skateboarders, basketball players, mothers with small children, radicals looking like 1960s retreads, spikey-haired punk rockers in torn black, skinheads in heavy working boots looking to beat up the radicals and punks, dreadlocked Rastafarians, heavy-metal bands, chess players, dog walkers - all occupy their spaces in the park, along with professionals carrying their dry-cleaned suits to the renovated "gentrified" buildings that are changing the character of the neighborhood.'

By night, Kifner notes, the contrasts in the park become even more bizarre:

'The Newcomers Motorcycle Club was having its annual block party at its clubhouse on 12th Street and Avenue B, and the street was lined with chromed Harley Davidsons and raised "ape-hanger" handlebars and beefy men and hefty women in black leather. A block north a rock concert had spilled out of a "squat" - an abandoned city-owned building taken over by outlaw renovators, mostly young artists - and the street was filled with young people whose purple hair stood straight up in spikes. At the World Club just off Houston Street near Avenue C, black youths pulled up in the Jeep-type vehicles favoured by cash-heavy teenage crack moguls, high-powered speakers blaring. At the corner of Avenue B and Third, considered one of the worst heroin blocks in New York, another concert was going on at an artists' space called The Garage, set in a former gas station walled off by plastic bottles and other found objects. The wall formed an enclosed garden looking up at burned-out, abandoned buildings; there was an eerie resemblance to Beirut. The crowd was white and fashionably dressed, and a police sergeant sent to check on the noise shook his head, bemused: "It's all yuppies."'

This is, of course, the kind of scene that makes New York such a fascinating place, that makes any great city into a stimulating and exciting maelstrom of cultural conflict and change. It is the kind of scene that many a student of urban subcultures would revel in, even seeing in it, as someone like Iain Chambers does, the origins of that distinctive perspective we now call 'the postmodern'.

'Postmodernism, whatever form its intellectualizing might take, has been fundamentally anticipated in the metropolitan cultures of the last twenty years; among the electronic signifiers of cinema, television and video, in recording studios and record players, in fashion and youth styles, in all those sounds, images and diverse histories that are daily mixed, recycled and "scratched" together on that giant screen that is the contemporary city.'

Armed with that insight, we could take the whole paraphernalia of postmodern argumentation and technique and try to 'deconstruct' the seemingly disparate images on that giant screen which is the city. We could dissect and celebrate the fragmentation, the co-presence of multiple discourses - of music, street and body language, dress and technological accoutrements (such as Harley Davidsons) - and, perhaps, develop sophisticated empathies with the multiple and contradictory codings with which highly differentiated social beings both present themselves to each other and to the world and live out their daily lives. We could celebrate the bifurcations in cultural trajectory, the preservation of pre-existing and the creation of entirely new but distinctive 'othernesses' within an otherwise homogenising world.

On a good day, we could celebrate the scene within the Park as a superb example of urban tolerance for difference, an exemplar of what Iris Marion Young calls 'openness to unassimilated otherness'. In a just and civilised society, she argues, the normative ideal of city life:

'instantiates social relations of difference without exclusion. Different groups dwell in the city alongside one another, of necessity interacting in city spaces. If city politics is to be democratic and not dominated by the point of view of one group, it must be a politics that takes account of and provides voice for the different groups that dwell together in the city without forming a community' (p. 227).

To the degree that the freedom of city life 'leads to group differentiation, to the formation of affinity groups,'(p. 238) of the sort which Kifner identifies in Tompkins Square, so our conception of social justice 'requires not the melting away of differences, but institutions that promote reproduction of and respect of group differences without oppression' (p. 47). We must reject 'the concept of universality as embodied in republican versions of Enlightenment reason' precisely because it sought to 'suppress the popular and linguistic heterogeneity of the urban public' (p. 108). 'In open and accessible public spaces and forums, one should expect to encounter and hear from those who are different, whose social perspectives, experience and affiliations are different'. It then follows, Young argues, that a politics of inclusion 'must promote the ideal of a heterogeneous public, in which persons stand forth with their differences acknowledged and respected, though perhaps not completely understood by others' (p. 119).

In similar vein, Roberto Unger, the philosophical guru of the critical legal studies movement in the United States, might view the park as a manifestation of a new ideal of community understood as a 'zone of heightened mutual vulnerability, within which people gain a chance to resolve more fully the conflict between the enabling conditions of self-assertion; between their need for attachment and for participation in group life and their fear of subjugation and depersonalization with which such engagement may threaten them' (p. 562). Tompkins Square seems a place where the 'contrast between structure-preserving routine and structure transforming conflict' softens in such a way as to 'free sociability from its script and to make us available to one another more as the originals we know ourselves to be and less as the placeholders in a system of group contrasts'. The square might even be interpreted as a site of that 'microlevel of cultural-revolutionary defiance and incongruity' which periodically wells upwards into 'the macrolevel of institutional innovation' (p. 564). Unger is acutely aware, however, that the temptation to 'treat each aspect of cultural revolution as a pretext for endless self-gratification and self-concern' can lead to a failure to 'connect the revolutionary reform of institutional arrangements with the cultural-revolutionary remaking of personal relations'.

So what should the urban policy-maker do in the face of these strictures? The best path is to pull out that well-thumbed copy of Jane Jacobs and insist that we should both respect and provide for 'spontaneous self-diversification among urban populations' in the formulation of our policies and plans. In so doing we can avoid the critical wrath she directs at city designers who 'seem neither to recognize this force for self-diversification nor to be attracted by the aesthetic problems of expressing it'. Such a strategy can help us live up to expectations of the sort which Young and Unger lay down. We should not, in short, aim to obliterate differences within the park, homogenise it according to some conception of, say, bourgeois taste or social order. We should engage, rather, with an aesthetics which embraces or stimulates that 'spontaneous self-diversification' of which Jacobs speaks. Yet there is an immediate question-mark over that suggestion; in what ways, for example, can homelessness be understood as spontaneous self-diversification and does this mean that we should respond to that problem with designer-style cardboard boxes to make for more jolly and sightly shelters for the homeless? While Jane Jacobs has a point and one which many urbanists have absorbed these last few years, there is, evidently, much more to the problem than her arguments encompass.

That difficulty is highlighted on a bad day in the park. So-called forces of law and order battle to evict the homeless, erect barriers between violently clashing factions. The park then becomes a locus of exploitation and oppression, an open wound from which bleed the five faces of oppression which Young defines as exploitation, marginalisation, powerlessness, cultural imperialism and violence. The potentiality for 'openness to unassimilated otherness' breaks apart and in much the same way that the cosmopolitan and eminently civilised Beirut of the 1950s suddenly collapsed into an urban maelstrom of warring factions and violent confrontations, so we find sociality collapsing into violence. This is not unique to New York City but is a condition of urban life in many of our large metropolitan areas - witness events in the banlieus of Paris and Lyons, in Brussels, in Liverpool, London and even Oxford in recent times.

In such circumstances Young's pursuit of a vision of justice that is assertive as to difference without reinforcing the forms of oppression gets torn to tatters and Unger's dreams of micro-revolutions in cultural practices which simulate progressive rather than repressive institutional innovation become just that - dreams.

The very best face that we can put upon the whole scene is to recognise that this is how class, ethnic, racial and gender struggle is, as Lefebvre would put it, being 'inscribed in space'. And what should the planner do? Here is how a subsequent article in the New York Times reflected on that dilemma:

'There are neighborhood associations clamouring for the city to close the park and there are others just as insistent that it remain a refuge for the city's downtrodden. The local Assemblyman, Steven Sanders, yesterday called for a curfew that would effectively evict more than a hundred homeless people camped out in the park. Councilwoman Miriam Friedlander instead recommended that Social Services, like healthcare and drug treatment, be brought directly to the people living in the tent city. "We do not find the park is being used appropriately", said Deputy Mayor Barbara J. Fife, "but we recognise there are various interests." There is, they go on to say, only one thing that is a consensus, first that there isn't a consensus over what should be done, except that any new plan is likely to provoke more disturbances, more violence.'

On June 8th, the question was resolved by evicting everyone from the park and closing it entirely 'for rehabilitation' under a permanent guard of at least twenty police officers. The New York authorities, situated on what Davis (1990, 224) calls 'the bad edge of postmodernity', militarises rather than liberates its public space. In so doing, power is deployed in support of a middle class quest for 'personal insulation, in residential, work, consumption and travel environments, from "unsavoury" groups and individuals, even crowds in general'. Genuinely public space is extinguished, militarised or semi-privatised. The heterogeneity of open democracy, the mixing of classes, ethnicities, religions and divergent taste cultures within a common frame of public space is lost along with the capacity to celebrate unity and community in the midst of diversity. The ultimate irony, as Davis points out is that 'as the walls come down in Eastern Europe, they are being erected all over (our cities)'.

And what should the policy-maker and planner do in the face of these conditions? Give up planning and join one of those burgeoning cultural studies programmes which revel in chaotic scenes of the Tompkins sort while simultaneously disengaging from any commitment to do something about them? Deploy all the critical powers of deconstruction and semiotics to seek new and engaging interpretations of graffiti which say 'Die, Yuppie Scum'? Should we join revolutionary and anarchist groups and fight for the rights of the poor and the culturally marginalised to express their rights and if necessary make a home for themselves in the park? Or should we throw away that dog-eared copy of Jane Jacobs and join with the forces of law and order and help impose some authoritarian solution on the problem?

Decisions of some sort have to be made and actions taken, as about any other facet of urban infrastructure. And while we might all agree that an urban park is a good thing in principle, what are we to make of the fact that the uses turn out to be so conflictual and that even conceptions as to what the space is for and how it is to be managed diverge radically among competing factions? To hold all the divergent politics of need and desire together within some coherent frame may be a laudable aim but in practice far too many of the interests are mutually exclusive to allow their mutual accommodation. Even the best shaped compromise (let alone the savagely imposed authoritarian solution) favours one or other factional interest. And that provokes the biggest question of all - what is the **conception** of 'the public' incorporated into the construction of public space?

To answer these questions requires some deeper understanding of the forces at work shaping conflict in the park. Kifner identified drugs and real estate - 'the two most powerful forces in (New York City) today'. Both of them are linked to organised crime and are major pillars of the political economy of contemporary capitalism. We cannot understand events within and around the park or strategise as to its future uses without contextualising it against a background of the political-economic transformations now occurring in urban life. The problems of Tompkins Square Park have, in short, to be seen in terms of social processes which create homelessness, promote criminal activities of many sorts (from real estate swindles and the crack trade to street muggings), generate hierarchies of power between gentrifiers and the homeless, and facilitate the emergence of deep tensions along the major social fault-lines of class, gender, ethnicity, race, religious, life-style and place-bound preferences.

2. Social Justice and Modernity

I now leave this very contemporary situation and its associated conundrums and turn to an older story. It turned up when I unearthed from my files a yellowing manuscript, written sometime in the early 1970s, shortly after I finished **Social Justice and the City**. I there examined the case of a proposal to put a segment of the Interstate Highway System on an East-West trajectory right through the heart of Baltimore - a proposal first set out in the early 1940s and which has still not been fully resolved. I resurrect this case here in part to show that what we would now often depict as a quintessentially modernist problem was even at that time argued about in ways which contained the seeds, if not the essence, of much of what many now view as a distinctively postmodernist form of argumentation.

My interest in the case at that time, having looked at a lot of the discussion, attended hearings and read a lot of documentation, lay initially in the highly differentiated arguments, articulated by all kinds of different groups, concerning the rights and wrongs of the whole project. There were, I found, seven kinds of argument being put forward:

1) An **efficiency** argument which concentrated on the relief of traffic congestion and facilitating the easier flow of goods and people throughout the region as well as within the city;

2) An **economic growth** argument which looked to a projected increase (or prevention of loss) in investment and employment opportunities in the city upon improvements in the transport system;

3) An **aesthetic and historical heritage** argument which objected to the way sections of the proposed highway would either destroy or diminish urban environments deemed both attractive and of historical value;

4) A **social and moral order** argument which held that prioritising highway investment and subsidising car owners rather than, for example, investing in housing and health care was quite wrong;

5) An **environmental/ecological** argument which considered the impacts of the proposed highway on air quality, noise pollution and the destruction of certain valued environments (such as a river valley park);

6) A **distributive justice** argument which dwelt mainly on the benefits to business and predominantly white middle-class suburban commuters to the detriment of low income and predominantly African-American inner city residents;

7) A **neighbourhood and communitarian** argument which considered the way in which close-knit but otherwise fragile and vulnerable communities might be destroyed, divided or disrupted by highway construction.

The arguments were not mutually exclusive, of course, and several of them were merged by proponents of the highway into a common thread - for example, the efficiency of the transport system would stimulate growth and reduce pollution from congestion so as to advantage otherwise disadvantaged inner-city residents. It was also possible to break up each argument into quite distinct parts - the distributive impacts on women with children would be very different to those on male workers.

We would, in these heady postmodern times, be prone to describe these separate arguments as 'discourses', each with its own logic and imperatives. And we would not have to look too closely to see particular 'communities of interest' which articulated a particular discourse as if it was the only one that mattered. The particularistic arguments advanced by such groups proved effective in altering the alignment of the highway but did not stop the highway as a whole. The one group which tried to forge a coalition out of these disparate elements, (the **Movement Against Destruction**, otherwise known as MAD), and to provide an umbrella for opposition to the highway as a whole turned out to be the least effective in mobilising people and constituencies even though it was very articulate in its arguments.

The purpose of my own particular enquiry, was to see how the arguments (or discourses) for and against the highway worked and if coalitions could be built in principle between seemingly disparate and often highly antagonistic interest groups via the construction of higher order arguments (discourses) which could provide the basis for consensus. The multiplicity of views and forces has to be set against the fact that either the highway is built or it is not, although in Baltimore, with its wonderful way of doing things, we ended up with a portion of the highway that is called a boulevard (to make us understand that this six-lane two-mile segment of a monster cut through the heart of low-income and predominantly African-American West Baltimore is not what it really is) and another route on a completely different alignment, looping around the city core in such a way as to allay some of the worst political fears of influential communities.

Might there be, then, some higher order discourse to which everyone could appeal in working out whether or not it made sense to build the highway? A dominant theme in the literature of the 1960s was that it was possible to identify some such higher order arguments. The phrase that was most frequently used to describe it was **social rationality**. The idea of that did not seem implausible, because each of the seven seemingly distinctive arguments advanced a rational position of some sort and not infrequently appealed to some higher order rationale to bolster its case. Those arguing on efficiency and growth grounds frequently invoked utilitarian arguments, notions of 'public good' and the greatest benefit to the greatest number, while recognising (at their best) that individual sacrifices were inevitable and that it was right and proper to offer appropriate compensation for those who would be displaced. Ecologists or communitarians likewise appealed to higher order arguments - the former to the values inherent in nature and the latter to some higher sense of communitarian values. For all of these reasons, considerations of higher order arguments over social rationality did not seem unreasonable.

Dahl and Lindblom's **Politics, Economics and Welfare**, published in 1953, provides a classic statement along these lines. They argue that not only is socialism dead (a conclusion that many would certainly share these days) but also that capitalism is equally dead. What they signal by this is an intellectual tradition which arose out of the experience of the vast market and capitalistic failure of the Great Depression and the Second World War and which concluded that some kind of middle ground had to be found between the extremism of a pure and unfettered market economy and the communist vision of an organised and highly centralised economy. They concentrated their theory on the question of rational social action and argued that this required 'processes for both rational **calculation** and effective **control**' (p. 21). Rational calculation and control, as far as they were concerned, depended upon the exercise of rational calculation through price-fixing markets, hierarchy (top-down decision-making), polyarchy (democratic control of leadership) and bargaining (negotiation) and such means should be deployed to achieve the goals of 'freedom, rationality, democracy, subjective equality, security, progress, and appropriate inclusion' (28). There is much that is interesting about Dahl and Lindblom's analysis and it is not too hard to imagine that after the recent highly problematic phase of market triumphalism, particularly in Britain and the United States, that there will be some sort of search to resurrect the formulations they proposed. But in so doing it is also useful to remind ourselves of the intense criticism that was levelled during the 1960s and 1970s against their search for some universal prospectus on the socially rational society of the future.

Godelier, for example, in his book on **Rationality and Irrationality in Economics** savagely attacked the socialist thinking of Oscar Lange for its teleological view of rationality and its presumption that socialism should or could ever be the ultimate achievement of rational life. Godelier did not attack this notion from the right but from a Marxist and historical materialist perspective. His point was that there are different definitions of rationality depending upon the form of social organisations and that the rationality embedded in feudalism is different from that of capitalism which should, presumably, be different again under socialism. Rationality defined from the standpoint of corporate capital is quite different from rationality defined from the standpoint of the working classes. Work of this type helped fuel the growing radical critique of even the non-teleological and incrementalist thinking of the Dahl and Lindblom sort. This critique suggested that their definition of social rationality was connected to the perpetuation and rational management of a capitalist economic system rather than with the exploration of alternatives. To attack (or deconstruct, as we now would put it) their conception of social rationality was seen by the left at the time as a means to challenge the ideological hegemony of a dominant corporate capitalism. Feminists, those marginalised by racial characteristics, colonised peoples, ethnic and religious minorities, echoed that refrain in their work, while adding their own conception of who was the enemy to be challenged and what were the dominant forms of rationality to be contested. The result was to show emphatically that there is no overwhelming and universally acceptable definition of social rationality to which we might appeal, but innumerable different rationalities depending upon social and material circumstances, group identities and social objectives. Rationality is defined by the nature of the social group and its project rather than the project being dictated by social rationality. The deconstruction of universal claims of social rationality was one of the major achievements and continues to be one of the major legacies of the radical critique of the 1960s and 1970s.

Such a conclusion is, however, more than a little discomforting. It would suggest, to go back to the highway example, that there was no point whatsoever in searching for any higher order arguments because such arguments simply could not have any purchase upon the political process of decision-making. And it is indeed striking that the one group that tried to build such overall arguments, MAD, was the group that was least successful in actually mobilising opposition. The fragmented discourses of those who sought to change the alignment of the highway had more effect than the more unified discourse precisely because the former were grouped in the specific and particular local circumstances in which individuals found themselves. Yet the fragmented discourses could never go beyond challenging the alignment of the highway. It did indeed need a more unified discourse, of the sort which MAD tried to articulate, to challenge the concept of the highway in general.

This poses a direct dilemma. If we accept that fragmented discourses are the only authentic discourses and that no unified discourse is possible, then there is no way to challenge the overall qualities of a social system. To mount that more general challenge we need some kind of unified or unifying set of arguments. For this reason, I chose, in this ageing and yellowing manuscript, to take a closer look at the particular question of social justice as a basic ideal that might have more universal appeal.

3. Social Justice

Social justice is but one of seven criteria I worked with and I evidently hoped that careful investigation of it might rescue the argument from the abyss of formless relativism and infinitely variable discourses and interest grouping. But here too the enquiry proved frustrating. It revealed that there are as many competing theories of social justice as there are competing ideals of social rationality. Each ideal has its flaws and strengths. Egalitarian views, for example, immediately run into the problem that 'there is nothing more unequal than the equal treatment of unequals' (the modification of doctrines of equality of opportunity in the United States by requirements for affirmative action, for example, recognise what a significant problem that is). By the time I had thoroughly reviewed positive law theories of justice, utilitarian views (the greatest good of the greatest number), social contract views historically contributed to Rousseau and powerfully revived by John Rawls in his **Theory of Justice** in the early 1970s, the various intuitionist, relative deprivation, and other interpretations of justice, I found myself in a quandary as to precisely **which** theory of justice is the most just. The theories can, to some degree, be arranged in a hierarchy with respect to each other. The positive law view that justice is a matter of law, can be challenged by a utilitarian view which allows us to discriminate between good and bad law on the basis of some greater good while the social contract and natural rights view suggest that no amount of greater good for a greater number can justify the violation of certain inalienable rights. On the other hand, intuitionist and relative deprivation theories exist in an entirely different dimension.

Yet the basic problem remained. To argue for social justice meant the deployment of some initial criteria to define which theory of social justice was appropriate or more just than another. The infinite regress of higher order criteria immediately looms as does, in the other direction, the relative ease of total deconstruction of the notion of justice as meaning anything whatsoever, except whatever people at some particular moment find it pragmatically, politically, or ideologically useful to mean. Competing discourses about justice were likely to be competing discourses about positionality in society.

There seemed two ways to go with that argument. The first was to look at how concepts of justice are embedded in language and that led me to theories of meaning of the sort which Wittgenstein advanced:

'How many kinds of sentence are there?....There are **countless** kinds: countless different kinds of use to what we call "symbols", "words", "sentences". And this multiplicity is not something fixed, given once for all: but new types of language, new language games, as we may say, come into existence and others become obsolete and get forgotten....Here the term **"language-game"** is meant to bring into prominence the fact that the **speaking** of language is part of an activity, or a form of life....How did we **learn** the meaning of this word ("good" for instance)? From what sort of examples? In what language games? Then it will be easier for us to see that the word must have a family of meanings.'

From this perspective the concept of justice has to be understood in the way it is embedded in a particular language game. Each language game attaches to the particular social, experiential and perceptual world of the speaker. Justice has no universal meaning but a whole 'family' of meanings. This finding is completely consistent, of course, with anthropological studies which show that justice among, say, the Nuer, means something completely different from the capitalistic conception of justice. We are back to the point of cultural, linguistic or discourse relativism.

The second path is to admit the relativism of discourses about justice, but to insist that discourses are expressions of social power. In this case the idea of justice has to be set against the formation of certain hegemonic discourses which derive from the power exercised by any ruling class. This is an idea which goes back to Plato who, in the **Republic** has Thrasymachus argue that:

'Each ruling class makes laws that are in its own interest, a democracy democratic laws, a tyranny tyrannical ones and so on; and in making these laws they define as "right" for their subjects what is in the interest of themselves, the rulers, and if anyone breaks their laws he is punished as a "wrong-doer". That is what I mean when I say that "right" is the same in all states, namely the interest of the established ruling class....'

Consideration of these two paths brought me to accept a position which is most clearly articulated by Engels in the following terms:

'The stick used to measure what is right and what is not is the most abstract expression of right itself, **justice**....The development of right for the jurists....is nothing more than a striving to bring human conditions, so far as they are expressed in legal terms, ever closer to the ideal of justice, **eternal** justice. And always this justice is but the ideologized, glorified expression of the existing economic relations, now from their conservative and now from their revolutionary angle. The justice of the Greeks and Romans held slavery to be just; the justice of the bourgeois of 1789 demanded the abolition of feudalism on the ground it was unjust. The conception of eternal justice, therefore, varies not only with time and place, but also with the persons concerned....While in everyday life....expressions like right, wrong, justice, and sense of right are accepted without misunderstanding even with reference to social matters, they create....the same hopeless confusion in any scientific investigation of economic relations as would be created, for instance, in modern chemistry if the terminology of the phlogiston theory were to be retained.'

It is a short step from this conception to Marx's critique of Proudhon who, Marx claimed, took his ideal of justice 'from the juridical relations that correspond to the production of commodities' and in so doing was able to present commodity production as 'a form of production as everlasting as justice'. The parallel with Godelier's rebuttal of Lange's (and by extension Dahl and Lindblom's) views on rationality is exact. Taking capitalistic notions of social rationality or of justice, and treating them as universal values to be deployed under socialism, would merely mean the deeper instanciation of capitalist values by way of the socialist project.

4. The Transition from Modernist to Postmodernist Discourses

There are two general points I wish to draw out of the argument so far. First, the critique of social rationality and of conceptions such as social justice as policy tools was something that was originated and so ruthlessly pursued by the 'left' (including Marxists) in the 1960s that it began to generate radical doubt throughout civil society as to the veracity of all universal claims. From this it was a short, though as I shall shortly argue, unwarranted step to conclude, as may postmodernists now do, that all forms of metatheory are either misplaced or illegitimate. Both steps in this process were further reinforced by the emergence of the so-called 'new' social movements - the peace and women's movements, the ecologists, the movements against colonisation and racism - each of which came to articulate its own definitions of social justice and rationality. There then seemed to be, as Engels had argued, no philosophical, linguistic or logical way to resolve the resulting divergencies in conceptions of rationality and justice, and thereby to find a way to reconcile competing claims or arbitrate between radically different discourses. The effect was to undermine the legitimacy of state policy, attack all conceptions of bureaucratic rationality and place social policy formulation at best in a quandary and at worst powerless except to articulate the ideological and value precepts of those in power. And some of those who participated in the revolutionary movements of the 1970s and 1980s considered that rendering transparent the power and class basis of supposedly universal claims was a necessary prelude to mass revolutionary action.

But there is a second and, I think, more subtle point to be made. If Engels is indeed right to insist that the conception of justice 'varies not only with time and place, but also with the persons concerned', then it seems important to look at the ways in which a particular society produces such variation in concepts. In so doing it seems important, following writers as diverse as Wittgenstein and Marx, to look at the material basis for the production of difference, in particular at the production of those radically different experiential worlds out of which divergent language games about social rationality and social justice could arise. This entails the application of historical-geographical materialist methods and principles to understanding the production of those power differentials which in turn produce different conceptions of justice and embed them in a struggle over ideological hegemony between classes, races, ethnic and political groupings as well as across the gender divide. The philosophical, linguistic and logical critique of universal propositions such as justice and of social rationality can be upheld as perfectly correct without necessarily endangering the ontological or epistemological status of a metatheory which confronts the ideological and material functionings and bases of particular discourses. Only in this way can we begin to understand why it is that concepts such as justice which appear as 'hopelessly confused' when examined in abstraction can become such a powerful mobilising force in everyday life where, again to quote Engels, 'expressions like right, wrong, justice, and sense of right are accepted without misunderstanding even with reference to social matters'.

From this standpoint we can clearly see that concepts of justice and of rationality have not disappeared from our social and political world these last few years. But their definition and use has changed. The collapse of class compromise in the struggles of the late 1960s and the emergence of the socialist, communist and radical left movements, coinciding as it did with an acute crisis of overaccumulation of capital, posed a serious threat to the stability of the capitalist political-economic system. At the ideological level, the emergence of alternative definitions of both justice and rationality was part of that attack and it was to this question that my earlier book, **Social Justice and the City**, was addressed. But the recession/depression of 1973-5 signalled not only the savage devaluation of capital stock (through the first wave of deindustrialisation visited upon the weaker sectors and regions of a world capitalist economy) but the beginnings of an attack upon the power of organised labour via widespread unemployment, austerity programmes, restructuring and, eventually, in some instances (such as Britain) institutional reforms.

It was under such conditions that the left penchant for attacking what was interpreted as a capitalist power basis within the welfare state (with its dominant notions of social rationality and just redistributions) connected to an emerging right wing agenda to defang the power of welfare state capitalism, to get away from any notion whatsoever of a social contract between capital and labour and to abandon political notions of social rationality in favour of market rationality. The important point about this transition, which was phased in over a number of years, though at a quite different pace from country to country (it is only now seriously occurring in Sweden, for example), was that the state was no longer obliged to define rationality and justice since it was presumed that the market could best do it for us. The idea that just deserts are best arrived at through market behaviours, that a just distribution is whatever the market dictates and that a just organisation of social life, of urban investments and of resource allocations (including those usually referred to as environmental) is best arrived at through the market is, of course, relatively old and well-tried. It implies conceptions of justice and rationality of a certain sort, rather than their total abandonment. Indeed, the idea that the market is the best way to achieve the most just and the most rational forms of social organisation has become a powerful feature of the hegemonic discourses these last twenty years in both the United States and Britain. The collapse of centrally planned economies throughout much of the world has further boosted a market triumphalism which presumes that the rough justice administered through the market in the course of this transition is not only socially just but also deeply rational. The advantage of this solution, of course, is that there is no need for explicit theoretical, political and social argument over what is or is not socially rational or just because it can be presumed that, provided the market functions properly, the outcome is nearly always just and rational. Universal claims about rationality and justice have in no way diminished. They are just as frequently asserted in justification of privatisation and of market actions as they ever were in support of welfare state capitalism.

The dilemmas inherent in reliance on the market are well-known and no one holds to it without some qualification. Problems of market breakdown, of externality effects, the provision of public goods and infrastructures, the clear need for **some** co-ordination of disparate investment decisions, all of these require some level of government interventionism. Margaret Thatcher may thus have abolished greater London government, but the business community wants some kind of replacement (though preferably non-elected) because without it city services are disintegrating and London is losing its competitive edge. But there are many voices that go beyond that minimal requirement since free market capitalism has produced widespread unemployment, radical restructuring and devaluations of capital, slow growth, environmental degradation, and a whole host of financial scandals and competitive difficulties, to say nothing of widening disparities in income distributions in many countries and the social stresses that attach thereto. It is under such conditions that the never quite stilled voice of state regulation, welfare state capitalism, of state management of industrial development, of state planning of environmental quality, land use, transportation systems and physical and social infrastructures, of state incomes and taxation policies which achieve a modicum of redistribution either in kind (via housing, health care, educational services, and the like) or through income transfers, is being reasserted. The political questions of social rationality and of social justice over and above that administered through the market are being taken off the backburner and moved to the forefront of the political agenda in many of the advanced capitalist countries. And it was exactly in this mode, of course, that Dahl and Lindblom came in back in 1953.

It is here that we have to face up to what Unger calls the 'ideological embarrassment' of the history of politics these last hundred years: its tendency to move merely in repetitive cycles, swinging back and forth between laisser-faire and state interventionism without, it seems, finding any way to break out of this binary opposition to turn a spinning wheel of stasis into a spiral of human development. The breakdown of organised communism in Eastern Europe and the Soviet Union here provides a major opportunity precisely because of the radical qualities of the break. Yet there are few signs of any similar penchant for ideological and institutional renovation in the advanced capitalist countries, which at best seem to be steering towards another bout of bureaucratic management of capitalism embedded in a general politics of the Dahl and Lindblom sort and at worst continue down the blind ideological track which says that the market always knows best. It is precisely at this political conjuncture that we should remind ourselves of what the radical critique of universal claims of justice and rationality has been all about, without falling into the postmodernist trap of denying the validity of **any** appeal to justice or to rationality as a war-cry for political mobilisation (even Lyotard, that father figure of postmodern philosophy, hopes for the reassertion of some 'pristine and non-consensual conception of justice' as a means to find a new kind of politics).

For my own part, I think Engels had it right. Justice and rationality take on different meanings across space and time and persons, yet the existence of everyday meanings to which people do attach importance and which, to them, appear unproblematic, gives the terms a political and mobilising power that can never be neglected. Right and wrong are words that power revolutionary changes and no amount of negative deconstruction of such terms can deny that. So where, then, have the new social movements and the radical left in general got with their own conception and how does it challenge both market and corporate welfare capitalism?

Young in her **Justice and the Politics of Difference** provides one of the best recent statements. She redefines the question of justice away from the purely redistributive mode of welfare state capitalism and focuses on what she calls the 'five faces' of oppression and I think each of them is worth thinking about as we consider the struggle to create liveable cities and workable environments for the twenty-first century.

The first face of oppression conjoins the classic notion of exploitation in the work place with the more recent focus on exploitation of labour in the living place (primarily, of course, that of women working in the domestic sphere). The classic forms of exploitation which Marx described are still omnipresent, though there have been many mutations such that, for example, control over the length of working day may have been offset by increasing intensity of labour or exposure to more hazardous health conditions not only in blue collar but also in white collar occupations. The mitigation of the worst aspects of exploitation has been, to some degree, absorbed into the logic of welfare state capitalism in part through the sheer exercise of class power and trade union muscle. Yet there are still many terrains upon which chronic exploitation can be identified and which will only be addressed to the degree that active struggle raises issues. The conditions of the unemployed, the homeless, the lack of purchasing power for basic needs and services for substantial portions of the population (immigrants, women, children) absolutely have to be addressed. All of which leads to my first proposition: **that just planning and policy practices must confront directly the problem of creating forms of social and political organisation and systems of production and consumption which minimise the exploitation of labour power both in the workplace and the living place.**

The second face of oppression arises out of what Young calls **marginalisation**. 'Marginals', she writes, 'are people the system of labour cannot or will not use'. This is most typically the case with individuals marked by race, ethnicity, religion, gender, immigration status, age, and the like. The consequence is that 'a whole category of people is expelled from useful participation in social life and thus potentially subjected to severe material deprivation and even extermination'. The characteristic response of welfare state capitalism has been to place such marginal groups either under tight surveillance or, at best, to induce a condition of dependency in which state support provides a justification to 'suspend all basic rights to privacy, respect, and individual choice'. The responses among the marginalised have sometimes been both violent and vociferous, in some instances turning their marginalisation into a heroic stand against the state and against any form of inclusion into what has for long only ever offered them oppressive surveillance and demeaning subservience. Marginality is one of the crucial problems facing urban life in the twenty-first century and consideration of it leads to the second principle: **that just planning and policy practices must confront the phenomenon of marginalisation in a non-paternalistic mode and find ways to organise and militate within the politics of marginalisation in such a way as to liberate captive groups from this distinctive form of oppression.**

Powerlessness is, in certain ways, an even more widespread problem than marginality. We are here talking of the ability to express political power as well as to engage in the particular politics of self-expression which we encountered in Tompkins Square Park. The ability to be listened to with respect is strictly circumscribed within welfare state capitalism and failure on this score has played a key role in the collapse of state communism. Professional groups have advantages in this regard which place them in a different category to most others and the temptation always stands, for even the most politicised of us, to speak for others without listening to them. Political inclusion is, if anything, diminished by the decline of trade unionism, of political parties, and of traditional institutions, yet it is at the same time revived by the organisation of new social movements. But the increasing scale of international dependency and interdependency makes it harder and harder to offset powerlessness in general. Like the struggle against the Baltimore expressway, the mobilisation of political power among the oppressed in society is increasingly a local affair, unable to address the structural characteristics of either market or welfare state capitalism as a whole. This leads to my third proposition: **just planning and policy practices must empower rather than deprive the oppressed of access to political power and the ability to engage in self-expression.**

What Young calls **cultural imperialism** relates to the ways in which 'the dominant meanings of a society render the particular perspective of one's own group invisible at the same time as they stereotype one's group and mark it out as the Other'. Arguments of this sort have been most clearly articulated by feminists and black liberation theorists but they are also implicit in liberation theology as well as in many domains of cultural theory. This is, in some respects, the most difficult form of oppression to identify clearly, yet there can surely be no doubt that there are many social groups in our societies who find or feel themselves 'defined from the outside, positioned, placed, by a network of dominant meanings they experience as arising from elsewhere, from those with whom they do not identify and who do not identify with them'. The alienation and social unrest to be found in many western European and North American cities (to say nothing of its re-emergence throughout much of eastern Europe) bears all the marks of a reaction to cultural imperialism and here, too, welfare state capitalism has in the past proved both unsympathetic and unmoved. From this comes a fourth proposition: **that just planning and policy practices must be particularly sensitive to issues of cultural imperialism and seek, by a variety of means, to eliminate the imperialist attitude both in the design of urban projects and modes of popular consultation.**

Fifthly, there is the issue of **violence**. It is hard to consider urban futures and living environments into the twenty-first century without confronting the problem of burgeoning levels of physical violence. The fear of violence against persons and property, though often exaggerated, has a material grounding in the social conditions of market capitalism and calls for some kind of organised response. There is, furthermore, the intricate problem of the violence of organised crime and its interdigitation with capitalist enterprise and state activities. The problem at the first level is, as Davis points out in his consideration of Los Angeles, that the most characteristic response is to search for defensible urban spaces, to militarise urban space and to create living environments which are more rather than less exclusionary. The difficulty with the second level, is that the equivalent of the 'mafiosi' in many cities (an emergent problem in the contemporary Soviet Union, for example) has become so powerful in urban governance that it is they, rather than elected officials and state bureaucrats, who hold the true reins of power. No society can function without certain forms of social control and we have to consider what that might be in the face of a Foucauldian insistence that all forms of social control are oppressive no matter what the level of violence to which they are addressed. Here, too, there are innumerable dilemmas to be solved, but we surely know enough to advance a fifth proposition: **a just planning and policy practice must seek out non-exclusionary and non-militarised forms of social control to contain the increasing levels of both personal and institutionalised violence without destroying capacities for empowerment and self-expression.**

Finally, I want to add a sixth principle to those which Young advances. This derives from the fact that all social projects are ecological projects and vice versa. While I resist the view that 'nature has rights' or that nature can be 'oppressed', the justice due to future generations and to other inhabitants of the globe requires intense scrutiny of all social projects for assessment of their ecological consequences. Human beings necessarily appropriate and transform the world around them in the course of making their own history, but they do not have to do so with such reckless abandon as to jeopardise the fate of peoples separated from us in either space or time. The final proposition is, then: **that just planning and policy practices will clearly recognise that the necessary ecological consequences of all social projects have impacts on future generations as well as upon distant peoples and take steps to ensure a reasonable mitigation of negative impacts.**

I do not argue that these six principles can or even should be unified, let alone turned into some convenient and formulaic composite strategy. Indeed, the six dimensions of justice here outlined are frequently in conflict with each other as far as their application to individual persons - the exploited male worker may be a cultural imperialist on matters of race and gender while the thoroughly oppressed person may be the bearer of social injustice as violence. On the other hand, I do not believe the principles can be applied in isolation from each other either. Simply to leave matters at the level of a 'non-consensual' conception of justice, as someone like Lyotard would do, is not to confront some central issues of the social processes which produce such a differentiated conception of justice in the first place. This then suggests that social policy and planning has to work at two levels. The different faces of oppression have to be confronted for what they are and as they are manifest in daily life, but in the longer term and at the same time the underlying sources of the different forms of oppression in the heart of the political economy of capitalism must also be confronted, not as the fount of all evil but in terms of capitalism's revolutionary dynamic which transforms, disrupts, deconstructs and reconstructs ways of living, working, relating to each other and to the environment. From the latter standpoint the issue is never about whether or not there shall be change, but what sort of change we can anticipate, plan for, and proactively shape in the years to come.

I would hope that consideration of the varieties of justice as well as of this deeper problematic might set the tone for our deliberations and, by appeal to them, we might see ways to break with the political, imaginative and institutional constraints which have for too long inhibited the advanced capitalist societies in their development path. The critique of universal notions of justice and rationality, no matter whether embedded in the market or in state welfare capitalism, still stands. But it is both valuable and potentially liberating to look at alternative conceptions of both justice and rationality as these have emerged within the new social movements these last two decades. And while it will in the end ever be true, as Marx and Plato observed that 'between equal rights force decides', the authoritarian imposition of solutions to many of our urban ills these past few years and the inability to listen to alternative conceptions of both justice and rationality is very much a part of the problem. For the conceptions I have outlined speak to many of the marginalised, the oppressed and the exploited in this time and place. For many of us, and for many of them, the formulations may well appear obvious, unproblematic and just plain common sense. And it is precisely because of such widely-held conceptions that so much welfare state paternalism and market rhetoric fails. It is, by the same token, precisely out of such conceptions that a genuinely liberatory and transformative politics can be made. 'Seize the time and the place' they would say around Tompkins Square Park and this does indeed appear an appropriate time and place to do so. If the walls are indeed coming down all over Eastern Europe then perhaps we can begin to bring them down in our own cities as well.

Acknowledgement

I am much indebted to Neil Smith for information and ideas about the struggles over Tompkins Square Park.

REFERENCES

Dahl, R. and Lindblom, C. (1953). *Politics, Economics and Welfare*. New York.

Davis, M. (1990). *City of Quartz: Excavating the Future in Los Angeles*. London.

Engels, F.

Godelier, M. (1972). *Rationality and Irrationality in Economics*. London.

Harvey, D. (1973). *Social Justice and the City*. London.

Harvey, D. (1989). *The Condition of Postmodernity*. London.

Jacobs, J. (1961). *The Death and Life of Great American Cities*. New York.

Kifner, J. (1989). 'No Miracles in the Park: Homeless New Yorkers amid Drug Lords and Slum Lords'. *International Herald Tribune*, August 1 1989, p. 6.

Marx, K. (1967). *Capital*, Vol. 1. New York.

Plato (1965). *The Republic*. Harmondsworth, Middlesex.

Rawls, J. (1971). *A Theory of Justice*. Cambridge, Mass.

Unger, R. (1987). *False Necessity: Anti-necessitarian Social Theory in the Service of Radical Democracy*. Cambridge.

Wittgenstein, L. (1967). *Philosophical Investigations*. Oxford.

Young, I. M. (1990). *Justice and the Politics of Difference*. Princeton, N.J.

PAPER BY THE SENATE OF BERLIN

**BERLIN: SOCIAL AND ENVIRONMENTAL RECONSTRUCTION
IN A UNIFYING REGION**

by

Edith Brickwell

1. Model City for the Problems of Conversion

In November 1989, in the days and nights when the wall opened, a shock wave of peace swept through the city of Berlin. People celebrated in the streets, an atmosphere of country fair and New Year's Eve sprang up. A hallucinating period of half a year followed, the citizens of Berlin were wondering about the 'Wende' - the change of tide, the new sense of freedom. A striving towards understanding, and a readiness to help were felt throughout the city. Berlin prepared to return to normality, to join the community of big cities.

However, when the GDR opened completely to the market, an economic shock wave seized the country. The run-down economy could no longer withstand the free competition of know-how, quality and price. The old system received its final blows. These facts brought a tremendous burden to both the inhabitants of the old Federal Republic and to the 'New Länder'. The tensions owing to different values, the dislocation of people and jobs, the crisis of identity, the sharing of funds - all these frictions of reunification are felt most distinctively in Berlin:

- Large enterprises are on the edge of breakdown. Their machines do not meet modern standards any more and they have not been maintained properly or renewed in time. Too many workers are badly trained, the products designed for a closed market in the eastern countries. The factories make their workers redundant and become derelict sites, with contaminated soil.

- Houses need repair desperately. Many flats are empty. The property situation is unclear. In many cases there are claims of former owners. If investors are found, the tenants often cannot afford the increased rent following modernisation, as salaries are still very low in the eastern part of the city.

- The eastern city's infrastructure is completely worn out; gas pipes are unsafe, water pipes leak, the district heating system needs repair and the power plants and heating stations have to be completely renewed as they do not meet environmental standards at all.

- Many people are losing their jobs and the unemployment rates are rapidly increasing. Almost every eastern family has experienced the threat of an unpredictable economic future. Looking for new jobs, they learn in many instances that their professional training and past professional experience are regarded as obsolete - in the western modern world the new citizens encounter different systems of thinking, marketing and machine operation, for which they have to retrain.

- Even weightier changes are in store for the young people - if they come from poor families in disadvantaged peripheral areas their path to integration may be very long. Gone are the menacing GDR police, the patronising socialist state, which once imposed on-the-job resocialisation. Western-standard social work is not yet fully operational as the whole administration has to be rebuilt in East Berlin. Meanwhile disoriented youths without roots express their fear in vandalism.

- In the west of the city business strives for quick money to be made in the east; these economic dynamics segregate social groups in West Berlin and widen the emotional gap between East and West. The pressures of the new functions as a capital raise prices and rents but not yet salaries. Individual income is decreased by the loss of former subsidies and by added taxes, to finance the tasks in the eastern areas.

The Berlin Wall has come down but you can still feel the potholes in the streets when you drive into the east. Berlin now realises its split economy and segregation of minds. The citizens of Berlin have to face the fact that they are back to the normality of a metropolis. They have to react to an accumulation of poverty factors and counterbalance social segregation. However, Berlin is the first European city which practices post-socialist conversion and social cohesion in the new framework of European unification - this means **social integration in a new dimension of quality, quantity and speed**.

2. Environment - A Field of Action for Strategic Intervention towards Social Cohesion

When we - the western-trained specialists - could first walk through the wall, we were appalled by the state of the environment in the eastern districts. Soil is heavily polluted by ninety years of uncontrolled industrial exploitation, urban greenery is hardly existent, industrial installations need radical change. This diagnosis calls for substantial environmental investments in the public and private sector.

In the private sector a heavy land use speculation is under way. As Berlin prepares for new functions as the capital of a larger Germany and the interface of east-west trading and integration, the pressure on land prices is high. The gigantic process of privatisation of the GDR economy undergone by the federal Treuhand Agency cannot counteract sufficiently.

Consequently, the Federal Government and the Land of Berlin have to organise strategic intervention. Public funds have to be made available for the poor quarters and a local business community has to be developed and assisted. The unemployed need to find a network for consultation, training and reintegration into the labour market.

In the context of urban renewal Berlin has developed a modest tradition of combining investments with social merits. The basic idea was to introduce actions for social reintegration into the world of development business. Investors in housing, infrastructure, commerce and industry were publicly subsidised to engage long-term unemployed, underqualified and handicapped people. Social integration was incorporated into urban renewal, people living on the fringe of a working and learning society were adopted into the centre of its activities. The method of urban and social reconstruction was the combination of public assistance programmes and private investment into coherent financing schemes for urban renewal projects.

The strategy of co-ordinated investments was developed gradually on a small scale at times when, in West Berlin, the squatters already occupied more than 2,000 houses. New solutions were sought as to how to appease youth - a home and a meaningful training were given to them, in the context of rebuilding the houses they occupied. In the framework of environmental measures for small and medium-size enterprises the thought of social integration, in combination with public investment subsidies, was further pursued, an increasing unemployment rate enhanced the means and public awareness for such programmes.

When the wall came down and the tremendous needs for investment and social reorientation in the eastern boroughs started to show, city politicians adopted the matching money strategy at large; now it was decided to co-ordinate all public funds to merge social, environmental and economic reconstruction in a new dimension. Reintegration of unemployed people should no longer remain a side track of social security activity. Large public and private activities such as subway construction, water pollution abatement, industrial rehabilitation, renewal of urban greenery, etc. are accomplished - at least in part - by specially funded unemployed. A portion of their work is devoted to professional training and qualification.

A 'Framework for Labour Policies' (1) gives the guidelines for direct job subsidies; its largest part (50% of the budget) is devoted to environmental measures. The 'Environmental Improvement Programme' (2), contains the co-ordinated investment projects; it was consequently developed by the Ministries of Labour and the Environment respectively. The programme has a scope of two billion Deutschmark over a period of seven years. It is designed to create 12,000 jobs, half of which are directly subsidised (3) over one to two year periods. The programme covers all important aspects of environmental improvement - activities to renew industrial installations; to modernise technical infrastructure and traffic; to clean the soil and water and to improve urban greenery.

It is a difficult task to start and run such a programme. Many new regulations have to be found and existing ones readjusted. For each type of project a model of how to match money has to be created. This is a matter of the art of finance and co-ordination. More complex problems of a social character stand behind the organisational schemes. Shall the programme management follow a top-down approach by way of colonising the 'new' areas of the city, or how are the ways of bottom-up - cross group co-ordination to be pursued?

The field of social tensions between east and west displays itself in a different texture than the one known from the classical urban renewal-model cities situation; it is less a 'vertical' set of bottom and top, rather a horizontal matter of sharing power between people with two different value schemes stemming from two divergent systems of professional experience. The people coming out of the eastern context have had ample training and qualifications, but on other kinds of machines, with differing production goals and a completely contrasting philosophy of work; all materials should be used and reused as much as possible; improvisation was highly appreciated, the abundance of human labour taken for granted. The western system, on the contrary, relies on international sharing of experience; the best technical solution is to choose the highest machine and material quality, demanding as little labour input as possible and offering a high output of commodities. Information has a very high value - the amount of materials, trips and environmental hazards connected with a certain technical scheme are regularly underestimated.

In the economic reconstruction of East Berlin these two worlds clash in a most direct form - whether new value systems will emerge remains to be seen. For the time being it is the 'eastern' partners who undergo an identity crisis and bear the load of anxieties, change and adaption. My guess is this will not last for long, as strong tensions are building up. Both sides will have to give up and change values. Hence, identities will be sacrificed during the merging process of the two parts of the city. The value of improvisation may be redetected in a world which needs the decrease of material flow for the sake of the environment. Technologies for the city which are not hi-tech, but environmentally and socially feasible, may call for reorientation of professional training also of the Westerners; a complex city society demands for new thinking, logic and managerial instruments. Both sides are involved in a struggle of learning and doing to break through to a new 'Upswing' (4). This way the identity of the future starts to build up.

The melting pot of Berlin is a laboratory for reconstructing Europe. Amsterdam and Paris, Portugal and Czechoslovakia will soon share this experience - on a much larger scale and in a far more complex way; Europe has to retrain its mind. Economic conversion cannot be an elitist take-over. Integration ought not to stay a matter of us and them. Europe is a matter of US.

Notes:

1. Arbeitsmarktpolisches Rahmenprogramm, the Senate of Berlin, decided upon in May 1991.
2. Ökologisches Sanierungsprogramm Berlin, the Senate of Berlin, decided upon in May 1991.
3. In the framework of so-called 'Arbeitsbeschaffungsmaßnahmen' - job provision activities - 90-100% of the costs of labour as well as costs for materials and machines up to 20%, or 30% of the labour costs are reimbursed by the Federal Employment Agency (Bundesanstalt für Arbeit). These jobs have to be additional to routine investments and in a non-profit context, e.g. non-profit agencies can send workers on this programme to rehabilitate schools, urban greenery, etc.
4. The 'Aufschwung Ost' - 'Upswing East' - is a federal financing programme for public expenditure, which is distributed between the New Länder according to their population rate. A fair amount of Berlin's share has been spent on environmental improvement (62 million Deutschmark).

SELECTED PAPERS AND CONCLUSIONS OF

THE WORKING GROUP

ON

TRANSPORTATION, ENVIRONMENT AND SOCIAL INTEGRATION IN CITIES

COMPOSITION OF WORKING GROUP 1

TRANSPORTATION, ENVIRONMENT AND SOCIAL INTEGRATION IN CITIES

Chairman: Prof. Enrique Calderón
Universidad Politécnica, Madrid

Rapporteur: Dr Margaret Grieco
University of Oxford

Expert Introducing the Working Group: Dr Laurie Pickup
Transport and Travel Research, Oxford

Speakers-Participants:

1. Dr Antje Flade
   Institut Wohnen und Umwelt, Darmstadt

2. Dr Klaus Schlabbach
   Town Planning Authority, Darmstadt

3. Mr Josep Maria Pascual i Esteve
   Barcelona City Council

4. Mrs Lia Vasconcelos
   New University of Lisbon

5. Dr William Cannell
   SAST/MONITOR, DG XII, Commission of the European Communities

6. Prof. Chris Jensen-Butler
   Institute of Political Science, University of Aarhus

TRANSPORT, ENVIRONMENT AND SOCIAL INTEGRATION IN CITIES

by

Laurie Pickup
Transport and Travel Research
Oxford

1. Introduction: Mobility as a Key European Issue

The rapidly growing European economy has brought with it an explosion in mobility. It has been estimated that a 1% growth of the GNP generates a 1.5% growth in passenger transport and up to a 3% growth in the transport of goods (European Commission, 1991). Transport now plays a very important role in the development of the European economy. It represents more than 6% of GNP, whilst more than 10% of the average family budget is devoted to transport. The increase in personal mobility in Europe and the desire for greater mobility has been one of the most noticeable social developments of recent decades. However, not all aspects of mobility have increased. Furthermore, the advantages and disadvantages of mobility have been unevenly distributed within European Society; this is of vital importance in developing policies for social cohesion. As the pressure on transport systems within European systems continue, Europe has been witnessing static or declining levels of mobility in housing and labour markets. Taken from a social perspective, mobility now represents an increasingly important dimension of what has been termed the emerging 'dual society' within European Community cities.

The freedom of mobility and the choice it provides clearly have important social, economic and psychological benefits to individuals. However, it needs to be stressed that, for satisfying most needs, mobility is a derived demand providing accessibility to opportunities. Greater mobility also involves considerable social and environmental costs which equally need to be recognised. Increased mobility is not necessarily 'a good thing' if the consequences of higher mobility for some produces both unacceptable social costs to the community at large and negative elements for social cohesion. It is important that it is viewed as a multifaceted issue and not solely as a transport issue. Mobility was an important issue in the Treaty of Rome. What is clear is that, from the policy perspective, mobility issues will be as prominent in discussions of European social cohesion beyond 1992 as they were when the original treaty was signed.

This chapter attempts to set the background for the transport aspects of this book. It firstly outlines the growth in European travel mobility and its consequent problems. It then focuses on the motivation for travel and discusses the groups defined as being transport disadvantaged. The final section discusses the forecasts for travel demand in Europe and the policy responses required in order to prevent the further social marginalisation of these groups (Pickup 1990).

2. European Cities – A Vast Canvas of Change

Most European cities face similar problems, namely the flight of capital and population, the decline in employment in traditional industries, the need to renew the urban fabric and infrastructure, and an increase in social and cultural questions caused by the concentrations of disadvantaged people within particular locations in the city. Coupled with these factors is a physical dimension as cities have an ageing capital stock with respect to housing, factories and infrastructure. Renewal programmes have generally not kept pace with this progress. Recently, there has been a switch back to rehabilitation and the notion of 'community' as local resistance to large scale development.

City functions have radically changed with more complex and diversified roles. Superimposed on these structural changes is the social perspective which is a crucial part of urban regeneration. Affluent and mobile middle classes are the catalysts for change with respect to housing and environmental conditions and in maintaining local services. However, there has been an increase in wealth inequalities as the population polarises into the mobile rich and the constrained poor. This social inequality has a spatial dimension (Banister and Pickup, 1989).

3. The Influence of Transport

Transport has been an important facilitator of change in European cities. By far the most important reason for this has been the rise in car ownership in all EC member states. This has radically altered the pattern of residences, jobs and services and has had repercussions for the viability of public transport modes. Resulting land use changes have also reduced the number of activities easily accessible on foot or by bicycle.

Car ownership has increased five-fold in the EC member states over the last thirty years. There are now some 120 million motor cars in Europe. Nevertheless, the level of car ownership still lags substantially behind the US average (300 versus 550 cars per 1,000 inhabitants), indicating that further growth can be expected. The car has altered the way we live and think and will continue to do so as car ownership levels increase. To the car user, it offers real advantages which alternative forms of transport can never match except in congested city centres. The car has a unique flexibility, offering door-to-door mobility, it has a high level of privacy and comfort and it really forms an extension of the personal (defensible) space of the home - part of the home than can be detached and re-attached at will.

The effects of these trends on travel patterns have been dramatic. For example, in the UK, total personal mileage between 1965 and 1985 rose by 60%. However, travel by bus and coach in 1985 was only two thirds of its 1965 level and rail use had also remained static over the period. The increase was entirely due to car use which doubled at the expense of only a 5% increase in total household expenditure on travel. People were making on average two more journeys per week in 1985/86 than they made in 1965, thirteen and eleven respectively; however, the average weekly distance travelled rose from 112 to 160 kilometres (UK Department of Transport, 1989).

The private benefits to car users witnessed by this growth in mobility conceal considerable costs. As a result of higher car ownership, public transport demand has fallen in some states. The decline reflects both a primary transfer of passengers from bus and rail to the car, and in secondary effects such as increased fares and decline in service levels to compensate for fewer passengers - the so-called 'downward vicious spiral' (Webster et al, 1985). This has adversely affected the opportunities of remaining public transport users. In addition, with city decentralisation, not only are average work journey lengths increasing, but the relative minority of commuters who travel much longer distances to work is also increasing. The provision of modern transport systems and infrastructure is enabling many workers, by choice or constraint, to reside further from their jobs as part of a commuter lifestyle (Pickup, 1987).

Whether commuting on a daily or weekly basis, the existence of substantial numbers of city commuters has done much to change the social structure of communities within the city hinterland from which they commute. What has been characteristic of recent increases in travel mobility is firstly the growth in orbital 'suburb to suburb' journeys, badly suited to public transport provision, and secondly the growth of discretionary mobility, consequent with more diverse family and friendship networks and the growth of the leisure society.

For freight transport the switch from rail to road modes and from public to private shippers reflects the advantages which accrue to the individual firm in having its own vehicle fleet with increased flexibility and control. The dispersal of industry to peripheral and road-accessible sites has made rail less appropriate. However, the public costs imposed by a road-based freight industry are considerable. Their impact, particularly the largest vehicles, is greater than that for cars in environmental, social and energy costs.

It is clear that the continuing growth in traffic volumes has not been matched by the growth in infrastructure provision. The European Conference of Ministers of Transport predicted in 1991 that 'bottle-necks will inevitably occur in land transport infrastructures in Europe' in the 1990s. These problems will exacerbate the negative social effects of road transport on human safety and on the environment (European Commission, 1991).

- Every year in the Community, around 55,000 people are killed on the roads, 1.7 million are injured and 150,000 permanently handicapped. The financial cost of this is estimated to be more than 50 billion ECU per year; the social cost cannot be measured.

- The cost of traffic in the Community is estimated to be around 500 billion ECU per year. A substantial part is due to congestion and poor routing, additional road building will not necessarily solve congestion as more journeys would be created as a result.

- Vehicle emissions contribute significantly towards the total of environmental pollution which is estimated to cost the European Community between 5 and 10 million ECU per year.

From the social perspective, superimposed on these other issues, is the basic inequality of the car. Not everybody has access to it and this will always be the case. Some will be too old or too young to drive, others will be constrained by disability, cost or gender from purchasing and running cars. Thus, there is polarisation between those with unrestricted access to a car and those with limited or no access - the 'transport disadvantaged'.

4. Transport Choices

Travel mobility and travel behaviour is a complex process. The demand for mobility derives from the underlying activity requirements of different social groups. Thus, a proper understanding of travel mobility issues requires an analysis of the ways in which the underlying activity of individuals and households interact, and this affects patterns of travel behaviour. The opportunities and constraints which affect the mobility levels of different social groups are not unique to travel, but are those factors which generally affect these groups in all areas of life. For example, mobility levels among the elderly and disabled are dictated by frailty, those of children by dependency and so on.

Gender and working status predominate as major determinants of travel behaviour. While the activity patterns of different social groups show a high degree of routine and habit, travel patterns exhibit considerable variability in both destinations visited and times travelled. Another aspect of growing importance in travel behaviour is the sequencing of activities in multi-stage journeys which underline the need to view elements of daily or weekly travel behaviour as interdependent (Grieco, Pickup and Whipp, 1989).

An important developing view on travel mobility is the idea that decisions to acquire or dispose of cars, and thus the decisions to use other travel modes, are not made on a daily or weekly basis. Rather, they are now seen as part of a longer-term decision when there is more strategic reappraisal of overall life circumstances. This may be a response to moving home or a change of job or household structure.

In addition to car acquisition, an important element has been the household level where mobility is distributed between household members. There is a clear pattern of principal users and supplementary users within households; the 'notion' that household members compete for car use may be misleading. Recent research in the United Kingdom has found strong personal attachments to cars (Stokes and Hallett, 1990). Important factors are the perceived rights to use the car and its ease of transferability between household members. In addition to these household factors, the supply of alternative transport modes is also relevant.

Car allocation decisions are thus household not individual decisions; they effectively determine the mobility levels of all household members. In addition to those in households for whom car ownership is simply too expensive, few people will have a realistic choice of travel mode.

5. Transport Disadvantage

Transport disadvantage is a relative term which relates strongly to access to cars. The increasing popularity of car use has reduced public transport use. Policies, while supporting public transport operations during difficult years with larger subsidies, have implicitly favoured car use subsidies by not charging motorists the full social costs of their road use. For some people, car ownership, and the higher mobility it offers, are matters of choice. Any disadvantage that results from the absence of a car is accepted in return for a higher disposable income which may accrue. However, for certain households, choice about car ownership is, in practice, virtually non-existent. There is a strong relationship between wealth and car ownership; the elderly and the poor constitute the majority of households for whom car ownership is not practical. Lifts in other people's cars do not compensate for the absence of a household car; such people make a high proportion of their journeys by bus or on foot. Both these groups may also experience problems in their use of other transport modes, due to low income and frailty which further limits their mobility.

In addition to the mobility problems of people not owning cars, a degree of deprivation is also apparent among those living in car-owning households who either cannot drive or who find a car unavailable at times when it is required, e.g. many women and young people.

6. Social Cohesion and Groups at Risk

Concepts of a dual society within Europe have been emerging for some years, associated with processes of social marginalisation and exclusion. Previous research by the European Foundation has attempted to define systematic processes which shape the levels of opportunity and living conditions of urban residents. Three basic processes are identified: segmentation, segregation and marginalisation. The compound effects of these processes place many social groups at differing degrees of risk: groups such as the unemployed, low income families, young and old, migrant workers and so on. Risk is greatest for those persons who fall into several groups simultaneously (Burton et al, 1986).

Travel mobility is a clear factor defining social segments; it is also important in the socio-spatial process of segregation. Transport disadvantaged persons are also those suffering general social marginalisation. Marginalisation refers to a set of interrelated processes which are creating new forms of poverty with Europe, i.e. the long-term unemployed, the young never employed, the low mobile poor elderly, single parent families, etc. Such groups have been shown to suffer from persistent exclusion. Such social groups, though disparate in character, are forming an expanding minority of people whose lifestyles are qualitatively distinct from the rest of society. Race, class, and gender also cut across such groups, further complicating their definition.

These groups, not surprisingly, are those who suffer the greatest mobility disadvantages and whose lifestyles are affected as a result. Policies have tended to focus on specific needs of certain groups rather than an overall approach to the problem. However, this policy can further the process of marginalisation by explicitly identifying and labelling certain groups of disadvantage. The rest of this section focuses on those population groups who are marginalised as a result of their lower travel mobility, pointing to the key characteristics of their disadvantage.

6.1 The long-term unemployed

Of 16 million unemployed in the EC in 1987, 8 million had been out of work for one year or more, a figure which had doubled since 1983.

The issues facing the long-term unemployed involve many problems relating to loss of skill and economic changes within local economy. Declining mobility is an element in the progressive alienation of such workers for both job and social networks. Declining income also limits the ability of the long-term unemployed to consider a residential move as a solution. For most of the long-term unemployed, adjustment to their circumstances involves making the best use of their potential mobility within the local labour market.

Job search is a difficult process for the long-term unemployed. In addition to deficiencies in skill and general job shortage, the long-term unemployed become separated from the working environment and the formal and informal networks of job information it contains. Over time, their reliance for information falls back on job centres or private employment agencies. Workers' available travel mobility influences the extent of the area in which jobs are sought. Most of the long-term unemployed are limited to the opportunities provided by the public transport network. Research in Manchester (Hedges and Hopkin, 1981), showed that travel mobility and travel costs influenced job search patterns of the unemployed rather than the number of job opportunities they were aware of. Work by Quinn (1986) underlines the additional impact of environmental knowledge in job search among the long-term unemployed. Workers he studied sought jobs only in familiar locations. Particularly among young long-term unemployed workers, jobs were not sought in some accessible areas due to an inadequate knowledge of the city. This underlines the importance of the support role played by information in creating new job opportunities. In addition to benefits which might be available for attending interviews, the searches of the long-term unemployed would be assisted by concessionary fares on public transport particularly for those resident on peripheral housing estates where costs of travel are proportionately higher in most cases.

An important aspect of mobility deprivation among the long-term unemployed is the knock-on effect which the resultant social isolation has for the well-being and cohesion of whole communities. Figure 1 shows a range of quotes from detailed interviews with long-term unemployed and low income families on outer housing estates in Merseyside (Pickup, 1988). The statements clearly underline the extent to which low travel mobility and labour market exclusion combine to affect the life and outlook of the whole community. Such estates were planned in an era where planning policies supported the provision of cheap public transport.

Figure 1: Transport and Social Marginalisation on Merseyside, UK

> 'People can't be marooned on an estate and they also need better facilities. They still need the means of getting out. A lot of young people...there will be an explosion, I can see it coming; evenings and weekends they're marooned here, they feel left out.'(R1). 'You need to get away sometimes even if you do not have all the facilities, you still need to get away occasionally for a break and if there was a better bus service, it would be happening more often.'(R2)

'Transport affects your whole way of life; it's part of the whole thing, it's interwoven with everything, the social life, the way of life.'(R1). 'It becomes an enclosed community doesn't it?'(R2). 'You can't have one without the other, if you've got bad bus fares and services, every other part of your life is going to be hampered by it.'(R1). 'Geographical mobility is a necessity. Now all right, we've got sports facilities and that type of thing but then, by having that sort of mentality, you're a prisoner and I think the only means we've got is the bus service for getting out of the estate.'(R3).

'The problem is why travel when you've got no money. You can't go anywhere, do anything, just stay at home don't you? A lot of people aren't used to travelling now. Before deregulisation (deregulation), there is a tradition around here that people don't go far from their home place anyway. A lot of people are used to being like that.'

'It's just one other factor, unemployment hit us, this (higher bus fares) has hit us, what next.'(R1). 'They've been kicked in the teeth and kicked in the teeth so often and this was just the straw that broke the camel's back; it's not one thing on its own.'(R2)*

Source: Pickup, 1988.

The added value of social trips to this group is often underestimated. For example, a study of the OECD on the effects of economic recession on travel behaviour felt that the long-term unemployed 'will have less reason to travel to spend their benefits' (Bly, 1984). In contrast, research in the Netherlands by Baanders et al (1984) found that the unemployed made more journeys due to fear of becoming isolated. Transport costs were thus excluded from any economies they made. Studies conflict as to the impact of unemployment on expressed travel mobility. On public transport, the loss of commuting trips is partially offset by increasing discretionary travel, although as the Figure indicates, the tendency is for a very local lifestyle to be adopted within walking distance of home; a lifestyle in which apathy, alienation and inertia flourish.

6.2 Low income families

The numbers of individuals living in households where the net income was below half of the mean income of their country were compared for all EC states in a recent study (Room, 1989). Between 1975 and 1985, the study found that the number of the EC residents living below the poverty line rose by 5.3 million, 83% of growth had occurred since 1980. While in 1975, the poor in the EC comprised 12.8% of the population, it had risen to 13.9% by 1985.

---

*   The terms (R1), (R2) and (R3) refer to different members of the discussion groups.

The effects of income are less straightforward. Such complexity arises because income affects all social groups, and therefore compounds other mobility constraints which may exist. Furthermore, the impacts of low income affect all other items of household spending. Thus the results of increased financial pressure may not result in a reduction in mobility but in a redistribution of other expenditure. The nature of poverty thus makes the tracing of cause and effect complex (Pickup, 1988).

Regarding travel mobility, low income families have received rather less attention than might have been expected. The relationship between car ownership and wealth is well established. Among the low paid it is unrealistic to think of car ownership as the result of a free decision and they are generally excluded from this form of mobility. Furthermore, many low income car owners have difficulty in paying for running and maintenance costs and only use their cars for essential trips. This in turn reduces the likelihood of non-car owning family and friends requesting lifts.

Low income households are therefore mainly captive to the slower and less flexible modes; public transport, cycling and walking. Many are disadvantaged by high public transport fare levels. Policies within many member states to subsidise public transport operations has done much to cushion the effects of increasing operating costs on the less wealthy bus, tram and rail user.

A detailed study of lifestyles among low income households in Merseyside, UK (Pickup, 1988) revealed that mobility was seen as a vital part of the functioning and survival of the local community - shown in Figure 1. It also showed how the poor budgeted for their bus fares to get around - shown in Figure 2. Essentially the ways of coping with the increased costs of mobility were:

(i)   To consolidate longer trips into several trips for many purposes, making use of reduced price travel tickets for unlimited daily travel.

(ii) To travel less, to make short walk journeys in the local area, to travel as a family group, to walk longer distances.

(iii) Quite often, the cost of occasional journeys such as medical, hospital visiting and job search were prohibitive or only possible by borrowing money.

While some of the poor did budget for essential trips such as for access to school or work, most paid for travel 'out of pocket'. This made families susceptible to lack of money at the end of their state benefit period so money was borrowed, journeys were cancelled or long walk trips made instead. Particularly vulnerable in this respect were journeys to visit friends and relatives (particularly older dependent parents), seen as very important journeys but foregone if money was tight. Furthermore, given the low quality of neighbourhoods, many trips were arranged when people could be accompanied and important networks of social support were established to cope with travel events such as emergencies which required transport or friendship networks around those who had cars and could accompany/be accompanied by others (Grieco et al, 1989).

Figure 2: Budgeting for Travel Mobility - the Poor on Merseyside

Hardship

Borrow money - 'Well you know how it is, say I've a few pounds left if I've to go into town; well I scrape what coppers I've got on me and I may go to me mother's and she'll give me a couple of bob for me bus fares to go the next day'.

No money - 'I do a lot of walking now, at the weekend mostly. I get me benefit on a Thursday, but fortnightly. So in other words the following week, say I got no money that week, I do a lot more walking than the week before cos I had money then. In that week I get me money, I travel around on buses but when it starts getting low I do walk it the following week. I walk from here to me mother's (Aintree), I've timed it, an hour and ten minutes, I walk to Fazakerley but that only takes me 25 minutes. If I had the money I'd get the buses but you see I can't afford some of the bus fares. When me money comes through I get Zone tickets (i.e. Saveaway Tickets) make me visits.' Do you find it difficult budgeting for bus fares? 'Well, that's where the walking comes into it see.'

'I wanted to change to weekly but he wanted to know why, I said I couldn't cope with it. He said put it in the bank. The first week you're OK, for the second week you're paupers. I've had to walk cos I've had no money, but very often though.'

No budgeting

'I couldn't say I put anything aside for bus fares. I can't even think like that.'

Budgeting

'Well like we're on benefit but like I say you gotta pay them if you want to go somewhere haven't you? I get benefit every two weeks, that's why I shop you see with the taxi. I've always got pence in me pocket, I'm a very good budgeter. All the slum you get just put all that away in a jar and you manage.'

Source: Pickup, 1988.

6.3 The young

The mobility situation of children is clearly dominated by their dependency; that of teenagers and young adults is more concerned with the transition to independent living. Their situation is associated both with the quality of urban and rural life and the change from full-time education to the labour market.

The variety of life experienced by young children is dependent on their parents and other adult family members. Many are restricted to the immediate home and local environment as a result of the problems parents face escorting them on longer journeys; problems which are much reduced where the family has a car available for such visits. Research in London (Hillman et al, 1973) showed that the age of children affected the frequency with which mothers escorted them on public transport; particularly where prams and pushchairs were involved. Mothers escorting children were more critical of poor service quality and access to bus stops than were bus users in general.

Although children can only travel by car when both a vehicle and a driver is available, the disadvantage may only affect certain types of journey. Children's lower mobility is recognised in the distribution of schools in most member states, they are not usually responsible for shopping, longer visits being made as part of a family group. However, they are likely to require independent mobility for some social and leisure activities to broaden the playing environment. In the absence of a car, they are dependent on walking, buses, trams, cars or (in the case of teenagers) cycles. The presence of several cars in a household does not necessarily provide children with greater car availability.

The structure of recreational provision is not well suited to the mobility levels of children, who will probably wish to use the facilities independently. Research by Town (1980) has shown that children aged five to ten years from households headed by unskilled and semi-skilled workers have significantly less expressed mobility for social and recreational purposes than do other households, with a higher proportion of their journeys being made on foot.

Lower relative mobility is thus one component restricting the socio-cultural environment of children in deprived areas. A low journey rate for recreational purposes may of course reflect lack of interest in the activity rather than a lack of travel. However, it has been recognised in many educational area projects that one cause of poor educational performance among young children is the narrowness of their home environment, coupled with their ability to play constructively (Town, 1980).

A similar argument can be advanced to explain the lower rate of social travel by young children. It has been shown that children from 'deprived' backgrounds tend to develop fewer and less stable friendships. Except in rural areas, the opportunities for making friends locally will mean that the availability of motor transport is not a prerequisite for making some social journeys. Travel mobility is not the only cause of a local lifestyle being adopted by children from marginal social groups and a number of factors affecting the family residential and employment circumstances are also important to consider in the wider context.

6.4 The elderly

Europeans of both sexes are now living longer; the European population is ageing. While the forecasts for different EC member states fluctuate, predictions indicate a steady growth in the elderly population throughout Europe particularly after 2000. An important demographic feature of most member states is the increasing proportion of 'very old' people over 75 years. In Denmark, for example, the proportion of people aged 85 and over is projected to rise from 7.2% to 11.6% between 1985 and 2000. Much of this is the result of increasing life expectancy among women (Paoli, 1989.)

While the proportion of car licence holders in old age continues to grow rapidly, most pensioners are reliant on public transport to travel beyond walking distance. Concessionary fares for the elderly cushion the impact of travel costs on mobility. However, further problems result from declining health and physical capabilities; such factors may limit the ability to drive, although, since the elderly grew up at a time when car ownership was less common, many have never driven at all. Declining health also affects walking ability. Such reasons as the height of the entrance step and the problems of reaching a seat within a moving vehicle are also important factors they consider in travelling. The same health problems are likely to affect both bus use and walking, as a result, those old people with walking difficulties are also those most likely to be unable to use buses; these old people are also more likely to live alone, and to have lowest incomes.

Where mobility among the elderly is particularly low, the demand for additional mobility is limited. This is marked among the elderly disabled, who require special design features of vehicles and door-to-door transport service. One study of this group noted that they only desired additional mobility for one or more shopping and social trips per week (Hopkin and Town, 1978). The reason for this appears to be that the constraints on mobility extend to the facility itself; i.e. access to buildings at the destination or the ability to conduct the activity. In this case, improved transport alone is not enough. Their low mobility aspirations possibly also reflect the extent to which they recognise that there are practical and financial limits on what can be provided. Particular problems arise here in providing access to dispersed locations such as hypermarkets or hospitals.

Studies of mobility among the very old state that they 'do not go out as often as they would like'. While improvements to public or special needs transport are cited as ways in which their limited mobility could be enhanced, the majority of reasons for not travelling relate to the need to be accompanied or their need to care for another elderly person which ties them to the home. The caring activities carried out by the elderly themselves is an important role often going unrecognised. The mobility and life quality of the elderly is very dependent on the social and organisational network surrounding them. For example, old people who live in multi-generational households are less likely to shop or go out for social visits than those who live alone or with another elderly person.

6.5 Women

It is argued that women's low mobility is a product of their gender role, a role which affects all areas of their life-style and not merely their travel circumstances. While studies have implicitly assumed that women's low mobility is a product of, and a response to, their social role, few studies have placed an evaluation of their circumstances explicitly in this wider context to taken account of women's changing roles and aspirations. Some feminists have argued that this lack of explicit recognition of women's social position in research has lead to a false assessment of their circumstances.

There exist well established tendencies for women's labour participation to increase in all EC member countries. This is in response to economic pressures and the choice to pursue a job or career at the same time as the peak child rearing age. The fastest rise in employed women is among the twenty-five to forty-five year age group; i.e. women with decreasing child care responsibilities, and also women with younger dependent children. Family structures are changing accordingly. Much of the impetus for the growth in employed mothers has been growth in part-time job opportunities. Essentially, the increase in women's paid employment has been of a type which would not adversely affect maternal and other domestic commitments.

Women's residential and employment mobility is usually constrained by the nature of their job within the family. Thus, outside the relatively small group of professional women workers, many are constrained in their job search to a fixed residential location. Indeed, many women returning to work after child-rearing find that a residence which has been an adequate family home environment is not accessible for local job markets given the time constraints on their activities and the low travel mobility they suffer.

Despite women's low mobility, the rise in the number of working women, particularly employed mothers, has substantially increased women's travel needs. A housewife returning to part-time work increases her daily travel by 30% on average. Decisions to re-enter the labour force thus include an important travel time component.

Several studies (e.g. McDowell, 1981) have argued that the built environment has been slow to respond to the spatial implications of the growth in working women. By changing the context of their lives, women have placed new demands on the planned environment. For example, the increasing number of working mothers has radically altered patterns of family life and the whole pattern of social interaction within residential areas. In addition, the previously 'private' domestic role has been partially transferred into the 'public' sphere changing the travel requirements of women and the timing and location of the journeys they make (Grieco et al, 1989).

Where planning agencies are continuing to centralise activities on a larger scale (e.g. the construction of district general hospitals on urban perimeter green field sites), the additional costs imposed on individuals are not fully taken into account. These costs not only involve travel costs and the amount of time consumed, but also the increased problems in the scheduling of activities to gain access to more dispersed facilities. For gaining access to some facilities, such as hospitals, additional problems in rescheduling activities can lead to additional anxiety and stress (Pickup, 1988).

Within households, there would appear to be a growing latent demand for car use among wives. For example, when a car was available it was used. However, these arrangements would still deny women the use of the car for regular commuting needs. In addition to the independence and convenience which accrue from car availability, safety emerges as a significant factor. Access to a car provides women with a 'defensible space' for travelling. It may free them to make journeys to certain locations and at certain times of the day when journeys would not otherwise have been undertaken. Furthermore, there is a tendency for women in certain social groups to acquire driving licences at a faster rate than women generally (e.g. women from ethnic minority groups).

While many women do organise lifts to work, the very flexibility in working hours which has provided women with greater job opportunities militates against organising regular lifts. If women are to obtain a better matching of work and domestic timetables this will inevitably lead to a demand among working mothers for greater parallel flexibility in commuting modes of the sort that only private transport can currently offer. While all the evidence suggests that women's access to cars is likely to increase in coming years (and this will both help and be a response to their employment circumstances), the majority of women still cannot drive a car and the cost of learning to drive remains substantial. The more optimistic picture among those households where wives are the main users of the household car must not cloud the poorer situation of the majority of women who cannot drive. Increasing numbers of working women rely to a greater extent on public transport than men to meet their commuting requirements. Work on women's mobility by Pickup (1985) suggests that within woman's limited labour market, they could substantially increase incomes if able to commute beyond the local area and furthermore, that they are constrained from doing so by gender role activity constraints rather than travel costs.

There are three types of low travel mobility which arise among women as a result of their gender role. The first derives from the impact of their family role on patterns of women's car availability. The second relates to the impact of gender related tasks (both home and non-home based) on women's access to opportunities. The third relates to the problems deriving specifically from the conditions under which women travel; escorting children and the growing fear of physical assault which deters many from going out at all, particularly by public transport.

Consolidation, reallocation, delegation or loss of tasks is necessary when women consider returning to the labour market; even a part-time job requires reallocation of up to thirty hours of domestic activities each week. While the relationship between time spent in child care and employment is strongly negative for women (Jones et al, 1983), the relationship between domestic constraints and their job choices is less clear. Some housework activities can be easily rescheduled between fixed activities. Others, like preparing meals, in some communities assume the importance of a fixed constraint against job choice. The consequence of activity organisation for the well-being and health of women also should not be underestimated. It is clear that tightly scheduled activity patterns have adverse effects on the well-being of women both in the short term and longer term. The European Foundation has undertaken research on this issue (Costa, 1986; Hildebrandt, 1986). Studies were undertaken in the Netherlands and Italy of the effects of long and short work journeys on the health of workers. Results confirmed that the incidence of reported health complaints were greater among women travellers. Most complaints were psychosomatic indicating the presence of an overall more stressful situation than men travelling in similar commuting situations.

Escorting very young children is particularly disadvantageous to mothers. While some paratransit services for the disabled admit women in the advanced stages of pregnancy, young mothers escorting children with prams or folding pushchairs also have many difficulties using conventional public transport. While better shops or crèche facilities may be available by using public transport, the added problems of escorting children lead to a preference for fewer, more local journeys which is not the case for women car users. The problems posed for women by escorting, coupled with the reliance many women have on public transport, leads to them preferring the immediate local environment which, for housewives, can contribute to the problem of social isolation (Pickup, 1985). In such circumstances, daily local trips by housewives to shops and schools have an important social function for them in contrast to employed women for whom such journeys tend to be more functional.

Another important aspect of women's travelling is the fear of physical assault or sexual harassment while travelling; women require defensible space. Such fear of attack prevents many women from going out unaccompanied and particular fear exists over the use of public transport. The scale and extent of such perceptions is important (Grieco et al, 1989) given the 'necessary economies' in staffing that operators are making on their services. To combat these problems, there have been a few experiments to introduce 'safe taxi' schemes for women and 'women only' cars have been provided on some metro systems.

7. Future Strategic Policy Directions

Unless ameliorative measures are taken the growth in mobility anticipated throughout the EC in coming decades will only serve to exacerbate the social inequities in transport, which currently exist and have been described in previous sections. However, it is clear that attitudes in this area have recently changed and that potential solutions are being widened by the availability of new technologies.

Goodwin et al (1990) for the UK, defines a distinct 'watershed' in transport policy thinking. The traffic forecasts for the UK published in 1989 indicated increased traffic levels of between 83% and 142% for the period 1988 - 2018, i.e. broadly double the current levels of mobility.

In response to these forecasts and combined with an increasing concern for the environment and the quality of urban life, policy was seen to change and to move much closer to a consensus.

The implications of traffic forecasts are clear. It is simply not possible to fit the forecast volumes into the projected infrastructure. 'It follows logically that (a) whatever road construction policy is followed, the amount of traffic per unit of road will increase - congestion will get more severe or more widespread, and (b) **demand management** would therefore become the centre of transport policy; if supply cannot be matched to demand, demand has to be matched to supply' (Goodwin et al. 1990).

It is therefore likely that future transport policies will place greater emphasis on the integration of the overall system and that public transport will become centre stage in policy strategies in European cities. Local initiatives will be tailored to local requirements with certain common themes:

- A very substantial improvement in the quality and scale of public transport provision, in some cases by new light rail or other high capacity reserved track systems and in most by extensive bus priority measures. This is almost completely agreed in principle, though there is not yet agreement on how to achieve it.

- Traffic calming, both as a set of detailed engineering techniques to reduce traffic speed in residential and central areas (by speed humps, chicanes, restricted road width, etc.) and also as a general strategy to tilt the balance of advantage in favour of pedestrians and sometimes cyclists. These measures, together with pedestrianisation of a scale now more familiar in European than British cities, are designed to improve the quality of life rather than mobility as such and are a necessary component in compensating for the loss of some expectations of car access.

- Advanced traffic management systems, including automatic driver guidance and integrated signal control, to get the most efficient use out of the existing network, no longer defined as the maximum throughput of vehicles, but allowing for a deliberate safety margin between traffic levels and capacity and also making provision for priority for the most efficient classes of vehicle or other local priorities (often mentioned are buses, delivery lorries, emergency services and disabled travellers).

- There is an increasing interest in the contribution that road pricing could play in knitting together the other policies (e.g. by providing some margin of unused road space with which to deliver the environmental improvements and public transport priorities) and, unlike all physical methods of restraining car use, producing a large revenue which could be used to fund other improvements. Road pricing is politically controversial and is likely only to be acceptable if it is carried out as part of a total programme of improvements, with safeguards to ensure that the revenue is used for this programme and that groups who lose out are more than compensated with other benefits. It has another advantage; by ensuring that the prices that are charged for transport services are approximately in line with their costs, the market can work more efficiently as between the different methods of transport and the resulting traffic levels will be those that are economically merited.

- Given this logic, any assessment of the need for new road construction would follow from a consideration of how much traffic it is desirable to provide for, which will be influenced by the combined effects of the policies described. There will still be occasions when new road construction is clearly justified - for example, in connecting a new industrial or residential development to the network - but construction 'to meet demand' is no longer the core of a transport strategy. Past policies of 'do nothing' or 'do minimum' are no longer tenable. Radical moves are required with potentially difficult decisions.

- Many of the new policies advocated will apply the latest developments in new transport information technologies. Advanced road Transport Telematics (ATT) can be defined as the application of advanced telecommunications technologies in the transport sector; it covers a broad range of technologies which in turn can serve a broad range of transport and transport related functions. Innovations and cost reductions in information technology, telecommunications and broadcasting potentially offer new effective means of achieving transport objectives. If brought together to provide integrated advanced communications with better control and information systems, they will enable new, more flexible and more responsive forms of traffic management and safety systems to be created to the benefit of all road users. Not only does ATT broaden the range of transport policy options, it also enables authorities to monitor the travelling environment, identify problems quickly, and make an appropriate response. For the traveller, it also provides the possibilities for greatly improved information on travel conditions and travel opportunities. The important point about ATT is that it opens up new solutions to existing problems particularly in the areas of demand management.

8. Conclusions

In introducing this topic area, this chapter has outlined the nature of the growth in urban travel mobility in European cities, specifically its social dimension. The focus has been on identifying certain population groups in some way disadvantaged as a result of past transport policies.

It is clear that travel disadvantage, compounded with the other disadvantages such people face, serves to marginalise significant population minorities, and reduce their opportunities relative to the more mobile.

It is clear that the emerging professional and political concern on urban transport policy will favour these groups in society and thus contribute to social cohesion. It is also clear that development of new technology will assist in opening up new solutions and policy options.

What is needed is an expansion of current work on the social dimension of transport to produce concrete guidelines at a European level in order to enable the explicit inclusion of social objectives in integrated transport strategies in European cities. Such guidelines should not merely be in the form of general social targets and strategies but should also include practical design, cost and operational items with the intention of assisting marginalised transport groups. A great deal could be achieved in this area and the next stage is to draw up a practical agenda to take it forward at a European level.

REFERENCES

Baanders, A., Kramer-Nass, J. and Riujgrok, C.J. (1984). Income Decline and Travel Behaviour; Some Recent Dutch Findings. In G.R.M. Jansen, P. Nijkamp and C.J. Ruijgrok eds. <u>Transportation and Mobility in an Era of Transition</u>. Amsterdam, North Holland Elsevier Science Publishers.

Banister, D. and Pickup, L. (1989). <u>Urban Transport and Planning</u>. London, Mansell.

Bly, P.H. (1984). The Effect of the Recession on Travel Expenditure and Travel Patterns. In G.R.M. Jansen, P. Nijkamp and C.J. Ruijgrok eds, <u>Transport and Mobility in an Era of Transition</u>. Amsterdam, North Holland Elsevier Science Publishers.

Burton P., Forrest, R. and Stewart, M. (1986). Living Conditions in Urban Areas. <u>European Foundation for the Improvement of Living and Working Conditions</u>. Dublin, European Foundation.

Commission of the European Communities (1991). <u>Drive 91</u>. Brussels, EC Directorate-General XIIIF, Drive Office.

Costa, G. (1986). I risultati di uno studio italiano sugli effetti del pendolarismo sulle condizioni di salute e di sicurezza dei lavoratori. In C. Reale and V. Di Martino eds: <u>Il Pendolarismo: studio del suo impatto sulle condizioni di vita e di lavoro</u>. Roma, Istituto di Medicina Sociale.

Department of Transport (UK), (1989). <u>Transport Statistics: Great Britain</u>. London, HMSO.

Goodwin, P.B., Hallet, S., Stokes, R.G. and Kenny, F. (1991), <u>Transport: The New Realism</u>. London, Rees Jeffreys Road Fund.

Grieco, M., Pickup, L. and Whipp, R. (1989). <u>Gender, Transport and Employment</u>. Aldershot, Gower.

Hildebrandt, V.H. (1986). Results and Discussion of a Study on the Impact of Commuting on Health and Safety in the Netherlands. In C. Reale and V. Di Martino eds: <u>Il Pendolarismo: studio del suo impatto sulle condizioni di vita e di lavoro</u>. Roma, Istituto di Medicina Sociale.

Hedges, B. and Hopkin, J. (1981). Transport and the Search for Work: a Study in Greater Manchester. <u>Transport and Road Research Laboratory Supplementary Report</u>, 639, Crowthorne, TRRC.

Hillman, M., Henderson, I. and Whalley, A. (1973). Personal Mobility and Transport Policy. <u>Political and Economic Planning Broadsheet</u>, 542, London, P.E.P.

Hopkin, J. and Town, S.W. (1978). Travel Patterns among Elderly People: a Study in Guildford. <u>Transport and Road Research Laboratory Report</u>, LR850, Crowthorne, TRRL.

Jones, P., McDix, M., Clarke, M.I. and Heggie, I.G. (1983). <u>Understanding Travel Behaviour</u>. Aldershot, Gower.

McDowell, L. (1981). Capitalism, Patriarchy and the Sexual Division of Space. <u>Paper presented to the Institute of British Geographers Annual Conference</u>. University of Kent, London, IBG.

Paoli, P. (1988). Ageing and Work. <u>European Foundation for the Improvement of Living and Working Conditions</u>. Dublin, European Foundation.

Pickup, L. (1985). Women's Gender Role and its Influence on their Travel Behaviour. <u>Built Environment</u>, 10, (1), 61-69.

Pickup, L. (1987). Commuting and its Consequences in the European Community. <u>European Foundation for the Improvement of Living and Working Conditions, Consolidated Report</u>. Dublin, European Foundation.

Pickup, L. (1988). A Study to Examine the Public Transport Needs of Low Income Households with Reference to the Impacts of the 1985 Transport Act on Merseyside. <u>Oxford University Transport Studies Working Paper</u>, 410, Oxford, TSU.

Pickup, L. (1990). Mobility and Social Cohesion in the European Community - a Forward Look. <u>European Foundation for the Improvement of Living and Working Conditions</u>. Dublin, European Foundation.

Quinn (1986). Understanding Accessibility: Problems of the Unemployed. <u>The Planner</u>, 72, (1), 25-27.

Room, G. (1989). Poverty and the Single European Market. Paper presented to the DG V seminar: <u>Social Dimensions of the Internal Market and the Positions of Special Category Groups</u>. Brussels, Commission of the European Communities, 24th February.

Stokes, R. G. and Hallet, S. (1990). Attitudes to Car Ownership: the Link with Car Advertising. <u>Oxford University Transport Studies Unit Working Paper</u>, 562, Oxford, TSU.

Town, S.W. (1980). Non-transport Influences on Travel Patterns. <u>Transport and Road Research Laboratory Supplementary Report</u>, 605, Crowthorne, TRRL.

Webster, F.V., Paulley, N., Bly, P.H., Dasgupta, M. and Johnston, R.H. (1985). <u>Changing Patterns of Urban Travel</u>. Paris, OECD, European Conference of Ministers of Transport.

TRANSPORT POLICY AND SOCIAL INTEGRATION IN CITIES

by

Chris Jensen-Butler
Institute of Political Science
University of Aarhus

1. Introduction

It is a well-known fact that technological developments in the transport sector have played a key role in urban development, both for urban systems and, more important for this paper, for the internal structure, both social and economic, of cities (Borchert, 1967, Yates & Garner, 1971). Likewise, urban transport policy, which has two main components, one being investment and transport provision policy and the other being pricing policy, has profoundly affected urban structure.

In the classical models of urban structure (Alonso, 1965, Muth, 1969, Evans, 1973) urban transport plays a central role in residential segregation. These models build upon maximisation of a utility function subject to a budget constraint. The basic model has the following form:

$$\text{Max } U = U(x, l, d)$$

subject to

$$y = p_1 x + p_2 l + p_3 d$$

Where x are goods, l is land and d is distance and p1-p3 are the unit prices of these elements. The model assumes a basic trade-off between transport costs (p3d) and housing costs, represented by housing area and rent (p2l) and it is relatively easy to show that given certain reasonable assumptions about income elasticities then higher income households will tend to locate in the outer areas of the city and poorer income households in the inner areas. Whilst this idealised model is clearly inadequate to explain social segregation in cities it serves to illustrate the fact that there is a basic relationship between transport costs and social segregation.

Other theories of social segregation in cities stress other explanatory variables, such as social distance or cultural distance. Nevertheless transport costs enter into many of the models proposed to explain segregation (for example, Timms, 1975).

The work of Hägerstrand (1971) relates the individual's activity space to spatial behaviour in cities, using time-space prisms and concepts of constraints on movement. This approach highlights the problem of equity. Different income groups have different activity spaces not least because of different levels of mobility, related in turn to income levels. Thus transport policy can be an instrument to further redistribution of income.

At the same time, transport can be viewed through an efficiency perspective. However, this perspective is in fact a twofold one. First, the transport sector can be seen in isolation. Here, standard economic theory demonstrates that under certain assumptions, the market solution to problems of equating demand and supply will maximise utility i.e. provide the most efficient solution. A second perspective is that of the urban economy as a whole. Here it is necessary to ask whether or not market solutions to the urban transport problem create efficient solutions for the urban economic system. Congestion and pollution suggest that this might not be the case.

A further problem when considering the relationship between transport provision and social segregation is the time scale involved. As we have seen, urban transport is a major factor structuring the city. However, the time scale involved for undertaking a transformation of urban transport systems is much shorter than that involved for changing urban structure. There is much more inertia in urban structure than in transport systems. In other words, the decisions made today concerning transport policy will create urban structures which will exist for many decades. An apparently optimal transport solution of today can contribute to creation of an urban structure which is inefficient and costly in the longer term. For example, low fares over long distances will encourage spread urban growth. Such a pattern may be inefficient under changed conditions, such as a new energy crisis.

2. The Urban Phenomenon Today

Before examining transport policy in cities some consideration of the general trends of urban development in relation to transport is necessary.

First, in the western world there has been a structural shift from industrial production to the production of services. Analysis of the nature and causes of this shift has been the source of a vast literature (for example, Fuchs, 1968, Gershuny, 1977, 1978) and it has a clear urban component. Manufacturing decline has been especially severe in European cities (Goddard, 1983, Fothergill & Gudgin ,1983) and cities have become first and foremost service centres. This phenomenon has also been related to that of counterurbanisation (Champion, 1989). For the transport sector this has resulted in a decline in the importance of freight transport in cities and an increase in passenger transport, particularly radial patterns of transport. At the same time industrial workers are increasingly faced with the reverse transport problem - outward commuting. Second, and related to the first point, is the fact that rising incomes and a high income elasticity of demand for cultural services, specialist personal services, and educational and health services have created new markets for this type of service, and these have been highly concentrated in the main urban areas. This fact too has strengthened the passenger transport element in urban transport and radial traffic flows to the centre. This type of demand has also been related to increases in use of cars.

Third, and again related to the first two points, the class divisions of society are changing. A major social cleavage is appearing between marginalised groups, who have low incomes, face insecure employment or unemployment, have poor quality housing, poor access to social services and education and are subject to cultural alienation. This group often occupies distinct areas of the city and has low mobility. Transport systems are not usually structured to link these groups to the urban economy or urban society.

Fourth, there are changes in the organisation and ownership of enterprises. One important vector of change is the growth in importance of small-scale flexible production, often involving the use of advanced technology, including information technology and telematics. The debate concerning the possible demise of Fordism, heralding the end of the era of mass production

(Piore & Sabel, 1984, Leborgne & Lipietz, 1988) and the beginning of a new era of production where the small flexible firm dominates has been extensive. Without wishing to take sides in this often muddy and as yet unresolved debate it is clear that changes in this direction are occurring. This in turn is related to the question of growth patterns for single plant and multiplant firms, local firms and externally controlled firms. In terms of urban transportation this implies increases in short frequent contacts between firms involving both goods and people. Congestion in the urban transport system clearly has negative consequences for this type of production system which requires the capability of rapid and efficient transport of small batches of goods, people and information in highly integrated networks of firms, often located in urban areas.

Fifth, time distance relationships have changed drastically during this century (Gaspar & Porto, 1984) and continue to do so. The transport revolution and not least, the telecommunications revolution, has provided hitherto unseen levels of flexibility with respect to locational patterns. It is by no means given that telecommunications and transport are substitutes, indeed, in many cases they appear to be complementary. What is however certain, is that they foster new patterns of location, both for sectors as a whole, and not least for enterprises, where the process of production can more easily be subdivided and the individual processes located optimally in space. Many aspects of production have been affected profoundly, for example the logistics revolution and just-in-time production have created new patterns of distribution and storage. In certain sectors and in certain parts of the production process agglomeration tendencies are growing again, related closely to the new flexibilities. This has consequences for urban transportation, for congestion and for pollution.

Sixth, an important vector of urban change is related to internationalisation of economic activity. This process of internationalisation has been furthered by institutional changes, such as those associated with the implementation of the single European market and the economic and monetary union will further this process (Emerson et al, 1988). The process has had a number of curious geographical effects. First and foremost, the importance of the region as an economic unit as the basis for decisions concerning production appears to have declined. Instead, there is an emerging important duality of the global and the local (see for example Lloyd & Dicken, 1986, Scott, 1988). Whilst the international level has assumed major importance, not least through the growth in importance of transnational companies, local differences in the production environment have assumed major importance for the actual implementation of the process of economic restructuring. In this context the European cities constitute some of the biggest 'localities' and their differences are of key importance for economic performance (see Cheshire, 1990, Lever, 1992). Internationalisation has thus created greater competition between different localities, especially cities, for investment and development as investors at the international level consider their spatial options in a wider framework than the national or regional perspective. Spatial competition in the new Europe is increasingly becoming competition within the European urban system rather than competition between regions. Larger regions are in economic and social terms frequently so socially and economically heterogeneous that they no longer are adequate as an analytical tool when considering development patterns. Locational decisions, both in terms of expansion and contraction of economic activity are now increasingly related to locality rather than region, as locational constraints, for example in relation to linked industries and business service are rapidly disappearing. As networks of firms develop within the context of flexible production, the cities, with their range of economic diversity and supply of goods and services, once again come into focus as production localities. The new forms of reconcentration (Leborgne & Lipietz, 1988) of economic activity will again favour the cities. The cities are also information-rich environments where innovation, especially product innovation, is especially favoured (Thwaites, 1982, Oakey et al, 1982). Finally, developments in transportation, for example the TGV network, and developments in telecommunications networks will affect development of urban areas. However, centrality can be modified in network topographical rather than geographical terms. Transport and communications are essential parameters in the future competition between European cities.

3. Public Policy - and the Transport Sector

When examining public policy, four basic underlying dimensions must be considered.

(i) The efficiency dimension

As will be seen, there are two different meanings of the concept of efficiency in connection with urban transportation. The first has its origins in economic theory where efficiency in allocation of resources is achieved via the market mechanism which will, under certain conditions, ensure a Pareto optimum. Thus, according to this argument, a free market for transport will create a situation where consumer utility is maximised and the most efficient suppliers are the ones who survive. The transport sector is thus seen in isolation in terms of its contribution to overall efficiency. However, there are conditions which can give rise to sub-optimal solutions, necessitating public intervention (see any standard text on public sector economics, for example Boadway & Wildasin, 1984). These conditions include:

- The existence of externalities, positive or negative. Externalities are of considerable importance in urban transport and include congestion costs, where divergence between marginal social and marginal private costs constitutes a negative externality. This is illustrated in Figure 1. Up to traffic flow f1 marginal social and private costs are equal and constant. Above f1 marginal private costs begin to increase, because of the time costs of congestion, but each additional traffic unit imposes costs on the other traffic users. The demand schedule D-D represents what the motorist is willing to pay for the use of the road. At traffic flow f3 there is a negative externality. If the flow was reduced to f2 the externality would disappear. Another important transport-related externality arises from emissions, causing serious environmental problems in cities. It is of course a feature of externalities that they affect other groups than those which generate the externality.

Figure 1   Road Congestion

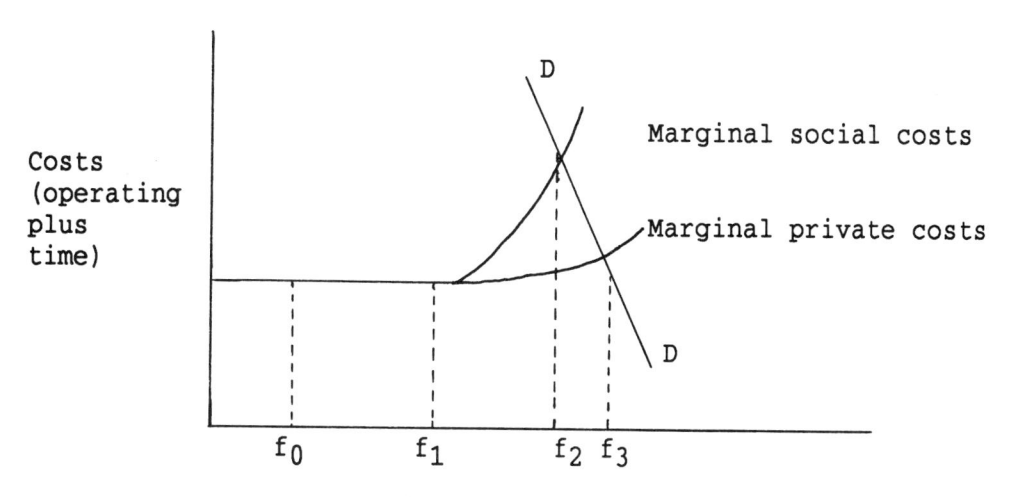

```
Costs
(operating
plus
time)
```

Marginal social costs
Marginal private costs

f_0 f_1 f_2 f_3

Traffic flow (vehicles per hour)

- The lack of perception of true costs affects the optimality of market solutions. Car owners notoriously lack perception of true costs. The existence of public goods, where consumption by one person does not detract from the benefit of others, or where there is the problem of the free-rider. Law enforcement and street lighting are two classical examples, and environmental amenity is rapidly becoming a public good. Again, this type of good is important in urban areas.

- The existence of natural monopolies, common in certain types of public utility, especially some urban transport systems, which render market solutions difficult or impossible.

- Where there are problems of indivisibility - a typical problem for large scale urban transport projects - marginal adjustments are not possible and the market breaks down.

Finally, in situations where equity problems are of importance, the market mechanism will not necessarily resolve these problems, not least because income distribution is taken as given.

Where one or more of these conditions apply, there is a case for public intervention on the basis of efficiency criteria - in other words, public policy, it can be argued, can create a more efficient (urban) economy than the market mechanism. This leads to the second interpretation of the efficiency criterion. The quest for efficiency in urban areas is one important dimension of public policy in cities. It can be many-faceted, including such options as the creation of efficient transport systems and the creation of developed cultural and service environments to attract (i.e. increase the utility) of the city to potential investors. This dimension has gained in importance through the concept of 'place marketing' (Burgess, 1982, Logan & Molotch, 1987, Shields, 1990, Ashworth & Voogd, 1990) where the city as an efficient and utility-maximising location is the central theme. Increasingly urban policy is directed to this end.

Fundamentally this type of policy relates to the question of overall economic efficiency in the urban system. It includes policies related to increasing labour and capital productivity and lowering of costs.

In the context of the future integrated Europe such policies appear to hold the key to economic success. As comparative advantage disappears in a unitary market with a common currency, the principle of absolute advantage, where productivity differences between localities are the central factor, will determine the fates of localities. The transport system is clearly an important element in this type of efficiency-based policy. Ensuring the rapid and efficient transport of people, information and freight in urban areas has become a major policy problem for many cities, particularly in connection with journey to work. Policies designed to improve efficiency in this sense are frequently not equitable. What is more, they often create negative externalities such as pollution, even if the congestion problem is (sometimes) solved.

(ii) The equity dimension

This dimension concerns the relationship between public policy and income distribution. It is important to distinguish between equity in social terms and equity in geographical terms. Urban areas are interesting because of the imagery of the association between these two types of equity. Urban management has typically had an important element of equity. Cheap urban transport, providing easy access to work, service and recreative areas, are examples of this dimension.

There are frequently conflicts between policies designed to increase efficiency and policies designed to create a more equitable income distribution, both in general and in the field of urban transport. The choice of trade-off is different in each European country and even between cities and the effects of this choice on urban economic fortunes is of considerable interest.

It is usually postulated in policy analysis that there exists a trade-off between efficiency and equity objectives, as illustrated in Figure 2. The broken lines illustrate the policy-makers' preference function permitting identification of optimal solutions. Public policy has an inherent spatial dimension and this spatial dimension itself implies income redistribution as income is not distributed evenly in space. Sometimes this effect can be indirect, as for example with the choice of spatial pricing policy for a new system of urban public transport. This choice always implies distributional considerations. Finally, it must be remembered that failure to take sufficient account of equity considerations in urban areas can have a negative influence with respect to efficiency. Social conflicts reduce the attractiveness of urban areas.

A major problem with equitable (especially low price) transport systems is that they can distort patterns of land use creating inefficient patterns of location of economic activity and housing, inefficiencies which can have serious consequences under changed circumstances (such as new energy crises).

Figure 2:   **Trade-off between Efficiency and Equity**

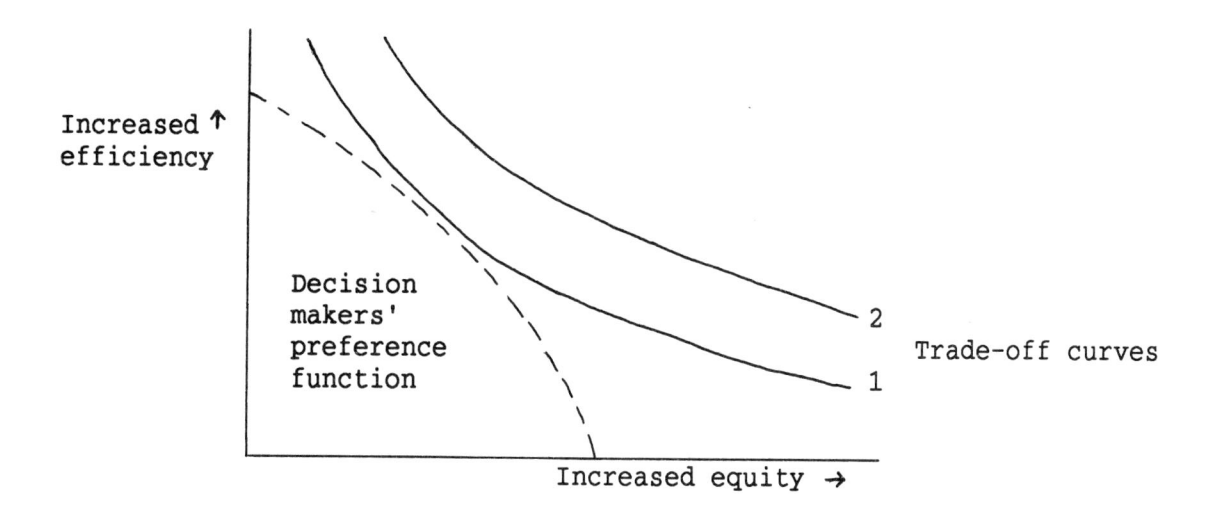

[Graph showing Increased efficiency on vertical axis and Increased equity on horizontal axis, with two trade-off curves labeled 1 and 2, and a dashed "Decision makers' preference function" curve.]

(iii) The externalities dimension

Externalities - particularly in urban areas - are inherently spatial. Policy-makers' awareness of the importance of negative externalities is increasing rapidly and control of these externalities is rapidly becoming a policy dimension in its own right. There is a conflict growing between externalities and policies designed to improve efficiency, and in some cases even equity. Negative externalities represent increasingly a major constraint on public policy and have thus become the target of public policy. Perhaps this represents the single most important shift in urban policy in recent years. Here urban transportation is one of the central policy areas in focus.

(iv) The budget dimension

Many European cities are facing fiscal crisis, related to changes in the social composition of urban areas, changes in the economic structure of urban areas and increasing demands for high-level service placed on urban areas. The response of the urban areas to fiscal crisis is various, ranging from cost reduction strategies to strategies designed to increase levels of economic activity and to change the social composition of cities. Urban public policy faces budgetary constraints and high opportunity costs. The interaction between budget constraints and policy choices is a major determinant of policy, not least with respect to transport provision.

3.1 Analysing transport policy

Public policy analysis, including transport policy, must be related to these four underlying dimensions, both when we wish to examine the basis and aims of policy and when we wish to evaluate its success. The importance of each underlying dimension varies from region to region, country to country and city to city. It also varies over time. It is this latter question to which we now turn.

4. Urban Transport Policy - the Long Term View

4.1 Equity considerations

From the 1930s until the 1980s urban transport policy clearly addressed the equity issue. Public transport and publicly owned transport played an important role in urban development. Often these policies were designed to patch up the worst deficiencies of the urban economic system in terms of redistribution of income, providing cheap travel to work from inner suburbs and easy access to service and recreative areas. This was often related to an ideology of greater equality of opportunity. Transport investments were financed via taxation and fares subsidised in the same way. However, the spatial economics of many fare systems often worked in such a way that fares per kilometre were higher for short journeys closer to city centres than for journeys to and from the more distant suburbs. Thus a more uneven redistribution of income was often involved in what seemed to be a more even redistribution. However, fare-cutting experiments were made in the 1970s in a number of countries, reflecting a clear equity dimension to policy.

At the same time the new urban middle class was de facto receiving income support as radial road development and suburban road development furthered urban sprawl.

Far from reducing social segregation, the increased mobility involved in this type of transport policy contributed to 'place differentiation', not least in social terms. Rapid access to the centre of cities from distant high income residential areas also was a feature of this period.

4.2 The quest for efficiency

During the 1980s a perceptible shift in policy emphasis appeared. The quest for efficiency became more apparent. Initially this was reflected in a transport policy which increasingly supported deregulation and privatisation, on market efficiency criteria. Thus the transport sector was increasingly viewed in isolation from the urban economic system. Even in public transport companies demands were made for changes in business strategy and principles. For example, many railway companies faced demands for establishment of net revenue maximising principles to replace budgetary cost minimising principles (incidentally frequently improving service provision at the same time, see Jensen-Butler & Jeppesen, 1987). This trend tended to ignore the problem of externalities and indivisibilities and also the fact that amenity, environment and fresh air were rapidly becoming perceived as public goods. It also ignored the fact that many features of urban transport render market solutions difficult. First, the main element of the urban transport problem is the journey to work. This is a special market situation in the sense that origins and destinations, at least in the short- and medium-term, are fixed. The only form of competition is between modes. But the competitiveness of each mode depends to a large degree upon the ability of the operators to co-operate and co-ordinate their supply, for example at transport interchanges. Secondly, the journey to work problem is a classical problem which lends itself to rational planning solutions. Transport flows, present and potential, are known, the problem can be viewed in purely operational terms and techniques of operations analysis used to optimise traffic flows. Most people would be willing to accept sacrifice of the relative comfort of their motor car for marked savings in transport time. And anyway why should public transport be low quality?

This period also witnessed decline in transport provision for the poor or disadvantaged. Privatisation and deregulation has eliminated many unprofitable services in urban areas and not least in the surrounding rural areas. This has contributed to the isolation of these groups and increasing segregation.

More recently, two new trends in urban transport provision are discernable, these being discussed below.

4.3 The problem of externalities

New policy signals are emerging in the transport sector. The internal combustion engine is a major source of atmospheric pollution and its effects are concentrated in urban areas. The larger the city the more serious the problem. At the national and international levels legislation and directives increasingly attempt to regulate the problem, for example the series of EC Council Directives on emissions during the 1970s and 80s. Tietenberg (1984) reviews emission control legislation in the US. However, these are general measures. The problem with atmospheric pollution is that its origin is usually concentrated and local, as is the case with the cities. Therefore many cities are realigning their transport policies to take account of the problem of negative externalities. This inevitably includes reduction of motor car access to cities and increasing priority to public transport.

A related problem is that of congestion. Many urban economies are being strangled and their economic efficiency is being lowered by congestion. Thus overall efficiency demands seem to be producing departures from market efficiency principles in the transport sector. However, the negative externalities associated with urban transport now that traffic volumes have passed key thresholds are of such a dimension as to render pure market solutions clearly sub-optimal.

This externality dimension cuts completely across the efficiency-equity trade-off. It is not immediately apparent that control of negative externalities will produce either more efficient or more equitable solutions. The outcome depends upon the specific context.

4.4 The new view of urban efficiency

In the Europe of the future competition between localities for economic growth will probably take the form of competition between cities. This competition will have a number of important dimensions all related to transport. One dimension is the overall productivity of the urban economy, where an efficient transport system plays a key role. A second dimension is the attractiveness of the city for investors and decision-makers as a place of residence and work. Environmental quality and access to advanced service and cultural facilities play an important role here. Again the relationship to the transport sector is clear. A third dimension is accessibility to the rest of the European (and world) urban system. Here again transport policy is of key importance. Scanty evidence suggests for example that the effect of development of the European TGV network will be to reinforce the position of the large and central cities in relation to the more peripheral (Abreu & Jensen-Butler, 1991). Also transport mode interfaces - a typical urban problem - will be of considerable importance. The capacity to travel rapidly and efficiently between major cities and also to complete the initial and final stages of the trip without undue delay will be an important component of urban efficiency and attractiveness. Fourth, it is clear from the logic of these arguments that the quality of public transport will be of considerable importance in the future. High quality public transport will be an important part of place marketing. In this sense quality includes not only speed and frequency but also the physical quality of the units involved and of the interfaces and also the question of personal security.

Again, this new view of urban efficiency tells us little about the consequences for changes in social or spatial equity. The marginalised urban groups will not be benefactors in this type of development. Indeed we will probably witness attempts to contain these groups physically rather than increase their mobility. The requirements of 'place marketing' indicate this.

5. Conclusions Concerning the Future of Transport and Urban Society

It seems clear that social segregation and its counterpart, social integration, (at least in spatial terms) is little affected by transport system developments. There are major forces at work in the economy and society which create these patterns and the main effect of transport policy is to determine their specific spatial configuration. The implication is therefore that urban transport policy will not in itself create a more or less integrated urban society. This also begs the question of the nature of social integration. Some of the more successful communities seem to have been ones where levels of social and economic homogeneity have been high. Social mix does not necessarily produce social integration in functional terms.

On the other hand it is clear that transport policy has important distributional aspects which should not be ignored. Any policy proposal can in principle be examined with respect to its effects on equity. Here it must be remembered that there can be important differences between spatial and social equity as any spatial fares policy indicates. At the same time it is important to remember that transport costs are a limited proportion of family budgets, which is why transport policy, however equitable, can scarcely resolve substantial equity problems.

It also seems probable that the broader view of urban system efficiency will prevail over the narrower view of market efficiency by sector. Negative externalities related to urban transport and efficiency requirements of other parts of the system will probably increase the demand for public transport and for well planned public transport. This suggests that the era of deregulation and privatisation in the transport field may be over. On the other hand we will probably witness efforts to improve service levels in public transport provision, involving increasing use of planning and management principles derived from the private sector in public sector companies. Perhaps this represents a type of convergence.

Atmospheric pollution will play an increasingly important role in urban transport policy, where both strategies of control and of taxation will be applied. The equity consequences of such policy remain unclear, though the inhabitants of central areas of cities will clearly benefit. It is perhaps illustrative to examine Thomson's (1977) schema of urban transport planning strategies, shown in Table 1. If the arguments of this paper hold then it seems that the strong-centre strategy will be the most important in the future, both for reasons of urban efficiency and competition and also because of the negative externalities involved. This strategy involves reurbanisation, the regeneration of the urban centre.

The marginalised groups in the cities seem to be one of the principal losers in transport policy - as indeed with most types of public policy.

The logistics revolution involving highly connected entities with frequent exchanges of small batches of goods, service and information will place new demands upon the urban transport sector, particularly highlighting congestion problems. The cities which resolve these problems will have the competitive advantage. Logistical problems in urban areas are also increasingly being seen as environmental problems (Hansson, 1991, Ruijgrok & Janssen, 1991).

New energy crises will increase the attraction of cities for residence (Christensen & Jensen-Butler, 1982). Urban transport systems are in general more robust with respect to fuel price increases than regional and rural transport systems. As new energy crises are inevitable, at some stage energy constraints will enter as a major policy parameter. Planning land use patterns in cities which are robust with respect to rising real energy prices will be a major factor contributing to equity in future decades. Energy efficient cities will be cities where levels of mobility are high. Lower transport prices have a clear redistributional effect.

The relationship between the urban transport system and the interurban transport system will assume increased importance as a part of the general competition between European cities. This implies a more integrated view of the links between the two types of system. It also implies a higher level of integration - social and economic - between cities rather than of social groups within cities.

Table 1

Urban Transport Planning Strategies

1. **Strong centre strategy: centralised cities**

Aim To maintain economic advantages of centralisation and minimise central city congestion.

Policy 1. Efficient public transport
2. Decentralisation of functions to nodal points to spread traffic loads.

Problems Peak hour congestion.

2. **Full motorisation strategy: decentralised cities**

Aim Retention of high levels of car accessibility throughout the system.

Policy Decentralised functional structure based upon urban freeways.

Problems Land and construction costs, long travel distances, energy costs, environmental impacts, lack of social identity, possible nodal congestion.

3. **Weak-centre strategy: inner centralised and outer decentralised cities**

Aim To retain commercial and social advantages of a city centre and ease of mobility throughout the suburbs.

Policy 1. Integrated system of radial and circumferential roads.
2. Supplementary commuter rail services to the centre.

Problems Tend towards decentralisation in the absence of sufficient investment in public transport and central redevelopment.

4. **Low-cost strategy: Third World cities**

Aim To alleviate congestion and assist economic development.

Policy 1. Improvements on the radial roads and public transport system.
2. Controls on central development and encouragement of decentralisation to peripheral nodes.

Problems City growth tends to be faster than levels of investment in transport infrastructure.

Source: Thomson 1977

REFERENCES

Abreu, D. de and Jensen-Butler, C.N., (1991). A evolução sócio-económica regional e a introdução de comboios de grande velocidade em Portugal. OPEUR, Lisboa, Portugal.

Alonso, W., (1964). Location and Land Use. Harvard University Press.

Ashworth, G.J. and Voogd, H., (1990). Selling the City. London.

Boadway, R.W. and Wildasin, D.E., (1984). Public Sector Economics. Little, Brown & Co., Boston.

Borchert, J.R., (1967). American Metropolitan Evolution. Geographical Review, 57, 301-323.

Burgess, J., (1982). Selling Places: Environmental Images for the Executive. Regional Studies, vol. 16, 1.

Champion, A.G., (Ed.), (1989). Counterurbanisation. The Changing Nature and Pace of Urban Deconcentration. Arnold, London.

Cheshire, P.C., (1990). Explaining the Recent Performances of the European Community's Major Urban Regions. Urban Studies, 27, 311-333.

Christensen, B. and Jensen-Butler, C.N., (1982). Heat Planning in Denmark. Progress in Planning, 17 (2).

Emerson, M. et al, (1988). The Economics of 1992. Oxford University Press.

Evans, A.W., (1973). The Economics of Residential Location. Macmillan, London.

Fothergill, S. and Gudgin, G., (1983). Trends in Regional Manufacturing Employment: The Main Influences, in Goddard, J.B. and Champion, A.G., The Urban and Regional Transformation of Britain. Methuen, London, 27-50.

Fuchs, V., (1968). The Service Economy. Columbia University Press.

Gaspar, J. and Porto, M., (1984). Telecomunicaçoes e desenvolvimento regional em Portugal. Revista de administração Publica VII, 26, 569-582.

Gershuny, J.I., (1977). Post-industrial Society: the Myth of the Service Economy. Futures, 9 (2) 103-114.

Gershuny, J.I., (1978). After Industrial Society: The Emerging Self-service Economy. Macmillan, London.

Goddard, J., (1983). Structural Change in the British Space-economy, in Goddard, J.B. and Champion, A.G., The Urban and Regional Transformation of Britain. Methuen, London, 1-26.

Hansson, L., (1991). Logistics, Air Pollution and the Cost Responsibility in Transport Policy. 119-138.

Hägerstrand, T., (1971). What about People in Regional Science? Papers of the Regional Science Association, vol. XXIV, 7-21.

Jensen-Butler, C.N. and Jeppesen, S.E., (1987). DSB's Regional Organisation. DSB, Copenhagen.

Leborgne, D. and Lipietz, A., (1988). New Technologies, New Modes of Regulation: Some Spatial Implications. Society and Space, Environment and Planning D, vol. 6 (3), 263-280.

Lever, W.F., (1992). Competition between European Cities. Unpublished manuscript, Working Group 4, RURE Project, European Science Foundation. Paper prepared for the RURE Conference in Budapest, February 1992.

Lloyd, P.E. and Dicken, P., (1986). Global Shift. Industrial Change in a Turbulent World. Harper & Row, London.

Logan, J. and Molotch, H., (1987). Urban Fortunes. The Political Economy of Place. Berkeley.

Muth, R.F., (1969). Cities and Housing. Chicago University Press.

Oakey, R.P., Thwaites, A.T. and Nash, P.A., (1982). Technological Change and Regional Development: some Evidence on Regional Product and Process Innovations. Environment & Planning A, 14, 1073-86.

Piore, M.J. and Sabel, C.F., (1984). The Second Industrial Divide. Possibilities for Prosperity. Basic Books, New York.

Ruijgrok, C.J. and Janssen, B.J.P., (1991). City Logistics and the Reduction of Urban Freight Trips, in Smit, H.G., Transport Developments in an Integrating Europe. European Transport Planning Colloquium Foundation, Delft, 139-156.

Scott, A.J., (1988). Flexible Production Systems and Regional Development: the Rise of New Industrial Spaces in North America and Western Europe. International Journal of Urban and Regional Research, vol. 12, no. 2, 171-185.

Shields, R., (1990). Places on the Margin. London.

Thomson, J.M., (1977). Great Cities and their Traffic. Gollancz, London.

Thwaites, A., (1982). Some Evidence of the Regional Variations in the Introduction and Diffusion of Industrial Products and Processes within British Manufacturing Industry. Regional Studies 16, 371-382.

Tietenberg, T., (1984). Environmental and Resource Economics. Scott, Foresman & Co., Illinois.

Timms, D.W.G., (1975). *The Urban Mosaic*. Cambridge University Press.

Yeates, M. and Garner, B.J., (1971). *The North American City*. Harper & Row, New York.

COMMUTING IN THE METROPOLITAN AREA OF LISBON:
EFFECTS ON THE QUALITY OF LIFE AND ON THE ENVIRONMENT

by

L.T. Vasconcelos
Science and Environmental Engineering Department
College of Sciences and Technology
New University of Lisbon

and

J.D. Geirinhas
UNINOVA, Institute for the Development of New Technologies

1. Background

Lisbon, like most European capitals, took a decisive step in the 'metropolitanisation' process between World War II and the 1970s, attaining spatial socio-economic levels never before observed. This increasing concentration continued during the 1970-1981 period as a result mainly of the greater employment supply. In 1970 the Metropolitan Area of Lisbon (MAL) housed 22% of the national population and ten years later this value rose to 26%.

Although small in area, about 2,600 km² (3% of the national territory), the MAL concentrates a significant part of the national socio-economic structure. In fact, in 1981, it sheltered ¼ of the national population, retained about 1/3 of national employment, providing for 2/5 of national employment in the tertiary sector (Vasconcelos et al, 1990) and had more than half of the headquarters of the main national societies located within the region (Baptista, 1987).

As regards productivity, recent estimates of the National Institute of Statistics show that more than 40% of the National Gross Value Added is concentrated in the two Districts of Lisbon and Setubal (1), accounting for 37% of the manufacturing industry and 49% of the tertiary sector (Mendes Baptista, 1989). Moreover, only Lisbon, Setubal and Oporto have per capita values of Gross Domestic Product higher than the national average (Mendes Baptista, 1989).

This situation resulted in a considerable concentration of population reflected in population densities (Figure 1) nine times higher than the average for Portugal, with 70% of its residents living in agglomerates of ten thousand or more inhabitants (Vasconcelos et al, 1990).

The growing spatial influence of the city of Lisbon over the surrounding region, and the steady increase in jobs and housing associated with its privileged position in the transportation network, generate a necessary growth in fluxes of people within the MAL, commuting between their homes and jobs, continuously aggravated by the response to new accessibility demands.

This is a dynamic self-reinforcing process with growing accessibility demands imposing enlarged road networks which, in turn, encourage further expansion. In the period between 1970 and 1981, the population growth in the municipalities of the metropolitan area was mostly around Lisbon with the population in this city remaining almost constant (Figure 2). On the other hand the employment balance supply/demand in 1981 was only in surplus for Lisbon and Setubal, with the other municipalities in the metropolitan area exhibiting deficits (2) (Figure 3), a fact that accentuates the commuting fluxes within the MAL. Curiously, more than half of the jobs in the MAL are located in Lisbon, and about 80% of them on the North bank of the Tagus river that crosses the MAL from East to West, dividing it into two parts of almost equal order. The result of the situation described is an increase in the number of commuters, in the distance travelled daily by them and in the number of vehicles in circulation.

Fig. 1: Population density (Pop/Km2)

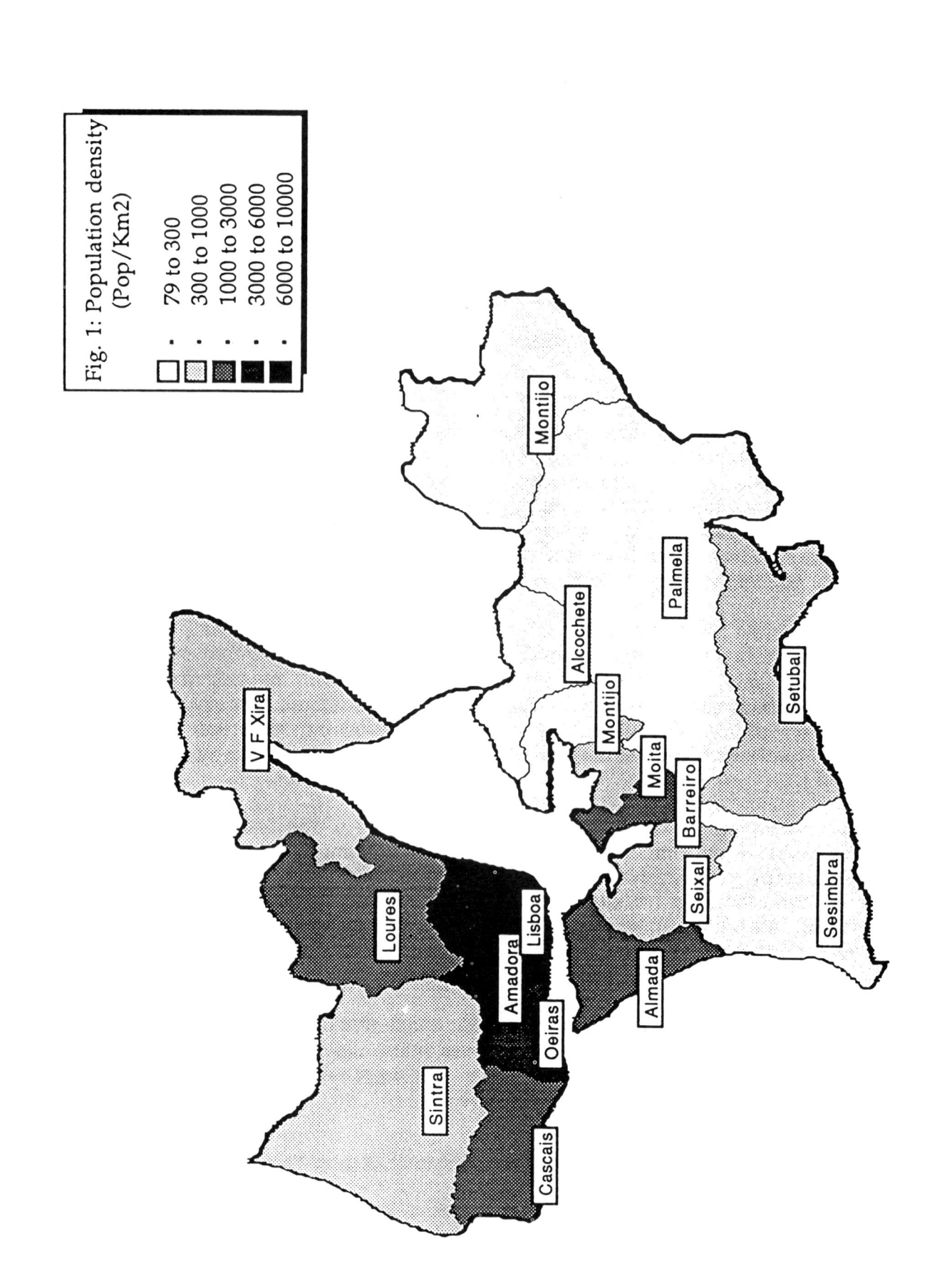

- 79 to 300
- 300 to 1000
- 1000 to 3000
- 3000 to 6000
- 6000 to 10000

Fig 2: Population
Growth Rate 70-81

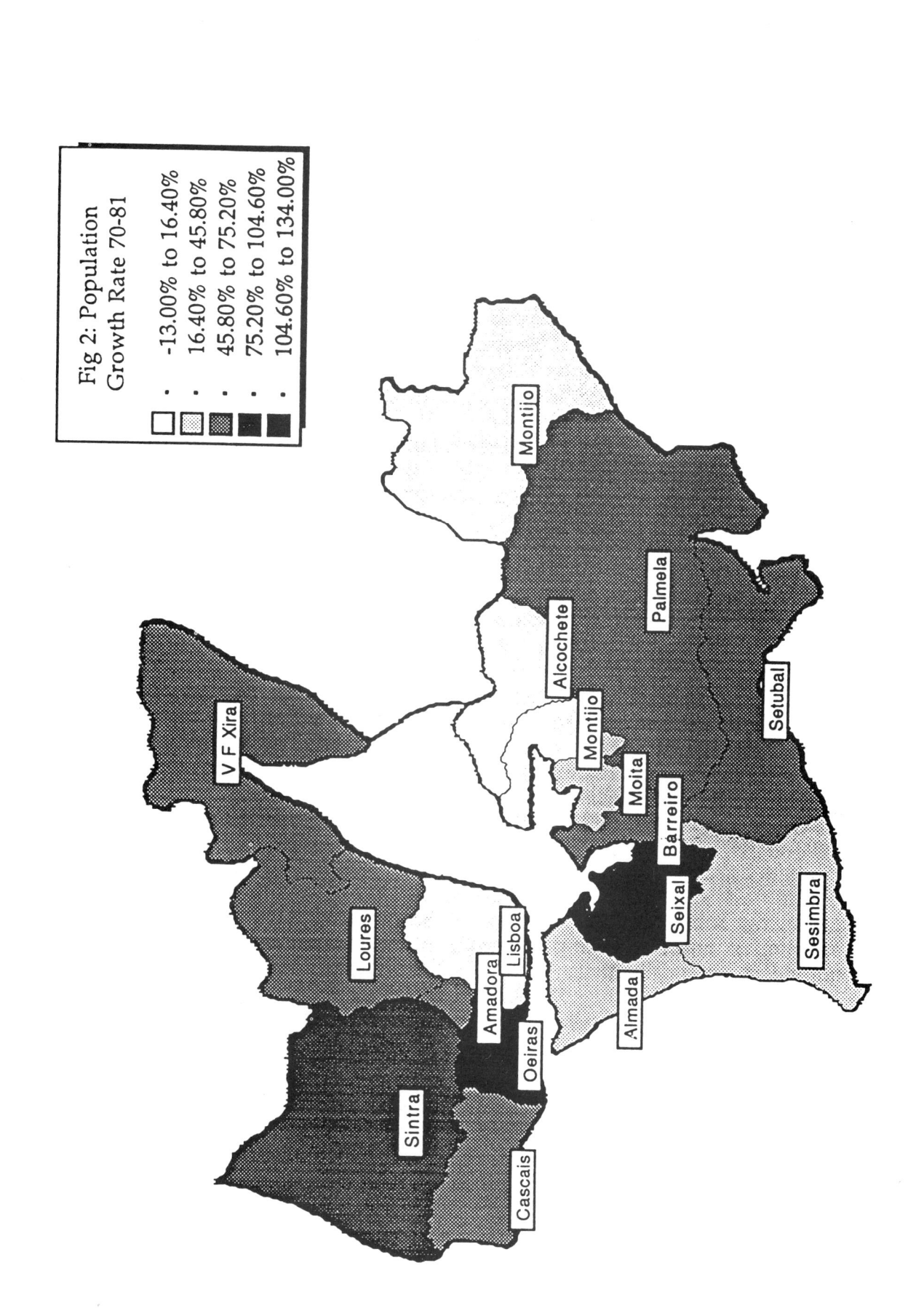

-13.00% to 16.40%
16.40% to 45.80%
45.80% to 75.20%
75.20% to 104.60%
104.60% to 134.00%

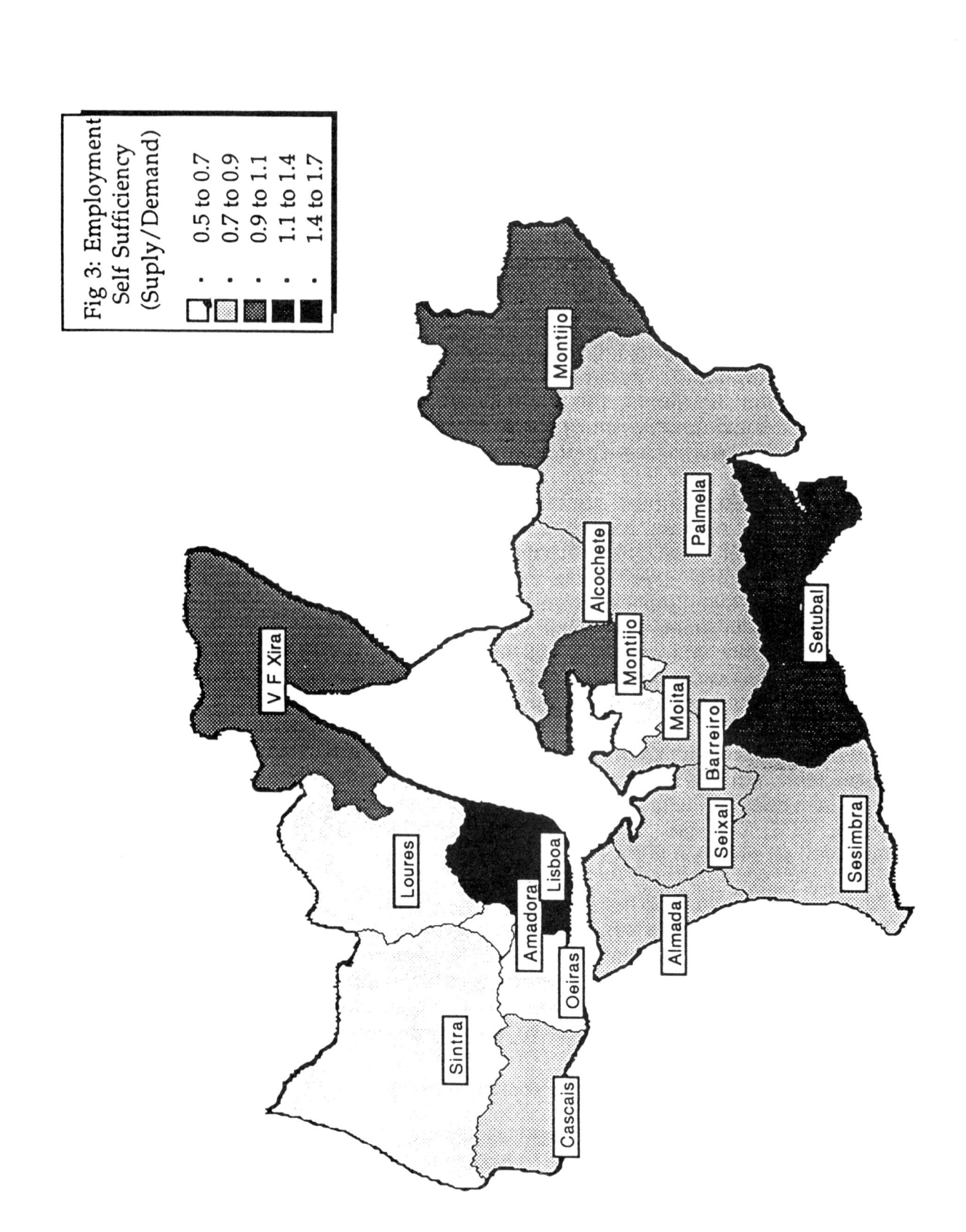

Fig 3: Employment Self Sufficiency (Suply/Demand)

- 0.5 to 0.7
- 0.7 to 0.9
- 0.9 to 1.1
- 1.1 to 1.4
- 1.4 to 1.7

The present paper reports on a rough quantitative assessment of the environmental impacts and of the effects on the quality of life of the residents resulting from the commuting fluxes described above.

2. Problem Statement and Objectives

The MAL (3) consists of sixteen local administrative units - municipalities - with varied economic dynamics, usually dependent on accessibility to their centres of activity, mainly Lisbon and Setubal. Most of the residents in the different municipalities are, in fact, under a strong attraction towards the city of Lisbon due to its privileged situation concerning employment supply and to its prominent position in the transportation network.

The distance travelled by the commuters, measured in terms either of money or time consumed, affects the quality of life of the MAL residents, implying a reduction in their leisure time. Work trips are an issue, although they frequently account for small shares of the total household trips, due to their specific characteristics concerning route, length and temporal clustering (Gordon et al, 1988). The constant expansion of the MAL inherent in continuing suburbanisation, results in a larger population living in remote places, implying a greater number of vehicles in circulation and increasing the number of commuting trips.

When the capacity of the road network is exceeded, congestion occurs, increasing commuting time. This environmental impact affects, in turn, the quality of life of the residents. The increasing number of vehicles on the road generates gas emissions and fuel consumption rises, affecting air quality and increasing demand on imported oil resources.

The issue under discussion is related to the increase in fuel consumption of vehicles occasioned by congestion. Two immediate consequences result: one mainly related to environmental concerns, namely the exploitation of non-renewable resources, with all the associated negative aspects; the other refers to the economic investment necessary to assure transportation. In the particular case of Portugal, the situation is even more serious than in most other countries, because energy consumption in transportation relative to the Gross Value Added is rather high, suggesting a lack of efficiency in the national transportation system (4).

In accordance with the PEN (5), the transportation sector in Portugal absorbs more than 1/3 of the total national energy consumption, a share that is expected to increase, with an almost total dependence on oil (98%) since coal use is inexistent and electricity only accounts for slightly over 1% (Almeida e Castro, 1990).

This is even more serious if, as it is suspected, there is a growing reliance on the private automobile (6), because it reduces the profitability of collective transportation, it affects the capacity and regularity of services and generates considerable energy spending and unwanted levels of air and noise pollution (Almeida e Castro, 1990).

Traffic has been the main contribution to the decreasing level of air quality, resulting mainly from the increasing number of vehicles, lack of improvement in the road network and a considerable proportion of old vehicles in circulation (SEARN, 1987). The comparison of the emissions of the different sectors in Portugal identifies transportation as the main responsible sector for NOx emissions (more than 60%), contributing considerably to HC emissions (92%), but only showing a small share of SO_2 emissions (4%) (SEARN, 1989). As regards Volatile Organic Components (VOC) it represents almost half of the total national emissions.

Several types of pollution (for example: air, water, soil and noise) can be associated with the situation just described. However, in the present study we only consider the issue of air pollution. For this average vehicle emissions (NOx, VOC, CO) are roughly quantified to provide information regarding the levels of air pollution in the region.

All the aspects focused here affect the quality of life of the population, either through damaging the environment, imposing extra costs or reducing individual economic, social and cultural opportunities by drastic reduction in available time. Unfortunately it is not possible to accurately estimate here the time consumed in daily commuting due to the unavailability of data regarding the fluctuations in traffic congestion and number of commuters during different periods of the day. A rough estimate is however attempted to provide for an idea of the significance of this factor.

Although the information under analysis refers to the year 1981, quantification of the trends observed since that date allow us to be sure that the present situation is certainly worse, as there has been a national increase of 58% in vehicles in circulation from 1980 to 1989, an increase of 78,000 vehicles annually (ACAP/AIMA, 1990).

Our main purpose in stressing the importance of the traffic problem is to mobilise interveners, pointing to more efficient alternatives which will necessarily include a better spatial management, more adequate transportation solutions and, possibly, the utilisation of new technologies allowing for decentralisation of job locations, lowering the need for commuting and decreasing the levels of pollution emissions.

3. Management Problems

An adequate Growth Management is essential to mitigate the negative aspects of the present situation and to provide a good framework for further development. This has to be done at the level of the whole metropolitan area and not, as it has been done until now, through localised interventions at the municipality level. Solutions like those discussed here, require implementation on a larger scale than the existing local administrative units.

The fact that transportation in the MAL did not accompany the demographic growth over time (Brito et al, 1987), the lack of an effective metropolitan entity of management over the whole region (Pereira, 1987, Portas, 1989) and the inexistence of a policy to articulate sectoral interventions (Brito et al, 1987) all contributed to the worsening of the inherited situation.

Obviously, it cannot be expected that management of the metropolitan area would achieve efficiency just from the sum of local policies, even if they are very successful (Pereira, 1987). Somewhere in the process there is a need to articulate the various interventions structured by some global criteria. The development of efficient policies for the metropolitan area requires a comprehensive approach considering the whole territory as a 'management unit' (Martins, 1987).

The need for a type of supra-municipal entity (which could result from an association of municipalities) with authority to manage and define strategies for the whole region (Abecassis, 1987, Borges, 1987) has been raised frequently by technicians and politicians (Abecassis, 1987, Borges, 1987, Lobo, 1987, Pardal, 1987) whenever they run into issues which have to be approached comprehensively.

In consequence of this growing awareness the national parliament (Assembleia da República) started a discussion on the type of administrative structure that should be implemented at the metropolitan level. However, such an entity has not yet emerged, making it rather difficult to intervene in the MAL, when macro-level problems so require. Nevertheless, the development of some infrastructures, like the highway Lisbon-Cascais, can mobilise a few municipalities in the region (Barreiros, 1988).

Recently, the enacted legislation of DL 338/83 recognised the need to elaborate a land use plan for the whole metropolitan area of Lisbon (Nunes da Silva, 1989). Disagreement of the municipalities over the attributions given to this plan by the Central Government generated a meeting of the Presidents of the administrative units of the MAL within 24 hours (Nunes da Silva, 1989). A consensus was reached about the necessity to create the Municipalities Association of the Metropolitan Area of Lisbon. This seems to be a new era for intervention in the MAL, leading to another type of communication between central and local entities in the planning context (Nunes da Silva, 1989).

4. Methodology/Application

The analysis of the fluxes resulting from daily commuting between home and job was assembled in charts showing origin and destination, at the municipality level for 1981 (date of the last population census). These charts refer to people using private cars, public transportation and other types of transport. All the data used were collected at the municipality level regarding daily values.

For estimating the distance travelled by commuters in the MAL charts were prepared referring to the existing fluxes, showing the commuting patterns among municipalities within the area (Figure 4).

Independently, a chart of the distances between the municipalities was obtained considering the main existent road network and computing the road length assuming the shortest path. For the municipality of Lisbon an average distance to arrive at the centre was considered after entering the city limits. A null distance is assumed for persons working or studying in their municipality of residence. The overlay of these two types of chart

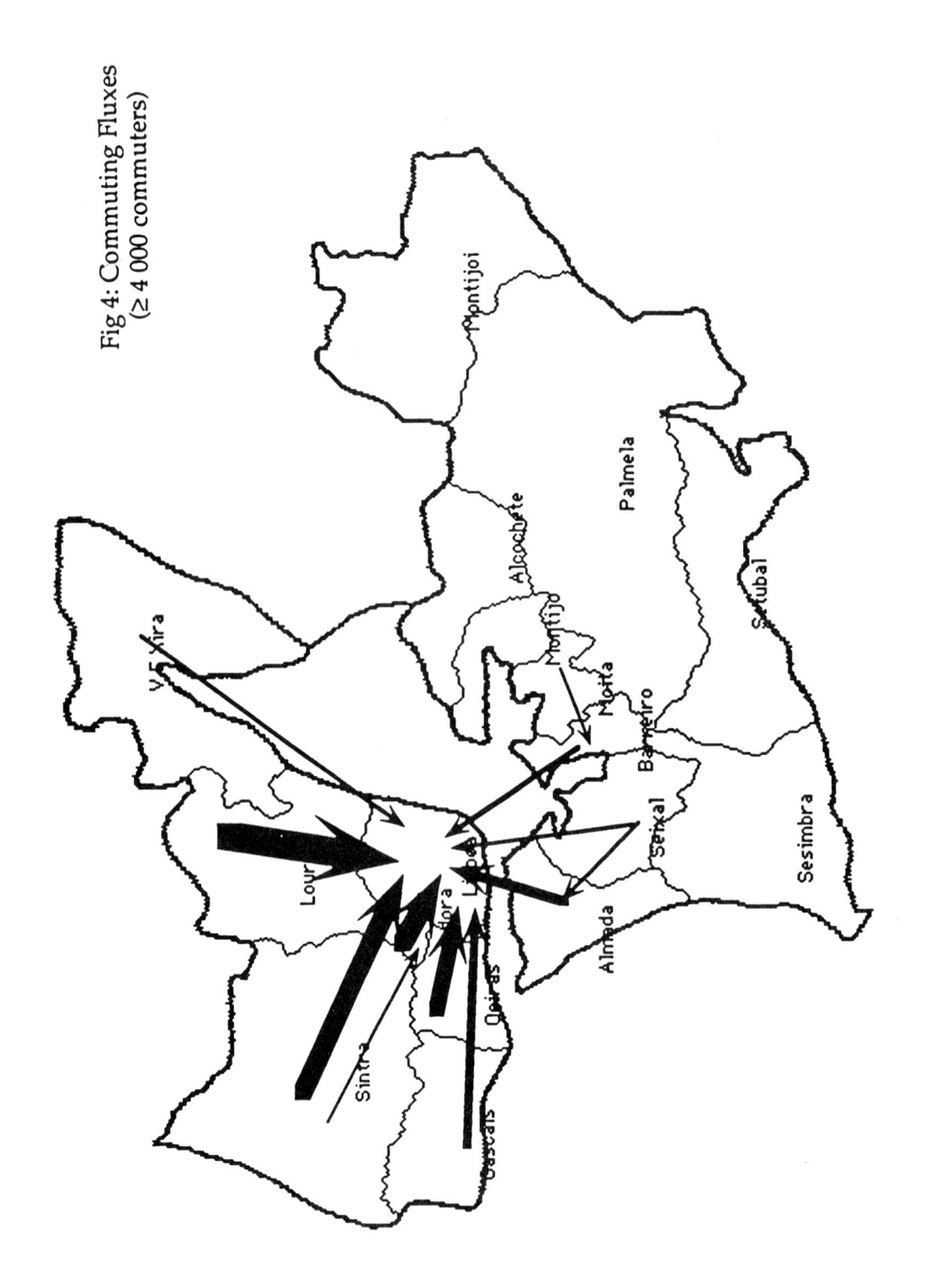

Fig 4: Commuting Fluxes
(≥ 4 000 commuters)

(number of people and distance) produced a third type, relative to commuting length, allowing for a comparison between the different administrative units. This distance is then divided by the municipal commuting population (Figure 5).

The daily commuting distance per capita allows for a rough assessment of the commuter time consumed by residents of each one of the municipalities. This in turn, informs on the reduction in the commuters' available time and the consequent negative impacts.

Computations of the total hours consumed in travelling by working commuters is also calculated, using an average speed of 30 km per hour (7). This is then converted into cost, assuming an average salary of 500$ (escudos) (8) per hour, to identify the cumulative cost of commuting time.

To assess the cost of transportation, two distinct steps are taken: for cars the approximate cost per kilometre travelled is considered (9) as 40$ (escudos) (10), and the calculations use an occupancy rate of 1.7 passengers per vehicle (11); for the group using collective modes of transportation an average value of 5,000$ (escudos) (12) monthly pass per user is assumed. The time consumed and the transportation costs result from the sum of these two values (Table 1).

The estimation of fuel consumption is a preliminary calculation for the overall assessment of emissions. An average value of fuel consumption (13) is considered and the amount of fuel spent on travelling is estimated.

The air pollution is then assessed using the amount of fuel consumption as the basis for calculation. Actually, averages of these values (14) are assumed for unity of fuel consumption of cars and buses. Furthermore, buses are assumed to use diesel and cars to consume only gasoline. This last assumption emerges from the fact that diesel cars account for only 5% of car sales (RevistACAP, 1991), although this share has been increasing lately.

5. Analysis of the Estimated Costs

Total daily commuting distances, estimated by the above procedure for the whole MAL, is about fourteen million kilometres, for its 340,000 commuters, which represent approximately 1/3 of the working population of the metropolitan region (Table 1).

The time consumed by the workers using cars and public transportation attains a daily total of 400,000 hours which represents a cost of about 50 million escudos (15). Although this reflects a daily value per commuter of only about one hour, a low estimate (16), its cumulative amount is rather impressive. For a more precise calculation congestion has to be taken into account and commuters divided into groups according to their chosen routes.

The values grow to more than 300 million escudos (17) if transportation cost is taken into consideration, equivalent to 1000$ (escudos) (18) per capita (Table 1).

Fig 5: Commuting Distance per capita

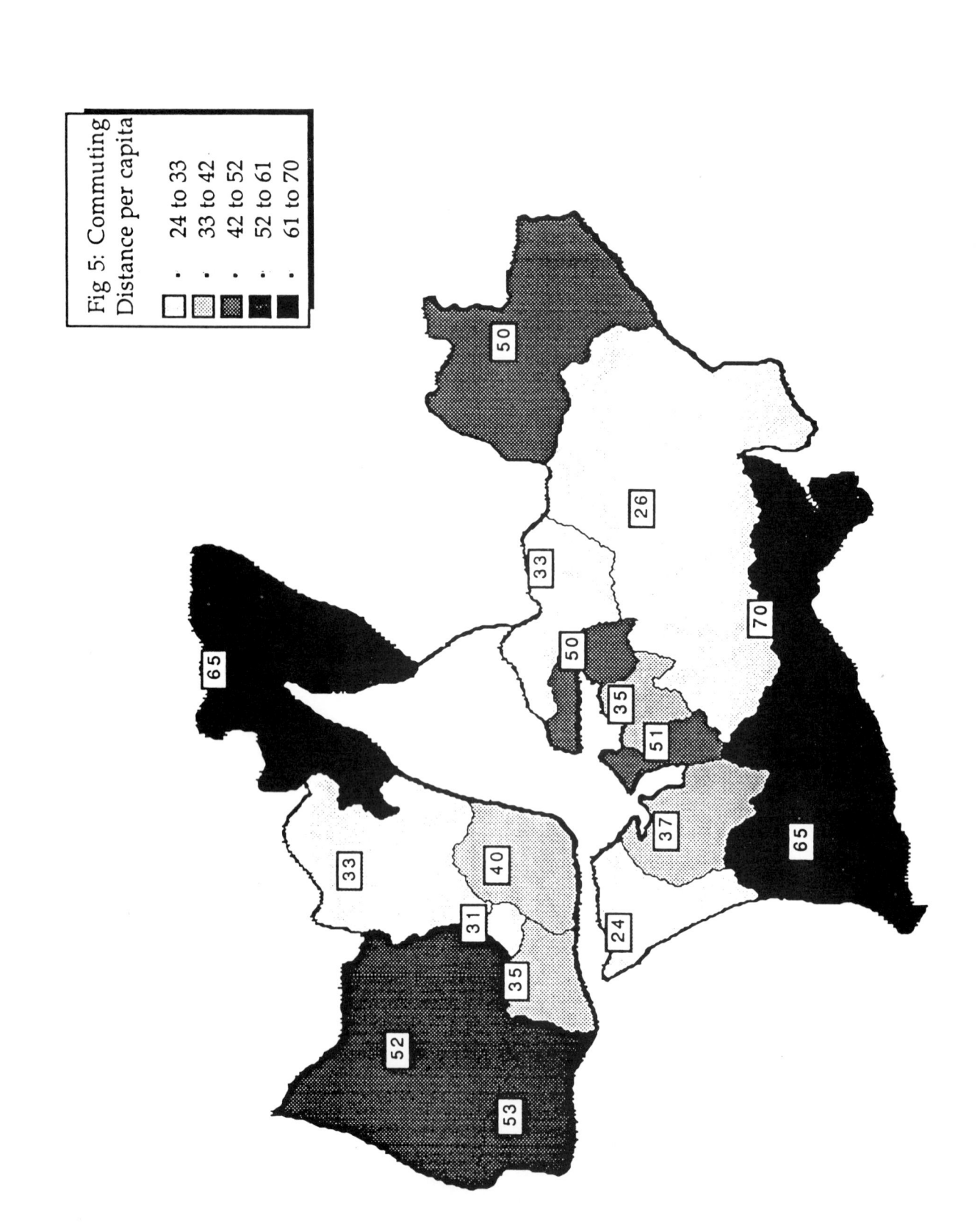

- 24 to 33
- 33 to 42
- 42 to 52
- 52 to 61
- 61 to 70

Table 1: Working Population Commuting Costs

	Commuters (10³)	Vehicles (Cars/Buses) (10³)	Total Km Commuters (10⁶)	Total Km Vehicles (10⁶)	Total Comm. Hours (10³)	Comm. Hour Cost (10⁶)	Transp. Cost (10⁶)	Total Cost (10⁶)
Car	52	30	2	1	67	33	47	80
Bus	252	–	10	–	330	165	63	228
Other	39	–	2	–	57	28	–	28
Total	**343**	**30**	**14**	**1**	**454**	**226**	**110**	**336**

Table 2: Total Fuel Consumption and Emissions of NOx, VOC and CO

Daily Values

	Fuel Consumption (litres)	NOx (Kg)	VOC (Kg)	CO (Tonne)
Car	121,431	2,951	4,891	16.08
Bus	228,284	11,962	1,348	3.98
Total	**349,715**	**14,913**	**6,239**	**20.06**

Annual Values

	Fuel Consumption (10⁶ l)	NOx (Tonne)	VOC (Tonne)	CO (Tonne)
Car	29	708	1,174	3,859
Bus	55	2,871	324	955
Total	**84**	**3,579**	**1,498**	**4,814**

The assessment provides some insight into the social impact on the quality of life. Actually, it represents the daily cost to commuters in time and transportation. This is reflected in the economic availability of the workers and in the amount of their leisure time, affecting more strongly the lower income groups due to their lower gains and the impossibility to compensate with alternatives, such as domestic help. Deprived groups are also driven out to less accessible places due to housing costs. This, associated with the strong reliance of these groups on public transportation, contributes to the cancelling of available opportunities.

Stress, anxiety, safety and other social and psychological factors, important to the assessment of these impacts, are not considered in the present study, although the scenario allows for the postulation of a very serious situation.

Fuel consumption in commuting accounts for 5% of diesel use and 3% of gasoline, when compared with the respective national consumption for transportation. Future national trends suggest a growing reliance on gasoline usage - a 43% increase from 1981 to 1987 - against the use of diesel which only rose 9%.

The contribution of the commuting vehicles (cars and buses) to the emission of air pollutants account for estimated annual values of 3,579 tonne of NOx, about 1,497 tonne of VOC and 4,814 tonne of CO (Table 2).

As regards per capita annual NOx emissions the values for the metropolitan area are rather low, 1.5 kg per capita if compared with the national average value of 11.8 kg (19). In spatial terms, however, it accounts for 1,385 kg/km^2, slightly over the average value for the country (1,240 kg/km^2). This discrepancy is due to several factors, namely the use of a restricted sample, since the estimation targets only passenger vehicles commuting among municipalities during the working year (240 days). Information on global emissions already suggests a growth (15% (20) from 1980 to 1983), confirmed by the increasing number of vehicles in circulation (about 60% from 1980 to 1989). It is curious to note that if this factor is analysed as an emission indicator, using as a basis the population responsible for the pollutant emission, the value rises to 10.4 kg per capita.

Regarding VOC emissions, although nature is the main source, traffic also contributes to the increase of this pollutant. In 1981 this value accounted for 2% of the total national value (21) for transportation emissions.

The values used for the analysis were processed in a personal computer allowing for easy updating of data as soon as the results of the next census of population are available. This is particularly interesting because it will provide information on the trends of the last ten years.

6. Final Remarks

In other countries, growing congestion and its negative effects have encouraged the rethinking of transportation policies. In fact, this jointly with the shift in public values, growing importance of socio-economic and environmental issues and their relation to traffic (Gakenheimer, 1978,

Martins, 1991), have generated controversy, calling attention to these issues and forcing politicians to act. Portugal is going through a similar process. It became quite important to evaluate the nature, magnitude and incidence of existing and expected social, economic and environmental effects, and to open this to discussion by the general public.

The objectives of any policy regarding transportation in a metropolitan area should attempt to assure urban mobility and increasing transport efficiency, while preserving environmental quality, and leading to energy saving. In 1970 road transportation was already consuming 21% of world oil production (Gakenheimer, 1978).

Several policies, which should be complementary, can be adopted to deal with this problem, namely:

- growth management intervening at the land use level to implement efficient location of employment versus housing, aiming at shortening distances;

- encouraging the use of public transportation through improvement of service (quality and efficiency), such as the implementation of special traffic lanes;

- as regards private cars, higher occupation rates should be encouraged to decrease the number of vehicles in circulation, contributing consequently to the decreasing of congestion and the lowering of emissions;

- technological innovation has a two-fold role to play: making vehicles more energy efficient and less air and noise pollutant, as well as contributing through new communication technology to the decreasing of commuter trips;

- congestion has also to be dealt with through restrictive policies in more affected areas and the channelling of the traffic and parking to peripheral areas with a good public accessibility service (Martins, 1991);

- staggering working hours (Gordon et al, 1988) to avoid temporal clustering.

Although there are some signs of a decreasing importance of the MAL in relative terms, there is not in Portugal another urban area similarly equipped to compete internationally. For this reason it is difficult to make predictions for the future of the region (Brito et al, 1987, Mendes Baptista, 1989). It seems reasonable, however, to assume a growing trend for the MAL although at lower growth rates than those observed previously.

A general overview of the commuting situation of the MAL with a rough estimation of some of its consequences has just been described. Although the calculations in time consumed are not very impressive, when converted into per capita values, the price of the hours consumed and the transportation cost attain considerable levels. This is a conservative assessment because it refers to 1981 data. Currently, there are indications that the situation has deteriorated with more cars in circulation and almost no significant change in road network capacity. The negative consequences seem to be overcoming the positive effects, contributing to the decline in the area viability. This situation requires urgent intervention.

Two issues call for special attention in the MAL: the lack of a management entity for the whole region and a radial road network pattern.

Concerning the regional management, the first step for an effective approach in this area is the establishment of a kind of management entity for the whole region (association, administrative structure, etc.). This seems to be emerging in accordance with recent developments. It is important to aim for a flexible entity able to achieve the involvement of groups and to reorganise the process according to the issue under discussion and the changing values and objectives of the relevant actors.

Decisions over mobility are the next step, as one of the priority aspects to be considered for a comprehensive planning and effective management of the MAL. A consensus on the metropolitan system of transportation has to be reached through a convergent negotiating process adopting interactive planning among different levels and sectors (Costa, 1988, Portas, 1989, Martins, 1991). This aims to reduce uncertainty on land use which affects and generates mobility of goods and people. It is important to involve the population to assure its commitment to the process (Martins, 1991).

Once consensus is reached, policies of the kind suggested here can be part of the negotiation process to achieve agreement on transportation and mobility strategies. Afterwards strategies should be progressively implemented and continuously adjusted to be successful. Furthermore, it is quite probable that the involvement of the different levels and sectors knowledgeable of the region would provide innovative strategies for the specific issues at stake.

The efficient management of the fluxes in a metropolitan area requires an integrated approach. Information to rationalise the situation is necessary at the different spatial levels to support the decisions.

The values obtained with this study show that the costs associated with commuting in the metropolitan area are considerable. Consequently, even small increases in efficiency can result in important savings at the regional level, making the control of factors related to the fluxes assume a key importance in the global management of the MAL.

Acknowledgements

The authors would like to thank their colleagues for their valuable collaboration: Julia Seixas, who provided the methodology for the estimation of emissions, and Helena Farrall and Leonor Amaral for the final proof-reading. L. T. Vasconcelos would also like to thank the National Institute of Scientific Research (INIC) for the grant to support her work.

Notes:

1. These administrative units (Distritos) contain the MAL.
2. Montijo shows a value close to one (0.98).
3. Mafra was not considered because its commuting pattern in 1981 as part of the MAL was not significant.
4. Portugal: 3.15 toe (tonne oil equivalent) per 1000 US dollars, France: 2.93, Federal Germany 2.88 (Almeida e Castro, 1990).
5. PEN - Plano Energético Nacional (National Energy Plan).
6. Due to car consumption in Portugal being similar to France and higher than Italy - 0.91 toe (Almeida e Castro, 1990).
7. Standard average speed in urban areas ranged from 15 to 30 km/hr (Almeida e Castro, 1990).
8. 3.4 US$.
9. In the public sector the price calculated per kilometre is 37.25US$, which includes the cost of fuel, maintenance and depreciation of the vehicle.
10. 0.3 US$.
11. Almeida e Castro, 1990.
12. 34 US$.
13. The average values considered are: 10 litres for 100 km for cars (value for 1980 for urban areas - PEN 90) and 18.5 goe (gross oil equivalent)/pkm for buses (DGTT).
14. For cars; NOx - 32.4 kg/tonne; VOC - 53.7 kg/tonne; CO - 3.93 tonne/TJI. For buses; NOx - 63.9 kg/tonne; VOC - 7.2 kg/tonne; CO - 0.35 tonne/TJI (DGQA, 2.90, Pollutant Emission).
15. 345,000 US$.
16. The average speed used was 30 km/h and the data referred to 1981 values.
17. 2,069,000 US$.
18. Approximately 7 US$.
19. OECD Environmental Indicators 1981.
20. According to the Environmental report on the 1987 'State of the Environment and Land Use' the national values of NOx in 1980 were 165,000 tonne and in 1983, 190,000 tonne.
21. The VOC value was 90,884 tonne in 1985 for the whole country.

REFERENCES

Abecassis, N. K. <u>Lisboa na Sua Area Metropolitana</u>. Paper presented in I Seminário Internacional Area Metropolitana de Lisboa. Que Futuro? Organizado FCSH/Universidade Nova de Lisboa (October 1987), 183-186.

Almeida e Castro, F. <u>Transportation and Energy Conservation in Transportation and Energy</u>. Course included in the European Programme of Specialisation in Combustion, Energy and Pollution organised by the IST/ITEC. COMETT-EEC 1990.

Baptista, E. <u>O Concelho de Loures na Area Metropolitana de Lisboa</u>. Paper presented in I Seminário Internacional Area Metropolitana de Lisboa. Que Futuro? Organizado FCSH/Universidade Nova de Lisboa (October 1987), 271-289.

Barreiros, J. Auto-Estrada Lisboa-Cascais. Um Atribulado Processo de Intervenção Urbanística in <u>Sociedade e Território</u> no. 7 (July 1988), 35-46.

Brito, R. et al. <u>Caracteristicas Gerais da População</u>. Paper presented in I Seminário Internacional Area Metropolitana de Lisboa. Que Futuro? Organizado FCSH/Universidade Nova de Lisboa (October 1987) pp. 127-141.

Costa, J. Congestão do Tráfego Rodoviário: Alternativas para a sua Redução in <u>Sociedade e Território</u> no. 7 (July 1988), 56-62.

Gakenheimer, R. (ed). (1978). <u>The Automobile and the Environment: An International Perspective</u>. MIT Press.

INE 1981, XII Recenseamento Geral da População e II Recenseamento Geral da Habitação.

Lobo, M. S. <u>Antecedents de Planeamento na Area Metropolitana de Lisboa</u>. Paper presented in I Seminário Internacional Area Metropolitana de Lisboa. Que Futuro? Organizado FCSH/Universidade Nova de Lisboa (October 1987), 143-149.

Martins, M. R. Conferência: 'Melhorar o Tráfego e a Qualidade de Vida nas Grandes Cidades' in <u>Sociedade e Território</u> no. 13 (July 1991), 130-132.

Mendes Baptista, A. J. Perspectivas de Desenvolvimento Económico da Area Metropolitana de Lisboa in <u>Sociedade e Território</u> no. 10, 11 (December 1989), 43-48.

Nunes da Silva, F. Area Metropolitana de Lisboa: que plano regional? in <u>Sociedade e Território</u> no. 10, 11 (December 1989), 121-122.

Pardal, S. C. <u>Ordenamento do Território e o Direito de Alteração do Uso do Solo</u>. Paper presented in I Seminário Internacional Area Metropolitana de Lisboa. Que Futuro? Organizade FCSH/Universidade Nova de Lisboa (October 1987), 157-161.

Pereira, M. Intervenções Autárquicas em Contexto Metropolitano. Paper presented in I Seminário Internacional Area Metropolitana de Lisboa. Que Futureo? Organizade FCSH/Universidade Nova de Lisboa (October 1987), 173-181.

Portas, N. Os Planos de Lisboa in Sociedade e Território no. 10, 11 (December 1989), 131-138.

Salgueiro, T. B. Os Transportes e a Organização do Espaço in Sociedade e Território no. 7 (July 1988), 47-55.

Searn-Mpat 1987, Relatório do Estado do Ambiente e ordenamento do Território.

Searn 1989, Ambiente 89.

Vasconcelos, L.T., et al. Resource, Health and Housing in Lisbon. Paper presented at the European Colloquium 1989 on the Project: European Academy of the Urban Environment, Urban Ecology, and Urban Open Space Planning, Berlin, December 1989.

Viegas, J. M. O Sistema Viário e de Transportes no Plano Geral de Urbanização do Porto in Sociedade e Território no. 7 (July 1988), 8-17.

MOBILITY PROBLEMS OF THE YOUNG

Antje Flade[*]
Institut Wohnen und Umwelt
Darmstadt

Based upon the thesis that the traffic environment of today impedes the mobility and the social integration of children, the question is pursued as to how the traffic environment affects the following groups: pre-school children, elementary school children and the age group from 10 to 14 years. Characteristics of these groups are: with the pre-school children, self-reliant mobility is extremely restricted, which has consequences upon their development, as well as upon the time budget of women; with elementary school children, the accident rate is the highest among all pedestrian accidents; the 10 to 14 year olds are in extreme danger when riding a bike. The hypothesis is that deficient integration of children into the traffic environment forms their socialisation in such a way that older children and adolescents strive for a motorised traffic participation. This hypothesis is proved by empirical data.

SOCIAL COHESION - THE REAL PROBLEM OF TRANSPORT PLANNING POLICIES

Klaus Schlabbach[*]
Town Planning Authority
Darmstadt

---

1. **Situation**

   Transport is an important aspect of everyday life and that is why transport policies are frequently discussed at the state, federal and local levels. In most European countries, transport planning still focuses on growing car ownership, new roads and truck freight movements.

   On the other hand, the structure of society is changing fast (e.g. increasing number of elderly people and one-person-households). And changes in the economic sector are important as well. This altogether leads to inequality in health, education, income, housing, employment and mobility as a common framework between regions, cities and districts.

2. **Analysing Transport Planning**

   Against this background, the improper use of cars, which will be defined by an individual and social approach, damages and polarises the society (rich/deprived). This will be evaluated by different criteria:

   - accessibility;
   - hierarchy of road network;
   - noise and air pollution;
   - social function of streets;
   - traffic safety.

   It is well known, for example, that people with less household income have to live in streets with more noise.

3. **Improvement by Example**

   Improvement can be made in six sectors:

   - public transport;
   - cycling;
   - pedestrians;
   - traffic calming;
   - parking restrictions;
   - land use and choice of location.

Many towns all over Europe are testing different measures of the above-mentioned sectors (Delft, Erlangen, Karlsruhe, Uppsala, Freiburg, Malmö, Bologna, Hannover, Göteborg, Zürich, Copenhagen, Saarbrücken, Amsterdam, Hamburg, Odense, Detmold, Den Haag, Rosenheim); details will be discussed. Latest research shows that about 50% of car traffic in large cities is suitable for diversion; under those circumstances public transport increases by 33% and cycling by 75%.

4. Cost and Effectiveness

Cost-benefit analysis for transportation systems is discussed. The main difference is between the individual and the social approach. Both approaches will be outlined for the former Federal Republic of Germany and the western part of Berlin.

CONCLUSIONS, RECOMMENDATIONS

by

Margaret Grieco
Transport Studies Unit
University of Oxford

The theme paper by Dr Laurie Pickup introduced the key transport characteristics of contemporary European cities; in particular, he drew attention to:

a) the growing problem of congestion and the emergence of demand management policies as a response

and

b) the importance of mobility (lack of mobility) as one indicator of an emerging dual and polarised society.

In this context, Dr Pickup drew attention to the potential of new transport, travel and passenger information technologies for addressing many of the identified mobility problems in European cities. These key themes made recurrent and repeated appearances throughout the subsequent workshop, sometimes as the content of the separately prepared deliveries by workshop members, sometimes as contribution to the discussion by the various workshop participants.

The presentation of papers took a mixture of forms: there were presentations which provided written papers to accompany deliveries, presentations which had accompanying data and overheads and inspired, but less formal, presentations by experts. There was a good and lively discussion which formed as important a part of the working group as did formal and quasi-formal papers and which ended with the joint construction of a listing of the key elements of discussion that should be reported back to the main plenary session.

This working group had the benefit of considering a highly diversified range of approaches on the topic of the Transport Environment and the Social Integration of Cities. We had available to us:

* conceptual papers which identified general transport organisational dynamics in the context of major societal changes such as social polarisation, demographic change, the emergence of the politics of the environment;

* a European policy paper concerned with the issues of the evaluation and implementation of transport technology programmes and which raised the important question of whether the various European technology programmes have fallen victim to an over-concentration on supply side activities at the expense of the proper consideration of social needs that technology should be harnessed to meet;

* a paper which demonstrated that the traffic environment of today impedes the mobility and social integration of children;

* papers on mechanisms for achieving shifts in transport behaviour towards more environment friendly modes as a general policy which drew particular attention to the need to adopt a social approach in evaluating the costs of the various alternative forms of transport provision;

* papers concerned with redesign of transport arrangements in particular cities (Lisbon and Barcelona).

Whilst the discussion itself was both detailed in terms of research and policy experience and findings, there were a number of bold and broad issues which emerged and which can usefully be reproduced here as understandings and recommendations emerging out of the working group.

1. Transport policy is not an effective tool for altering basic equity arrangements although transport organisation can enhance or amplify disadvantage.

2. Efficiency considerations can dominate equity considerations most particularly in situations where there is a transport crisis, for instance, in cities such as Lisbon. High levels of congestion have generated a clear recognition of the need for demand management policies in a number of European locations. Equally issues of safety and the environment have played a major role in placing demand management policies on the political agenda.

3. Within European transport policy, there has been a general movement away from an equity focus towards an efficiency focus which has in its turn been replaced by a negative externality focus. Currently, transport arrangements are increasingly viewed in terms of their contribution towards the competivity of cities. This is not to argue that such a movement in policy priorities is to be welcomed but merely to record the existence of such a dynamic.

4. The polarisation of mobility and accessibility experience which is occurring in Europe requires clear and immediate policy thinking. The urban expression of this process of polarisation is the 'fortress' image where whole communities are sealed into poorly resourced local environments and where they are by-passed in terms of access to high quality transport facilities. There is a danger of social explosion where such polarisation of mobility experience is permitted to occur.

5. Taking any one course of action in the transport area requires complementary, supporting and accompanying measures to be taken in other policy areas. In particular the group considered the relationship between housing dynamics and transport organisation. Housing dynamics have an impact on transport patterns, similarly transport dynamics have an impact on housing patterns.

6. Changing transport behaviour away from dependence on the private car and towards public transport, cycling and walking was deemed crucial by the

working group as a whole; in particular attention was drawn to the importance of breaking the automobile cycle by changing childhood constraints on mobility.

7. The improper use of cars damages the total society and polarises the society (rich/deprived). That this is the case can be established both from a social and individual approach in respect of a range of different criteria:

   * modal split;
   * accessibility;
   * hierarchy of road network;
   * noise and air pollution;
   * social functions of streets;
   * traffic safety.

   Given these considerations there is a need for careful transport policy design which operates so as to harness environmental friendly coalitions. At the very outset, there is a need for the social evaluation of the costs of the various alternative transport arrangements. In adopting such an approach, the following factors are of considerable importance:

   * Re-education of transport planners away from the perspective of the car culture.
   * The recognition of the important social impact of an integrated information approach in the public transport sector (in-home trip planning facilities, high quality real time public transport information).
   * Policy commitment to influence and change modal arrangements in favour of public transport (park and ride facilities, road pricing, etc.).
   * The recognition that different institutional arrangements around transport organisation and transport policy in different countries affect both policy formulation and its transferability.

8. There was a clear recognition of the need for an integrated urban systems approach to transport planning. The general understanding was that matters of transport circulation were problems in the domain of urban logistics rather than component problems for commercial resolution. There was an equal recognition that the relationship of the city to the region required considerable attention in the area of transport; the migration of problems from one urban location to another received group attention. In this context, it was noted that the removal of the old European boundaries would affect the old relationship of cities to their hinterlands along the borders, with the probability that the cities of the weaker border region would lose out in the competitiveness stakes. The old national protection afforded to such weaker cities by their borders would be removed and there will be a need within the European Community to develop policies for coping with the declines of such municipalities as they are opened up to the more competitive market forces. In line with the new territorial boundaries of Europe there will be needs for new transport alignments; existing

transport arrangements will require re-assessment as new 'natural' urban and regional units emerge.

9. There was a clear recognition of the importance of strategic transport planning in a context where there is a general European transport crisis in evidence. It was noted that special events or circumstances could generate the necessary social consensus to permit the rapid development and implementation of strategic transport plans; the forthcoming Olympics in Barcelona provided a very clear example of such a set of circumstances. It was noted that conflicting goals were very often a feature of the transport environment and Barcelona, despite its ability to reach a rapid consensus on some relatively radical demand management measures, was no exception.

10. Finally, we did not discuss the demography of ageing and its transport implications. The view of this rapporteur, though not necessarily that of the working group, is that such a topic might usefully serve as the focus of the next European Foundation initiative.

SELECTED PAPERS AND CONCLUSIONS OF

THE WORKING GROUP

ON

PREVENTING AND FIGHTING CRIME/DELINQUENCY AND THE URBAN ENVIRONMENT

COMPOSITION OF WORKING GROUP 2

PREVENTING AND FIGHTING CRIME/DELINQUENCY AND THE URBAN ENVIRONMENT

Chairman: Ms Mairín Quill, TD
Chairperson, Committee on Crime
Dáil Éireann, Dublin

Rapporteur: Mrs Sandra Walklate
University of Salford

Expert Introducing the Working Group: Mrs Lina Marsoni
Municipality of Milan

Speakers-Participants:

1. Mrs Maria Wissen
   ILRES, Luxembourg

2. Mrs Clelia Boesi
   Regional Government of Lombardy

3. Mr Vincent-Pierre Comiti
   Ministère des Affaires Sociales, Paris
   Representative of WHO

4. Mrs Lindsay MacFarlane
   Urban Affairs Division, OECD

5. Mrs Chara Paraskevopoulou
   Hellenic Agency for Local Authorities and Development

6. Mr Peter Lumsden
   Committee on Crime
   Department of Justice, Dublin

7. Ms Graziella Caiani Praturlon
   EUROPIL, Italy

CRIME PREVENTION FACING THE 1990s: ANOTHER VIEW

by

Sandra Walklate
Department of Sociology
University of Salford

This paper is concerned to examine the traditional concern with delinquency and the environment within crime prevention work. It is intended to argue that those traditional concerns have had a limited success and that a broader based understanding of the nature of crime, fear of crime, and the links between public and private experiences are necessary in order to establish a more complete crime prevention programme.

1. Introduction

The title of this workshop, focusing as it does on delinquency and the environment, reflects what have been the traditional and what are the continuing concerns of the crime prevention 'industry'. As Bottoms (1990) reports, 18% of males under 28 convicted of an offence by that age account for 70% of all known offences for that age group. In addition, it is well established that the peak age of offending for boys is 15 - 18 years, and for girls is 15 years; with half of all known offenders being aged under 20 years (1991: Home Office Research and Statistics Department: A Digest of Information on the Criminal Justice System.). The focus on delinquency would therefore seem justifiable.

A further concern has been reflected in the attention accorded to the environment. Again much criminological work from the Chicago School to Wilson and Kelling's 'broken windows' thesis (1982) has been concerned to establish the contribution of both physical and spatial factors towards the creation of a 'criminogenic' environment. Again a range of evidence would seem to justify the continued persuance of this theme. The purpose of this paper is not to deny the importance of these concerns, but to examine how an exclusive focus on them may discourage a broader and more imaginative approach to crime prevention.

2. Crime Prevention Themes of the 1980s

Davis (1991) states that:

'The dire predictions of Richard Nixon's 1969 National Commission on the Causes and Prevention of Violence have been tragically fulfilled: we live in "fortress cities" brutally divided between "fortified cells" of affluent society and "places of terror" where the police battle the criminalized poor......In many instances the semiotics of so-called "defensible space" are just about as subtle as the swaggering white cop' (ibid. pp. 225-6).

Whilst it might be possible to dispute the literary style and subsequent connotations of the observations made by Davis, what cannot be disputed is the extent to which the developments with which he is concerned form a real part of the '(post)-modern' North American environmental experience. These developments can be connected to what Currie (1988) has called the 'first phase' of community crime prevention. But what does this 'first phase' comprise?

The title of this paper is borrowed, purposefully, from a paper published in 1990 and written by Professor A.E. Bottoms. In this paper Bottoms offers an excellent summary of the nature of crime prevention initiatives which have developed in the United Kingdom and elsewhere during the 1980s. His discussion of these initiatives utilises the distinction which has been made between situational crime prevention and social crime prevention. Situational crime prevention measures focus on a particular kind of crime and the management of the immediate environment to prevent that crime. Social crime prevention measures deal with the 'fundamental causes' crime (Clarke, 1983). Each of these strategies have their problems.

Situational crime prevention measures raise the question of displacement, (Bottoms, 1990); presume an 'opportunistic' view of the cause of crime (Kinsey, Lea and Young, 1986) and subsume notions of victim blaming (Walklate, 1989). Hope and Shaw (1988) argue that social crime prevention measures, whilst initially concerned with the prevention of individual criminality, have latterly been concerned with the preventive role of the community. This latter concern has two strands to it; 'grass roots' responses and inter-agency responses.

The grass roots response has been typified in the United Kingdom by the increasing popularity of neighbourhood watch schemes. These schemes, which encourage local residents to become the 'eyes and ears of the police', have grown from one scheme in 1982 to 80,000 in 1990 (Jefferson and Shapland, 1990). The evidence to date concerning their effectiveness, however, clearly indicates that such schemes only appeal to certain sectors of the community; the predominantly white, middle class homeowner, (Dowds, Elliott and Mayhew, 1989, Donnison, Skola and Thomas, 1986, and Bennion et al, 1985); and if they achieve anything, it is in the area of fear reduction rather than crime reduction (Bennett, 1987).

Inter-agency responses attempt to bring together different agencies in the community to address a range of social problems in that community including crime. Such inter-agency activity suffers from a 'top-down' implementation style (Lewis and Salem, 1986); may be dominated by one agency, usually the police (Kinsey, Lea and Young, 1986); and can reflect agency conflicts over increasingly scarce resources and stereotypical images of what can be achieved in particular communities (Sampson et al, 1988).

In overviewing these developments Bottoms (1990) points favourably to two crime prevention initiatives which have deployed a mixture of situational and social crime prevention strategies. These two projects are: the Kirkholt Burglary Prevention Project based in Rochdale (Forrester et al, 1988) and the Hilldrop Project based in Islington, London (Lea et al, 1988). Both of these initiatives were introduced in high crime areas and employ a variation on the neighbourhood watch theme. The first established 'cocoon' schemes; the second a neighbourhood forum version. Both have also introduced target hardening and other crime prevention measures. The relative success of these mixed strategy initiatives leads Bottoms (1990) to argue for a 'strategy of careful and creative synthesis of situational and social approaches to crime prevention'.

There is, perhaps, little of surprise in an overview of crime prevention presented in this way. Bottoms (1990) is wary of the view that the rise of 'unstoppable' individualism is the root social cause of crime since this would result in a society:

'with massive security hardware protecting individual homes, streets, and shops, while all adult citizens would carry personal alarms, and perhaps guns, for individual protection while moving from place to place' (ibid. p. 20).

He reasonably concludes that what is needed is a 'balanced' crime prevention programme with an emphasis on 'social integration' and 'social relationships'. In some respects there is little need to dispute the spirit of this conclusion. However, it is significant that Bottoms reaches this conclusion without considering the problematic assumptions contained within the crime prevention strategies he considers or the extent to which his own conclusions stemming from them may also be problematic. This needs to be developed a little further.

Currie (1988), as suggested earlier, in overviewing the collection of papers edited by Hope and Shaw (1988) sidesteps the issue of situational or social crime prevention by arguing that there appears to be two phases in community crime prevention. These phases represent different conceptions of what a community is. It is worth quoting Currie (1988) at length on this since he raises some important questions which will be developed in this paper. He suggests that in these phases:

'their views of what it means to strengthen a community in order to fight crime differ sharply. Moreover, they differ in their view (and even more in their practice) on what kinds of communities should receive most attention, and similarly, on what kind of crime should be most heavily targeted by community prevention....or indeed whether reducing crime is the main priority at all. By the same token, the two "phases" differ in the degree to which they are concerned with the offender, or potential offender, as a focus of intervention. Finally, they differ on the balance to be struck between public and private responsibility for crime prevention and more generally for the enhancement of community life' (ibid. p. 280).

Phase one thinking is characterised by the defensible space, broken windows, neighbourhood watch equation, in which the view is that 'if people just get their act together they will at the very least feel better about their community and each other'(Currie, 1988, p.281). This, Currie argues, results in an emphasis on fear reduction strategies, perhaps to the expense of crime reduction strategies. In addition, phase one thinking fails to recognise that offenders are members, often, of the same community. Thus:

'There is no sense, for example, that the people you are dealing with might include a neighbour's kid who has a learning problem and hangs about on the corner because he is afraid to go to school, or your sister's abusive husband....hardly a stranger....but an intimate member of a local household' (ibid. p. 2281 -2).

These emphases amount to what Currie calls a lack of 'structural awareness'. Such an awareness is more characteristic of the second phase of community crime prevention. Different initiatives, however, reflect this 'structural awareness' in different ways; see for example, Bottoms and Wiles (1988) on community crime careers, and Curtis (1988) on employment opportunities and extended family structures.

Currie's distinction between phase one and phase two thinking does not equate with the bifurcation between situational and social crime prevention. Indeed rather like Bottoms (1990), Currie recognises that both situational and social crime prevention measures may or may not work in differential combinations. Currie's analysis, however, encourages much closer critical attention to be paid to the underlying sociological and criminological assumptions of these strategies. In particular he draws attention to:

i) whether crime prevention strategies reduce crime or reduce the fear of crime;

ii) what kind of crime is presupposed by such strategies, or perhaps more pertinently, what kind of crime is neglected by such strategies;

iii) the need to examine the resourcing base of such initiatives.

To this list I would add, that the crime prevention debate couched in the terms presented by Bottoms appears to fail to appreciate the complex nature of communities, their existing social networks and daily routines. These factors not only form the basis of individual's 'precautionary' behaviour (Stanko, 1987) but also the basis of the likely success of any initiative introduced into them. If these interrelated questions are explored then there develops a somewhat different picture of not only what is meant by crime prevention, but also what this might mean in the urban environment. One way of constructing such a redirection is to reconsider some of the issues raised by the fear of crime debate alluded to by Currie (1988).

3. The Fear of Crime Debate

In the 1980s much attention was paid to the question of whether it was crime or the fear of crime which constituted 'the problem'. As a part of this concern attention became focused on the role of the media in constructing and perpetuating the fear of crime. As a consequence the Home Office Standing Conference on Crime Prevention commissioned an independent report on the fear of crime, chaired by Michael Grade. This came to be known as the Grade Report (1989). This report states that:

'The media play a central role in forming impressions about crime. Television, radio and the press feed the public much of their information about - and images of - crime. The pressure to increase circulation or attract audiences leads to simplification, over-dramatisation and sensationalism. The media, especially the tabloid press, frequently aggravate and exploit the fear of crime' (ibid. p.23).

As much of the traditional social psychological research has shown, the formation of people's attitudes and perceptions is somewhat more complex that this quote suggests. But the quote does articulate a strand in the fear of crime debate which is concerned with the (ir)rationality of such fear. Thus fuelling the view that it is the fear of crime rather than crime itself which constitutes 'the problem'. A view, which in some ways was facilitated by the findings of the Home Office sponsored criminal victimisation survey with those same findings also clearly illustrating that such fear was not evenly distributed throughout society.

The First British Crime Survey found that 60% of elderly women who lived in inner city areas felt very unsafe when out on foot after dark. Maxfield (1984), analysing data for the second British Crime Survey, states that fear for personal safety is a feature of residents of densely populated urban areas, with 41% of women in cities feeling very unsafe walking alone at night in their neighbourhood. Asking similar questions, the 1989 International Crime Survey also found that fear was much higher among women than men and also higher among inhabitants of larger cities (Van Dijk et al, 1991, p.78); with the proponents of the local victimiszation surveys, (Kinsey, 1985, Jones et al, 1986, Crawford et al, 1990) going so far as to suggest that in inner city areas an implicit curfew operates for women. The problem is, of course, in relation to all these findings, that it is not necessarily the fear of (street) crime per se which produces the curfew on women (or the elderly). Fear of crime may constitute the expression of other perceptions of relationships and the neighbourhood. These issues have yet to be fully explored. (See below.)

Findings such as these, if read alongside some of the findings from the same data sources concerned with the risk from crime (see for example, Gottfredson, 1984) led to the conclusion that women's fears, (and those of the elderly) are irrational since they are the groups least at risk from crime. There is a certain circularity implied by this argument which also represents a tendency to read such findings in isolation from some of the other issues addressed by the surveys discussed above which have been revealed in subsequent analyses.

Worrall and Pease (1986) in re-analysing some of the British Crime Survey data, Jones, MacLean and Young, 1986, Crawford et al, 1990, and the International Crime Survey, Van Dijk et al, 1991, all found in differing degrees and with slightly different ways of analysing offence categories, that women were more at risk from street crime than men. This leads to Crawford et al (1990) to comment that:

'Crime is a product of inner city reality and Government policy not a figment of some editors imagination' (ibid. p.77.).

Thus clearly suggesting that fear of crime is not irrational and that women's fear of crime may well be related to their own public and private experiences of criminal victimisation, the notion that women's fears are irrational has contributed to the crime prevention debate in a particular way. Stanko (1991) states that:

'Crime prevention advice revolves around public crime. And while the police and criminal justice system are slowly becoming involved, private violence is still seen as something entirely different than public violence. Crime prevention advice, including much of the advice about avoiding sexual assault, focuses on the public domain. It is easier to give advice about checking the back seat of your car for intruders, or advising against standing at dimly lit bus stops than finding ways of advising women not to trust "so-called" "trustworthy" men' (1991, p.4).

Stanko (1990) offers a critical analysis of the kind of crime prevention advice which has been offered to women in recent years through Home Office and local authority documentation. This documentation, she argues, fails to address a number of questions. Firstly, much of the advice offered, as Stanko rightly points out above, focuses on the potential danger of strangers. Thus ignoring a wealth of feminist research which clearly shows that women have most to fear from men that they know. Secondly, it advises women on precautionary behaviour, thus paying little attention to the fact that women are well trained in precautionary tactics. (See Stanko, 1990, and also Crawford et al, 1990.). Finally, it fails to recognise that women's fear of sexual violence is the foundation of these strategies (Stanko, 1991).

The fear of crime debate, fuelled by a view that women's fears (and to a certain extent those of the elderly) were irrational, has been challenged. This challenge demands a closer examination of those publicly expressed fears. The continued elision within crime prevention initiatives between women's publicly expressed fear and their privately experienced victimisation is clearly problematic. It is, however, not intended to imply by this observation, that the focus on public space as an arena for the victimisation of women is misplaced. Some of the evidence cited above would clearly suggest that such a focus is worthwhile. Neither is it intended to suggest that those local authorities who have attempted to take seriously the gender issues related to crime and the fear of crime are misguided. The situational strategies of improving street lighting (Painter, 1988), the introduction of women-only taxi services, late night bus services and women-only sessions at leisure centres (examples of which are all cited by Comedia, 1991), may all have improved the quality of life for those women who have benefited from them. Indeed, these strategies certainly provide a different feel for, and appreciation of, the crime prevention issues facing the 1990s than the impression one might be left with from the overview presented by Bottoms (1990). It is intended, however, to use the issues raised by Stanko (1990) and others to suggest a re-orientation of the concerns of crime prevention.

Two important issues are raised by the feminist critique of conventional crime prevention. The first of these relates to the conceptual framework used by feminist work. Feminists talk of strategies of personal safety, not fear of crime. This emphasises positive strategies and the potential autonomy of women. Some work has already progressed our understanding of such strategies. What is of particular interest here, however, is the connections to be made between knowledge of these personal strategies and the broader conceptions of a 'public sense of well-being' (Taylor, 1991), both of which may influence the more traditional crime prevention framework.

The second issue relates to the question of crime prevention in the private domain. One strand of 'crime prevention' activity not commented on by Bottoms (1990), though recognised as important by Currie (1988) is reflected in the increasing criminal justice agency activity in the arena of domestic violence. Its separation from the mainstream activity of crime prevention officers, crime prevention literature, and from the broader academic literature on crime prevention, would serve to support Stanko's observation cited above. There has, however, been a flurry of activity on this issue both in the United Kingdom and elsewhere during the 1980s. An examination of responses to domestic violence highlights some important questions in relation to crime prevention in particular and women's fear of crime in general. Such an examination also has the potential for influencing the more traditional crime prevention network.

4. A Public Sense of Well-Being

Research currently being undertaken at the University of Salford is concerned to document some of the features of how 'the public' feel about public spaces. This research has been influenced by some of the issues relating to crime and the fear of crime discussed in this paper. It is, however, also influenced by a desire to understand the impact of the 'transformations of the urban landscape' (Taylor, 1990), and the sense that people may make of such transformations. The research has recently completed its pilot stage and is about to enter a more detailed comparative one, but the findings to date concerning people's sense of safety in different locations in Manchester raise some interesting issues for the questions under discussion here.

A survey of 767 train and bus users and shoppers showed that people in Greater Manchester have a very modest set of expectations of what could be provided for their use with respect to public transport systems. Though perhaps somewhat contrary to what some of the criminological literature might suggest, particularly of the Wilson and Kelling (1982) variety, whilst the majority of bus users (65%) regarded bus stations as 'dirty', 42% of those same respondents still regarded them as 'safe' or 'very safe' places to be (Taylor, 1991). Taylor (1991) goes on to suggest that:

'It seems quite apparent that the key issue for many citizens of this Northern industrial city is not **necessarily** or **primarily** the dilapidated condition, for example, of bus stations or trains: what seems to matter most is the "friendliness" of the staff and of other users of public services' (ibid. p.22.).

Indeed there appears to be a resigned acceptance of the presence of vandalism and graffiti. These findings are substantiated to a certain extent by the follow-up focus group interviews. In these interviews, which support the idea that there is more than one public each of whom have different expectations of public services, suggest that whilst there was little anxiety expressed about safety in relation to accidents, there was clear evidence of anxiety over safety expressed in other terms. Women, and the elderly, in particular, expressed anxiety in relation to the behaviour of other people, especially men (Taylor, 1991b).

This research clearly confirms some of the findings which were already known with respect to gender. In addition, however, it is also clearly putting the public's responses to the environment in a particular perspective. For 'the public' of Greater Manchester, what seems to matter most, is the friendliness of figures of authority in these public places alongside the behaviour of other people (men). This does not mean that the public of Greater Manchester are unappreciative of improvements to public space as the respondents' views of the refurbishments to Manchester Piccadily Station indicate (Taylor, 1991a). What these findings may suggest, however, is that the tolerance of the physical nature of public space is more specifically connected to the historical processes which are transforming public life in the UK; namely, the extension of the 'free' market economy. These developments, as a consequence, may well be marking a new phase in the 'community crime career' (Bottoms and Wiles, 1988) of certain localities within the region.

It is intended that this research engage in a comparative analysis of these ideas in an urban area with historically different physical and social characteristics. What it has illustrated in this context is not only the complexity with which human beings may interact with the physical environment but also the difficulty of assigning too great an importance to that physical environment. Its effects are difficult to chart. With respect to fear and safety it suggests that it is the behaviour of other people (men) that matter. With that in mind it is perhaps worthwhile considering some features of the recent policy activity which has focused on domestic violence.

5. A Private Sense of Well-Being

The issue of 'domestic' violence itself has moved through a number of phases; from 'wife battering' in the 1970s, to domestic violence in the 1980s, and towards the question of woman abuse in North America of the 1990s. It has also moved through different questions; from why doesn't she leave, to why does she stay, to why are men violent? Each of these phases and questions are telling in what they reveal, at different historical moments, about how this issue has been addressed.

In the United Kingdom at this point in time the policy response to domestic violence is perhaps centred in the middle stage. This is represented most keenly by the Home Office circular 60/1990 issued to all Chief Constables (and others) urging them to treat domestic violence as seriously as violence which occurs in the street, and reminding them of their powers under a range of statutory and common law legislation. The circular encourages a 'presumption to arrest' response in the case of domestic violence incidents.

This is not the place to discuss the strengths and weaknesses of such a policy response. Suffice it to say that there are many difficulties in a partial translation of an essentially North American response to domestic violence to the UK context (Morley and Mullender, 1991) and even more difficulties in ensuring that it works effectively; that is, in the interests of women. (See for example, the collection of essays edited by Hamner, Radford and Stanko, 1989.). The question of interest here is to consider this response in relation to crime prevention.

As a preventive response a 'presumption to arrest' policy represents an 'enforcement crackdown' style (Elias, 1986). The assumption being that the prioritisation of domestic violence as an offence alongside the use of the law as a symbolic indication that such behaviour is no longer acceptable, will result in discouraging individual offenders from re-offending. In the context of domestic violence this approach has been supported in policy terms by an incomplete reading of the deterrent effect of arrest under these circumstances as represented by the work of Sherman and Berk (1984), and by a belief in the symbolic power of the law. The question raised here is not so much to doubt the validity of either of those two positions (which can certainly be argued) but to emphasise the fundamental individualistic bias of a policy conceived solely in these terms. There is little evidence to suggest that the presence of the law, per se, and its use against individual offenders, has succeeded with respect to other offences either to prevent individual recidivism or to change collective attitudes. To summarise, it is interesting to note that the response to domestic violence as conceived in the United Kingdom has been formulated in a vacuum, with little recognition of what is already known concerning the effectiveness or otherwise of such policies and little concern to translate the **community** rhetoric of crime prevention, highlighted elsewhere in this paper, to the question of domestic violence.

Evidence from North America supports the view that a presumption to arrest policy is most effective when put into place alongside a range of other community based initiatives; refuge facilities for women and children, counselling initiatives for men etc. (See, for example, Jaffe et al, 1986.). Yet this understanding has not been embraced in the UK either on the basis of this evidence or on the basis of the evidence from other community based crime prevention initiatives. This, of course, assumes that such a policy has as its primary aim crime prevention. There is clear evidence from both my own empirical work in this area and from appreciating the overall trends in policing in the UK that other motivating forces are present. During the 1980s policing has been very much concerned with 'efficiency', 'value for money' and 'quality of service'. The willingness with which the police in particular have moved towards implementing responses to domestic violence are as much a product of these forces as they constitute a crime prevention response.

What this discussion of public and private senses of well-being clearly illustrates is the recognition that crime, and crime prevention, needs to be, and is beginning to be, conceived in much broader terms than that crime which occurs in public; and that, as in the consideration of public space above, gender is the key to understanding how to respond to both the public and the private arena. It also illustrates that the question of the resourcing of the 'public household' is an important determinant of not only how public space is changing, but also how responses to private space are being structured. How might an increased awareness of these issues impinge upon a crime prevention agenda?

6. Crime Prevention Facing the 1990s

In some respects this paper has moved a long way from the initial agenda discussed and presented by Bottoms (1990). The issues addressed represent a challenge to the crime prevention debate at a theoretical, empirical and policy level.

Giddens (1991) has argued that there are two key features to the present modern world; the globalisation of modernity and the radicalisation of modernity. By these Gibbens is referring to, on the one hand, not just the extension of capitalism but the transformation of time and space. A process which does not necessarily produce unity but may also produce fragmentation and marginalisation. And, on the other hand, it is important to acknowledge that we all live in post-traditional societies; the radicalisation of modernity. These processes of globalisation and radicalisation connect changes in interpersonal life with changes taking place in global life. One dimension to these changes is the question of violence and its resolution both interpersonally and globally. Giddens argues that the 'implicit democracy' presumed by the idea of a 'relationship' at the interpersonal level is producing gender transformations in Western society which are not unconnected to the options on the agenda at an international level. The relevance of appreciating such a theoretical perspective with respect to crime prevention are important.

Firstly, it draws attention to the need to challenge the historical separation of the public from the private in two ways. In the first instance it encourages the recognition that such a separation results in unnecessary and unproductive contradictions in understanding crime and the fear of crime with respect to gender. Challenging this separation would demand in the context of domestic violence, not just more resources from more refuges etc., but a serious educational package designed to encourage young men and women to re-evaluate their relationship with one another. (An example of such an initiative in New Zealand is cited by Stanko, 1990.) Thus ensuring that prevention advice with respect to interpersonal violence addresses the behaviour of men as well as women.

The second challenge it makes to the traditional distinction between the public and the private is in terms of not only reconstituting the debate concerning the nature of public provision and the responsibility for that provision (see, for example, Association of Metropolitan Authorities, 1990) but to consider the social effects of 'free market societies'. (Taylor, 1990). Such social effects would appear to be having both their public and private dimensions in terms of the constraints placed on policy initiatives and the implementation process.

Secondly, it draws attention to the complexity of understanding the relationship between any individual and their behaviour and the wider social context. Such complexities make themselves most keenly felt in the context of evaluating any crime prevention initiative as some of the examples cited above illustrate. If, however, the concern to take gender seriously in terms of crime prevention were considered then it would be important to recognise the variable mediating factors which would enhance or inhibit the success of an initiative. For example, a survey conducted in Tayside concerned with women and safety clearly illustrates the potentially complex interrelationship between where you live and how safe you feel (Tayside Womens' Forum, 1990). Thus a persons sense of well-being in public may well be mediated by not only their 'private' experiences but also the extent of their involvement with a range of formal and informal groupings within their community. All of which may, of course, have gender dimensions to them. (See Walklate, 1990, pp.37-39, for a further discussion of this in the context of the fear of crime.) This suggests that we do not know enough about the infrastructure of particular communities and what may or may not work within those communities. These questions constitute a clear empirical challenge to social scientists in monitoring and evaluating the impact of crime prevention initiatives.

The policy challenge is considerable. The disturbances which have occurred in England and Wales during September illustrate this challenge more adequately than any academic discussion. The problem of young men's behaviour is the key problem of criminology and crime prevention. If that behaviour is to be taken seriously as gender constructed behaviour then there may be many lessons to be learned from appreciating what feminism has already told us concerning the social control of young women. Thus complying with the view of Giddens (1991) that the translation of violence into discourse is a crucial process. Such a process, of course, is not always empowering, but the recent events in the United Kingdom clearly suggest that in terms of crime prevention the debate needs to move much further on from its traditional concerns with the relationship between delinquency and the environment. That relationship may well be there, but the arguments presented here would suggest that it needs to be formulated in substantially different terms.

7. Conclusion

Whilst this paper has attempted to summarise a diverse range of issues and material, it is hoped that it has presented a view of the crime prevention for the 1990s in somewhat different terms than that posed by Bottoms (1990). It is interesting to note that in some respects the implications of the argument presented here lead to a similar conclusion to that offered by Bottoms (1990); that is that the crucial issue for crime prevention lies in finding strategies for the improvement of social integration and social relationships. However, that conclusion has been reached by considering a different theoretical, empirical and policy agenda than that presented by Bottoms (1990). The questions raised by understanding the interrelationship between public and private life and the significance of gender to those relationships takes crime prevention beyond the realms of the environment and delinquency and yet simultaneously subsumes them in an agenda couched in terms different to those with which this paper began. Challenging what is meant by crime and crime prevention and the impact of the nature of the public household on those issues may still return us to the question of the behaviour of men, but hopefully, by taking such a challenge seriously the quality of life for all sections of society can be improved.

REFERENCES

Association of Metropolitan Authorities (1990). *Crime Reduction; Framework for the Nineties*. London, AMA.

Bennett, T. (1987). *An Evaluation of Two Neighbourhood Watch Schemes in London: Executive Summary*, Final Report to the Home Office Research and Planning Unit. Cambridge, Institute of Criminology.

Bennion, C., Davis, A., Hesse, B., Joshua, L., McGloin, P., Munn, C. and Tester, S. (1985). *Neighbourhood Watch: The Eyes and Ears of Urban Policing?*, Occasional Papers in Sociology and Social Policy No.6. University of Surrey.

Bottoms, A. E., (1990). Crime Prevention Facing the 1990s, *Policing and Society*, vol.1., no.1., 3-22.

Bottoms, A.E. and Wiles, P. (1988). Crime and Housing Policy: A Framework for Crime Prevention Analysis, in T. Hope and M. Shaw (eds) *Community and Crime Reduction*, London, HMSO, 84-98.

Clarke, R.V. (1983). Situational crime prevention; its theoretical basis and practical scope, in M. Tonry and N. Morris (eds) *Crime and Justice: An Annual Review of Research* vol. 4. Chicago, University of Chicago Press.

Comedia (1991). *Out of Hours: Summary Report*. Calouste Gulbenkian Foundation.

Crawford, A., Jones, T., Woodhouse, T. and Young, J. (1990). *The Second Islington Crime Survey*. Middlesex Polytechnics: Centre for Criminology.

Currie, E. (1988). *Two Visions of Crime Prevention* in T. Hope and M. Shaw (eds) op. cit., 280-92.

Curtis, L. (1988). *The March of Folly: Crime and the Underclass*, in T. Hope and M. Shaw (eds) op. cit., 180-203.

Davis, M. (1990). *City of Quartz*. London, Verso.

Donnison, H., Skola, J. and Thomas, P. (1986). *Neighbourhood Watch: Policing the People*. London, The Libertarian Research and Education Trust.

Elias, R. (1986). *The Politics of Victimisation*, Oxford. Oxford University Press.

Forrester, D., Chatterton, M. and Pease, K. (1988). *The Kirkholt Burglary Prevention Project, Rochdale*, Crime Prevention Unit Paper 13. London, HMSO.

Giddens, A. (1991). Lecture presented to the Soviet Sociologists Summer School, University of Manchester, September.

Gottfredson, M. R. (1984). *Victims of Crime: the Dimensions of Risk*, Home Office Research Study no. 81. London, HMSO.

The Grade Report (1989). Home Office Standing Conference on Crime Prevention, Report on the Working Group on the Fear of Crime. London, HMSO.

Hamner, J., Radford, J. and Stanko, E. A. (1989). Women, Policing and Male Violence. London, Routledge.

Hope, T. and Shaw, M. (1988). Community Approaches to Reducing Crime in T. Hope and M. Shaw (eds) op. cit., 1-29.

Jefferson, T. and Shapland, J. (1990). Criminal Justice and the Production of Law Order and Control: Trends in the 1980s in the UK Paper presented to GERN seminar on the Production of Order and Control. CESDIP, Paris, October.

Jones, T., Maclean, B. and Young, J., (1986). The Islington Crime Survey. Aldershot, Gower.

Kinsey, R., (1984). Merseyside Crime Survey: First Report. Liverpool, Merseyside Police Authority.

Kinsey, R., Lea, J. and Young, J., (1986). Losing the Fight Against Crime. Oxford, Blackwell.

Lea, J., Jones, T., Woodhouse, T. and Young, J. (1988). Preventing Crime: The Hilldrop Environmental Improvement Survey, First Report (Middlesex Polytechnic, Centre for Criminology)

Lewis, D. A. and Salem, G. (1986), Fear of Crime: Incivility and the Production of a Social Problem, (New Brunswick, N.J., Transaction.)

Maxfield, M.G. (1984), Fear of Crime in England and Wales, Home Office Research Study no. 78, (London, HMSO)

Mayhew, P., Elliott, D., and Dowds, L. (1989), The 1988 British Crime Survey, Home Office Research Study no. 111, (London, HMSO)

Morley, R. and Mullender, A. (1991), Hype or Hope? The Importation of Pro-Arrest Policies and Batterers Programmes from North America or Britain as Key Measures for Preventing Violence Against Women in the Home, paper presented to the Law and Society Association and Research Committee on the Sociology of Law of the I.S.A. Joint Meetings, Amsterdam, June.

Painter, K. (1988), Lighting and Crime Prevention: the Edmonton Project, (Middlesex Polytechnic, Centre for Criminology).

Sampson, A., Stubbs, P., Smith, D., Pearson, G., Blagg, H. (1988) Crime, Localities, and the Multi-agency Approach, British Journal of Criminology, 28, pp. 478-493.

Sherman, L.W. and Berk, R.A., (1984).The Specific Deterrent Effects of Arrest for Domestic Assault. American Sociological Review, 261-72.

Stanko, E.A. (1987). Typical Violence, Normal Precaution: Men, Women, and Interpersonal Violence in England, Wales, Scotland and the USA in J. Hanmer and M. Maynard (eds) Women, Violence, and Social Control. (London, Macmillan, 122-34.

Stanko, E.A. (1990). When Precaution is Normal: A Feminist Critique of Crime Prevention in L. Gelsthorpe and A. Morris (eds) Feminist Perspectives in Criminology. (Milton Keynes, Open University Press) pp. 173-183.

Stanko, E. A. (1991). Address to Preventing Crime Against Women Conference, London, Hammersmith, April.

Taylor, I. (1990) Introduction: The Concept of 'Social Cost' in Free Market Theory and the Social Effects of Free Market Policies, in I. Taylor (ed) The Social Effects of Free Market Policies, Brighton, Harvester/Wheatsheaf, 1-26.

Taylor, I. (1991a) The Experience of Order and Disorder in Free Market Societies: New York and Manchester, paper presented to the ESRC seminar series on Citizenship, Civil Society and Social Cohesion, London, February.

Taylor, I. (1991b). Not Places in Which you'd Linger: Public Transport and Well-being in Manchester. Department of Sociology, University of Salford.

Tayside Women's Forum. (1989). Women and Safety: Summary Report, Dundee, Tayside Regional Council.

Van Dijk, J. Mayhew, P. and Killias, M., (1991). Experiences of Crime Across the World: Key Findings of the 1989 International Crime Survey, Deventer, Kluwer.

Walklate, S. (1989). Victims, Crime Prevention and Social Control, paper presented to the British Sociological Association Annual Conference, Plymouth, March.

Walklate, S. (1990). Researching Victims of Crime: Critical Victimology, Social Justice, vol. 17., no. 3., 25-42.

Wilson, J.O. and Kelling, G. (1982). Broken Windows, Atlantic Monthly, March, 29-37.

Worrall, A. and Pease, K. (1986). Personal Crime against Women, Howard Journal of Criminal Justice, vol. 25., no. 2., 118-24.

PREVENTING AND FIGHTING CRIME/DELINQUENCY AND THE URBAN ENVIRONMENT

by

Peter Lumsden
Committee on Crime
Irish Parliament

In the time available it has not been possible to prepare a comprehensive paper on all of the listed aspects of the above topic. The preparation of such a paper would be a major undertaking because of the very broad scope of the subject. However, given the fact that certain aspects of the topic have recently been the subject of the attention of the relevant Irish Authorities, this paper concentrates on aspects of juvenile/delinquent crime as follows:

1. the Garda Síochaná (Irish Police) Juvenile Liaison Officer Scheme;

2. the Garda Síochaná Schools Programme, and

3. community-based initiatives to rehabilitate young offenders.

1. Juvenile Liaison Officer Scheme

This is an extra-statutory scheme to divert juveniles principally in the major urban areas of the country, from the judicial system. It provides for the cautioning and supervising of young offenders of 17 years or under as an alternative to prosecution. It is a requirement of the scheme that the juvenile admits the offence and that the parents or guardians agree to co-operate with the Gardaí (Irish Police Force) in accepting advice about the child. While the consent of the injured party is not a condition for inclusion in the scheme, any views expressed are taken into consideration.

1.1 Number of cases being dealt with under the scheme

The number of new admissions to the scheme in recent years is as follows:

	Total	DMA Only*
1986	2,718	1,306
1987	3,709	1,255
1988	3,032	1,108
1989	2,716	928

* DMA = Dublin Metropolitan Area

1.2 Functions of the JLO

The function of the Juvenile Liaison Officer is to maintain contact with each juvenile assigned to him, with the intention of weaning him/her away from involvement in crime. The juvenile may be one who has committed an offence and, having been warned, has been informally committed to the care of the officer. The Juvenile Liaison Officer may also be given the care and guidance of a young person who, though not known to have committed an offence, may be regarded as a potential delinquent by reason of unsatisfactory behaviour, such as persistent truancy, running away from home, staying out late at night, being unruly at school or at home, behaving in a disorderly manner, or frequenting undesirable places. Such cases come to notice through teachers, parents, school attendance officers, or other Gardaí. There are 83 Juvenile Liaison Officers in the Garda Síochána at present. They are members of the Garda rank (basic rank) and are assigned to 37 major centres of population, as follows:

Location	No. of Members Assigned
Dublin	38
Cork	4
Limerick	2
Galway	2
Kilkenny	2
Waterford	2
Other Provincial Areas	33 (1 Garda at each centre)

1.3 Recent reforms

1991 saw the implementation of the first major reforms of the Garda Juvenile Liaison Scheme since its inception in 1963. These reforms are intended to improve the effectiveness of the JLO scheme and to ensure that it is available for all suitable young offenders. The new measures put in place this year include:

i) Establishment of a **National Juvenile Liaison Officer** to monitor and co-ordinate all matters relating to juveniles on a national scale. This office reports to the Chief Superintendent in charge of Community Relations and its Director is the Superintendent in charge of the Community Relations/JLO section in the Dublin Metropolitan Area Headquarters in Harcourt Square.

ii) Reform of the **reporting and supervision arrangements** for Juvenile Liaison Officers. The Garda management at District Officer level (generally Garda Superintendents) now have greater responsibilities in terms of ensuring reporting arrangements and overseeing case supervision by Juvenile Liaison Officers at a local level. The intention is to 'target' the young offenders who require the greatest level of attention, encouragement and counselling.

iii) **Variation of the duration of the period of supervision** by Juvenile Liaison Officers of their young charges. Examination of this issue has shown that a more flexible approach was required in this area. Young offenders require variable periods of counselling and support, depending on circumstances. From now on, JLO supervision will be more closely tailored to the needs of the young people concerned. As long as the child is at risk, he or she will receive visits from the Juvenile Liaison Officer, but no longer. The two-year supervision period which has generally obtained up to now is no longer being applied in rigid fashion.

iv) **Weekend and evening working by Juvenile Liaison Officers.** Given the family situation of the young people involved in this scheme, the Garda Commissioner came to the view that there should be scope for members of the Juvenile Liaison Service to visit the young people under its supervision at a time when their parents are most likely to be available, i.e. in the evenings and at weekends. JLOs are now available to families at these times.

v) **Training of Juvenile Liaison Officers.** Members of the Gardaí who carry out this special work all receive a degree of preparation by way of training courses which cover the main elements of social work. The aptitude of the members of the Force who seek to fill Juvenile Liaison posts is very much taken into account when they are selected. Nonetheless, it was felt that their preparation and training requires to be enhanced and deepened in the future and a new training course for these officers has commenced in the Garda College.

The intention of these various measures is that the 'caution' rather than prosecution option will increasingly be pursued to the fullest extent possible from now on by the Garda Síochána. Guidelines for the implementation of the new measures are set out in a manual which was issued recently to all Garda Juvenile Liaison Officers to assist them in their work. A new information leaflet for parents whose children have been cautioned under the JLO scheme has been made available.

2. Garda Schools Programme

2.1 Establishment

The Garda Schools Programme was set up in January 1990 in two schools in Tallaght, a suburb of Dublin, and later extended to twelve schools in Coolock, Dublin, two in Portmarnock, Dublin and two in the Southill area of Limerick. The project was established with the assistance of St. Patrick's College, Dublin and has been the subject of favourable evaluation by Professor Mark Morgan from the college. This evaluation has confirmed the potential of the project to influence youngsters for the good before they ever become involved in criminal activity.

2.2 Purpose

The purpose of the Garda involvement in the schools is to develop positive attitudes towards law enforcement and the Gardaí. Research has shown that young males can develop negative attitudes towards police and the law at an early age. A Garda survey bore out this conclusion and persuaded the Gardaí that an intervention by them at 4th/5th class level in the primary school has the potential to make a positive impression on potential delinquents and deflect them from becoming involved in vandalism and crime.

2.3 Scope

The project involved specially prepared classroom visits by selected and trained members of the Garda Síochána. Some project work is done outside the classroom in school playgrounds and on trips organised by the Gardaí. There are opportunities for the pupils to take part in sport and other activities organised by the Gardaí in conjunction with local clubs and societies. A number of specially fitted minibuses from the Garda fleet have been made available for the purpose and other Garda/Community relations purposes.

2.4 Expansion

Plans are at an advanced stage to extend the school project further to other areas considered suitable to benefit from it.

3. Community-Based Initiatives to Rehabilitate Young Offenders

The Probation and Welfare Service and the Garda Síochána are actively involved with non-statutory organisations in the implementation of community-based programmes designed to effectively steer youngsters away from re-offending. Two specialised remedial projects are underway at Cherry Orchard, Dublin, (WHAD) and Southill, Limerick (OUTREACH), which aim to tackle head-on the delinquent lifestyle of small groups of young offenders. Other projects which are more broadly based are in operation in Coolock/Darndale, Killinarden and Ronanstown (all suburbs of Dublin). A short note on each of these projects follows.

3.1 Cherry Orchard and Southill Projects

The aim of these projects is to reduce the re-offending rate of young people who have been identified as being at risk. Each project is run by a management committee comprising representatives of local residents and non-statutory bodies, Gardaí, Probation and Welfare Service, etc. The cost of full-time Youth Workers is met by grants from the Department of Justice. Project activities include counselling of young offenders, group exploration of criminal/delinquent behaviour and its consequences, leisure activities and community projects.

3.2 Coolock/Darndale Project

A pilot project was also organised recently in the Coolock/Darndale area by two Probation and Welfare Officers with the enthusiastic co-operation of local Gardaí who work as Juvenile Liaison Officers.

A group of young probationers between the ages of 13 and 16 years attended on-going group sessions conducted on Wednesday afternoons, when they were on a half-day from school. Some of the activities were held in a sports hall and a hostel in the area, so re-enforcing the neighbourhood nature of the project. Many activities were involved, e.g. group discussions, educational videos, bowling, snooker and other leisure-time pursuits.

3.3 Killinarden/Ronanstown Youth Projects

A year-long community development programme in these two Dublin communities is being funded by the Department of Justice and supported by the Garda authorities and the Probation and Welfare Service in association with the Tallaght Youth Service and the Catholic Youth Council. The Department of Justice is making £55,000 in central Government funding available for this programme which will include support for youth activities, recreational, sporting and social events. Special provision is being made within the programme for a counselling service for young people who may be at risk. There will be a particular focus on meeting the needs and interests of young travellers in the Killinarden and Ronanstown areas.

There is a determined commitment in place to meet the needs of the youth of both areas by all the voluntary and Government agencies involved. The grant made by the Department of Justice will fund two co-ordinator posts for one year in both areas. These co-ordinators employed through the Catholic Youth Council and the Tallaght Youth Service will liaise with the Gardaí and ensure that Garda community support activities are relevant to local needs.

4. Conclusion

In conclusion it should be noted that a bill is being prepared at present entitled 'The Juvenile Justice Bill' which will replace the Childrens Act, 1908. This new legislation will cover comprehensively all aspects of the law relating to the protection of children and young persons. It is expected to come into force in the course of next year.

ROLE OF THE STATE AND LOCAL AUTONOMIES: NEW RIGHTS AND NEW POWERS
A PILOT STUDY: PROGRAMME FOR NOMADS AND SEMI-NOMADS, FANTASY OR REALITY?

Clelia M. Boesi*
Region of Lombardy
Milan

CONTENT

1. Foreword

2. In the context of evolution and development of new social problems. New poverty.

3. Central and local level and lack of representation.

4. Analysis of the institutional crisis from the point of view of the population and of its representatives in a highly marginal social area: the nomads and the semi-nomads.

5. Outline for a legislative project and programme for a highly marginal sector of the population.

    5.1 Definition of strategies: with the interested populations or for the interested populations.

    5.2 Institutional Methodology: intra-, inter- and extra-institutional.

    5.3 Actions on the programme and experimentation.

    5.4 Human and Economic Financial Resources: what is the potential of the enterprise?

6. Conclusions

    6.1 Global or Sectoral Projects.

    6.2 Metropolitan areas and marginalisation: is it possible to forecast the population?

    6.3 Urban development and underdevelopment can co-exist: what is the limit of tolerance and the possible rules?

7. Conclusions

    The paper will include condensed social data.

HEALTH, HABITAT AND EQUITY

Vincent-Pierre Comiti
Ministry of Social Affairs, Paris
Representative of WHO

A recent report of a committee of experts in the World Health Organisation (The Hygiene of the Environment in Urban Planning, 1991) clearly presented the health components in urban areas. 'The health of an urban population is strongly determined by physical, social, economic, political and cultural factors related to the urban environment. These factors include the processes of social regroupment, of migration, of modernisation and of industrialisation, as well as urban lifestyles which can vary according to the climate, the terrain, the population density, the housing infrastructure, the industrial infrastructure, the distribution of income and the transport system. The impact of urban processes on public health cannot simply be the sum of the effects of the various factors considered individually, because after all these factors are highly interconnected.'

The theoretical and practical aspects of the links between health and housing are treated in the WHO's document 'Health and Housing'. This publication insists on the fact that excellent housing can benefit physical and mental health, give a certain psychological security and reinforce the links between inhabitants by favouring the expression of individuals. The concept of equity is therefore essential for housing planning and rehabilitation processes.

The 44th World Health Assembly in 1991 has clearly indicated the links between the WHO strategy of 'Health for Everyone', the necessity of public participation, the indispensable intersectorality of actions and the problems caused by urbanisation. 'There are many national governments, engaged in having "Health for Everyone" as a clearly social objective. The WHO strategy "Health for Everyone" up to the year 2000 requires public participation and intersectoral action for the improvement of health, especially of the most disadvantaged groups. In a world of rapid urbanisation, it is up to cities and their elected administrative bodies to take measures in this direction.' The disadvantaged groups, such as the elderly, the handicapped or those with reduced mobility have specific needs which are not always taken into account. Physical accessibility in planning is a concept which has to be integrated in all housing and urban plans.

The link between housing and health goes far beyond the strict framework of pathology linked to housing or the environment and it includes problems linked to the planning of workplaces or the localisation of commercial spaces and it has to take into account as diversified factors as the aesthetics of the sites, the comfort of the housing, the accessibility to cultural life or the choice in lifestyles.

There is a strong trend of social dichotomy. The wealthy people deserve the green spaces and minor pollution; the poor deserve housing in old run-down city centres or near industry. This spatial division increases the already existent inequalities.

Article 11 of the International Pact relating to economic, social and cultural rights (in force since 1976) defines housing as a fundamental right: 'The States signing this Pact recognise the right of everybody to a satisfactory level of life for himself and his family, meaning adequate food, clothing and housing as well as constant improvement in his living conditions'.

Various WHO programmes (Hygiene and Ecology, Healthy Cities, Primary Health Care) co-operate to this end. These actions, based notably on the opening of structures and the bringing together of professionals coming from different horizons have to avoid, among others, a difficulty identified by Roderick J. Lawrence ('Housing and Health' in 'World Health', March-April 1991). This difficulty concerns the minima criteria of quality related to a large number of environmental factors: 'However, if we examine the criteria from the point of view of their internal logic and their objectives, we are aware that what has dominated their elaboration were priorities of economic, technological and political order and that the lifestyle, the domestic economy, the beliefs and the well-being of the population concerned did not really have much weight'.

The notion of sustainable development has to be fully integrated into the framework of urban development, in order to achieve:

- a maximum of diversity, notably architectural;
- a maximum of integration in the site;
- a minimum of use of non-reusable energies;
- a maximum of recuperation and recycling.

These developmental axes have to be taken into account from the design stage. It is also essential, as highlighted by R.J. Lawrence, to proceed to an equitable breakdown of resources by always taking into account the environment. 'The existence of inadequate housing is not only a problem of architectural or technical order, but it constitutes, fundamentally, the expression of economic and political difficulties linked to the equitable utilisation of natural resources and the respect towards the environment.'

Various interesting studies (e.g. Vincenzo Calo: 'Health and the City') show the diversity of problems. Pollution, noise, stress may need specific responses, but the interdependence between the various factors has always to be taken into account. One factor can, in fact, cancel the effect of another.

From any point of view, it is therefore extremely important for the health factor to be taken into account in policies affecting urban areas, where problems sometimes erupt in violence.

HOUSING, SOCIAL INTEGRATION AND LIVABLE ENVIRONMENTS

Lindsay MacFarlane[*]
OECD Urban Affairs Division
Paris

The paper focuses on two main issues:

1. the plight of those most in need - suffering from poverty and even homelessness and who seem to be increasingly excluded from society as a whole; and

2. the housing 'affordability' problem as it affects low and moderate income groups who today are often unable to find reasonably priced rental accommodation or to buy their own home on a site reasonably close to their place of employment.

These two interrelated problems are widespread in OECD countries and appear to be linked both to changes in housing policies and to the evolution of the macro economic context, particularly structural changes in cities.

One of the factors which compounds the difficulty of dealing with the problem of exclusion from housing and even from society as a whole is the wide variation in the characteristics of the types of persons affected. For this reason, the paper highlights the multi-disciplinary and spatially targeted approaches involving more than housing policies alone, such as that being applied in France. Such strategies may be required if any sustainable improvement in the social condition of disadvantaged groups or in the areas they live in is to be effected.

The paper also argues that a more holistic approach, in line with that advocated by Canada, should be applied in formulating housing policies in order to give more priority to factors associated with housing, such as easy access to transport or jobs and to longer term considerations affecting, for example, social integration and the environment. It is therefore suggested that the planning process should take more account of social and economic redistributive effects as well as environmental consideration.

The paper also highlights the need for governments to convince housing finance institutions to become the partners of governments and to remodel their policies in order to help meet the credit needs for housing the homeless, low income families and first time home buyers. It is suggested that there is a need to involve housing finance managers more with community and informal sector organisations and to become more responsive to the needs of lower income groups.

The paper points out that another policy area deserving greater attention is the impact of certain other policies, such as fiscal policies and land market policies, formulated outside the housing sector but which affect importantly the price and availability of housing.

ETHNIC MINORITIES: THE PROBLEM OF GYPSIES

Lina Marsoni[*]
Municipality of Milan

This paper deals with the problems of discrimination of vulnerable ethnic groups and the role of their emancipation for social urban development. The cultural values of ethnic minorities and the role and attitude of public authorities are highlighted through the case of gypsies, the landless minority. The paper gives a comprehensive overview of the reasons which place gypsies on the margins of modern society and analyses their friction with 'normal' citizens. An endeavour for action is given by the example of the city of Milan, whose actions aim to improve the living conditions of gypsies living in its territorial district.

REVITALISATION THROUGH INTEGRATED SOCIO-ECONOMIC APPROACHES. THE INTERNATIONAL EXPERIENCE. LOCAL PARTNERSHIPS AND TRANSNATIONAL NETWORKS.

Chara Paraskevopoulou[*]
Hellenic Agency for Local Development and Local Government
Athens

In this paper I am going to present the main socio-economic problems which characterise the Prefecture of Attika in general.

My presentation will focus on the area of Western Attika, an area of 450,000 inhabitants, with low standard of living indices and with the majority of the population belonging to low income groups and living in a poor ekistic environment.

The numerous industrial units existing in the area have turned these districts into reception areas for those coming to the capital in search of work. As a result, the area has a high concentration of new entrants to the immigrant work force; of minorities (gypsies, Pontian Greeks from the Soviet Union, etc.) and, in general, population groups whose main characteristics are their low educational level, lack of specialised vocational training, high unemployment rate and problems of integration into the city's social fabric.

Within the above framework, a number of national and local agencies as well as voluntary organisations have co-ordinated their actions and taken the initiative to promote projects aimed at improving the living and working conditions in the area.

Also, the experience of other European Countries with similar problems has been taken into consideration through our participation in European Networks, e.g. PETRA. Most of the projects that are going to be presented in the workshop have already been financed by the FSE or they are expecting to be financed under the transnational European Initiatives HORIZON and NOW.

The projects that will be presented the following main groups:

- ethnic minorities;
- disadvantaged groups;
- women.

CONCLUSIONS, RECOMMENDATIONS

by

Sandra Walklate
University of Salford

The one theme which held this diverse range of papers together was the theme of social integration, though each of the papers were suggesting different strategies towards achieving this goal. The group nevertheless had a productive discussion in which a genuine exchange of ideas took place. The discussion which took place proceeded on the basis of a number of assumptions some of which were explicitly agreed and some of which became apparent on reflection. It is important to note, however, that the group did express some disquiet with its working title and the assumption that 'gypsies' and 'crime' went together. This was felt to be discriminatory. In addition, the group felt it was unfortunate that more planners/architects were not present for the discussion.

The group proceeded on a number of assumptions:

1. It assumed that the environment encompassed not just the physical but the social, cultural and economic environment.

2. It assumed prevention constituted a genuine concern for crime prevention strategies and not 'after the event' prevention strategies.

3. The group assumed a primary target of young males for prevention work.

4. It assumed the importance of a 'political will' to implement any recommended strategies.

On the basis of these assumptions the group made a number of recommendations as potentially effective crime prevention strategies.

1. The need to create new forms of employment which were real, valued, and possibly environmentally sound (the Wise Project based in Glasgow was used as an exemplar). Such employment opportunities need not always be state sponsored but need to be real, i.e. **not** more training programmes.

2. The need to resource deprived areas recreationally and culturally. This would be state led. These two recommendations it was suggested would be backed by a number of subsidiary but interconnected strategies.

3. The need for inter-agency/partnership/intersectoral strategies, especially the police, education systems, social work agencies and the family. But also recognising the importance of a range of more informal groups/associations looking within communities who are often neglected in formal inter-agency work.

4. The need to recognise that different societies may be on a different (though related) trajectory concerning delinquency and crime prevention. Careful consideration and evaluations need to be made of questions of transferability of initiatives not only from society to society, but from community to community.

5. The need to recognise the potential value of using the mass media to portray more positive images of agency work and local communities.

The group concluded by stating that these recommendations were not made in the hope of reconstituting some bygone 'Golden Age' or in the belief of a new 'Utopia', but were based on a real recognition of the employment trends within the European Community and the belief that meaningful and valued employment was the creative key to social integration.

SELECTED PAPERS AND CONCLUSIONS OF

THE WORKING GROUP

ON

SOCIAL HOUSING AND QUALITY OF THE URBAN ENVIRONMENT

COMPOSITION OF WORKING GROUP 3

SOCIAL HOUSING AND QUALITY OF THE URBAN ENVIRONMENT

Chairman: Mr Olgierd Roman Dziekónski
Deputy Mayor of Warsaw

Rapporteur: Mrs Marie Ganier-Raymond
IFS, Berlin

Expert Introducing the Working Group: Prof. Uwe Wullkopf
Institut Wohnen und Umwelt, Darmstadt

Speakers-Participants:

1. Dr Paul Burton
   University of Bristol

2. Mr Claude Leroy
   A.I.Q.V., Paris

3. Dr Thomas Maloutas
   National Centre of Social Research, Athens

4. Mr Philip Potter
   Klaus Novy Institut e.v., Cologne

5. Mr José Garcia
   European Committee for Housing, Brussels

6. Mrs Francine Boudru
   FEANTSA, Brussels

7. Mr John Bell
   Community Development Foundation, London

8. Mr Rui Godinho
   Municipality of Lisbon

9. Mr John O'Connell
   Dublin Travellers Education and Development Group

10. Mr John Lomax
    Bank of England

11. Ms Maria Finzi
    EUROPIL, Italy

12. Mr Peter Fazakas
    Berzsenyi, Hungary

13. Mr Carlo Pignocco
    CISL-SICET, Rome

SOCIAL HOUSING AND THE QUALITY OF THE URBAN ENVIRONMENT

by

Uwe Wullkopf
Institut Wohnen und Umwelt
Darmstadt

socially disadvantaged groups. This is why the 'insertion' approach of the Social Division of the EC is an absolutely proper one; there is a strong synergy effect of a combination of local policies attempting to simultaneously improve social, working and housing conditions. For improving everything except for the housing conditions would in the case of many disadvantaged groups fail because the market alone is not capable of improving their housing sufficiently, and housing conditions are the major symbol of the success or failure of social integration as a whole.

4. Who Plays which Role in the Whole Game?

If one requests a better participation of the tenants in social housing estate management one must be honest enough to also mention some serious obstacles to this objective.

One issue here concerns the selection of new tenants for empty flats. There is clearly a danger of a 'creaming effect' in that existing neighbours tend to select their new neighbours preferably from among social strata which lie slightly above their own, with the result that minorities and households who have particularly difficult problems in finding a flat in the housing market tend to be excluded.

Another issue lies in the pure economics of determining rent levels and financial plans. If social criteria determine these decisions, the relatively most well-to-do tenant will, in the end, be charged for everything, and when he leaves the estate everything will break down; Or the government will be expected to pay for everything.

There is also a danger that a minority of tenant representatives tends to professionalise and to dominate the rest of the inhabitants, and in many cases behavioural rules related to the staircase are much better accepted if they come from a more or less anonymous landlord than if they come from one's not so beloved direct neighbour.

However, these cautionary remarks should not prevent the management from considerably improving tenants participation as, particularly in social housing, there is no other plausible way towards better adapting the supply to the real demand pattern and to enhance responsible behaviour among tenants.

In this context the role of the neighbourhood as a substitute for the diminishing functioning of the family as well as the public sector in providing social services, consolidation and hope, is frequently being discussed. Also, it is claimed that the neighbourhood could serve as a training camp for the unemployed and underprivileged to exercise persuasiveness and self-esteem. The counter-argument is that well functioning neighbourhoods are rather a middle class phenomenon and could not be expected to emerge when the inhabitants feel segregated from society. However, more research needs to be done on this subject matter.

Another issue is the organisational structure of the social housing enterprises. It is argued that they ought to imitate the structural change which has recently taken place in industry, namely a concentration of firms as far as overall financial responsibilities are concerned, and a deconcentration and delegation to the neighbourhood level of all decisions which have to do with allocations, lettings, the organisation of repairs and maintenance, estate-based capital repairs and improvements, caretaking, cleaning, environmental maintenance and so on. The argument against this is that in this way, competition is eliminated and thus good and bad management performance could not be distinguished from each other in time. Also, an equal treatment of different neighbourhoods ought to be provided.

Another important issue concerns the relation between public and voluntary social services and estate management. As mentioned above these tasks are highly interrelated, and perhaps new organisational forms need to be developed to better cope with this.

Turning now to the government side, there has been a tendency in several EC countries to decentralise social housing financing to lower government levels, which has the clear advantage that local needs can be better matched, but also the disadvantage that the goal of equal living conditions in all parts of a country may be neglected. This holds also true for the EC level; the more regional equality is striven for, the more must the higher level intervene. And to come back to the blue banana: if the demographic pressure upon this region is to be alleviated, growth poles must be created outside, and due to the above-mentioned synergy effect housing policies must be an integral part of such overall development strategies. Subsidiarity economies and scale economies do not exclude each other if integrated in a well reasoned strategy. As long as national governments hesitate to shift housing policy responsibilities to the EC level, the task remains nevertheless for the EC to stimulate innovation in the form of experiments, examples and international comparison. And this is what we must now do.

Notes:

1. A particularly convincing study of this subject seems to me Anne Power, Housing. A Guide to Quality and Creativity. Longman, 1991.

2. cf. Necdet Taymur, Thomas A. Markus and Tom Woolley, Rehumanizing Housing, Butterworths, 1988. Heidede Becker, Neubauerneuerung. Vom Rückbau zur Nachverdichtung, Berlin: difu, 1990.

1. **The Need for Social Housing**

One could divide the EC territory into three categories:

i. the 'blue banana', ranging from Southern England to Northern Italy, where most economic growth takes place and where the main social problem of housing lies in an excessive (and further increasing) portion of the total income of people in the lower strata being required for rent;

ii. the areas outside the 'blue banana' where flats are available in principle, but where the supply is of low quality ('unfit housing') and the living space per person is small; and

iii. an 'in-between' category where older quarters inhabited predominantly by the poor are threatened with conversion into offices or new housing with high rent levels, as happens for example in large agglomerations in Spain and Greece.

In each of these categories, the arguments in favour of social housing differ from each other:

a. within the 'blue banana', the main problem is not a housing shortage for everybody. The discussion of housing shortage in Western Germany, for example, has been strongly correlated with periods of high economic growth, whereas in recession periods complaints about increasing vacancy rates were predominant. This is because in periods with strong economic growth, households have a high demand for additional living space, which cannot be met by supply. The building process reacts only with a considerable time lag to changes in demand, and boom periods are in general characterised by high interest rates which make other investments particularly attractive. If the market reacts with strongly increasing rents - as is the case at present in Western Germany - social problems are created particularly within large, booming agglomerations, with long waiting lists for few social dwellings and an increasing number of homeless people. Individual rent allowances are for several reasons insufficient to cope with this problem. They are not claimed by all those entitled (in Western Germany, only by 40%), they do not encourage new construction, and over and above that, money is in many cases not the only necessary condition for households to gain ground in a narrow housing market. There are other barriers to overcome such as racial prejudice, particular demand structures of groups like the handicapped and large families not provided for by the market, or doubts in longer term solvency, for example of single parent families. Hence local authorities need a special housing stock to cater for the needs of these households.

b. Outside the 'blue banana', unfit housing and insufficiently large dwelling units, together with a lack of private housing investment (and perhaps private investment in general) are a token of poverty and social inequality. Social housing is part of a parcel of policies to enhance the attractiveness of the areas, and there is also a hope that growth in the building industry might stimulate economic growth in general.

c. For our third regional category, but also in connection with urban renewal measures, a further justification of social housing emerges: housing must be provided when people are relocated and flats are to be evacuated as a result in consequence of public works.

With these different types of need for social housing in mind, the political question remains how much of the total housing stock ought to be social housing; by definition rents are limited and tenants are selected from among those in particular need. In this connection it may be interesting to note that in Western Germany, social rental housing prevailed in the 1950s when the stock had been largely destroyed; there was an influx of large numbers of refugees and the capital markets did not yet work efficiently. The share of social housing construction among all new housing construction has since declined up to the late 1980s, when optimism about the efficiency of the free market was at its peak and most decision-makers in housing policy argued that only some 2-4% of all households would require social housing provision in the long-term. In the last few years, however, opinions have changed considerably, and with the perspective of a 'two-thirds society' and strong immigration pressure, the arguments in favour of a considerable stock of social housing units to be kept in the long-term, at least in the large agglomerations, have gained momentum. This raises the question whether social housing should be provided only for the poor (with the danger of creating ghettos) or for large parts of the population, and which rent level should be set. In Western Germany at least, the very poorest are still strongly under-represented in the social housing stock, so that the danger of ghettoisation is confined to but a few social housing areas. And as to rent level, there is a discussion as to which income groups living in social housing should pay market rents; and if all inhabitants were to pay market rents and the poor were individually subsidised, whether this would not label an ever increasing part of the population as belonging to the group of those who are dependent on donations from others.

2. Location, Design, Comfort

In the 1970s and 1980s, a rather ideological debate went on in many Western countries on the blessings of the filtering process according to which the more well-to-do would tend to move into new housing and would thus enhance the stock of older flats available for the poor. The reality has always been, however, that there has been a segregation between neighbourhoods, and, in large European towns particularly, certain neighbourhoods have been inhabited by the rich for many centuries (with very rich people living in very old houses) and other quarters by the poor, and that in these areas also, the new stock (e.g. the 'Mietskaserne' in Berlin) has been inhabited by the poor from the first day onwards. However, if one considers location not according to wealth but according to average household size, more central locations have been inhabited predominantly by one and two person households while larger households have preferred to live in the outskirts. Hence baby booms cause urban decay, and low fertility rates cause gentrification of urban quarters. And the very poor have been constrained to particular zones located, for example, in the proximity of polluting industries or in railway line triangles.

This market geography produces a series of social problems, such as the stigmatisation of people living in particular streets or quarters, the expulsion of poor households in gentrification processes, and accessibility limitations of poor families to labour markets, good schools, and even shopping facilities. Social housing areas, when located at the fringe of large agglomerations, have in many cases even aggravated the problems resulting from market location, instead of healing the locational deficiencies of the underprivileged.

Some particular aspects of this problem may be mentioned here: when women who have interrupted their career in order to care for small children wish to start to participate in the labour market again, preferably at first with part-time employment, they are to a large extent dependent on a functioning public transport system and on the proximity of labour demand. Living in the outskirts and faced with an overall shift in favour of the private car, reintegration into the labour market can be strongly hampered.

Another problem concerns the management of housing estates. There is a strong lack in many areas of integration of housing and social policies, and both respond rather inflexibly to the particular on-the-spot needs. Hence, the locational policies for day care centres or medical care units are insufficiently related to locational policies for particular households in social housing.

A rather sad story, at least in Western Germany, must be told about the design of social flats. They have almost always consisted exclusively of a living room, a bedroom for the parents, two very small rooms for two children, a kitchen and a bathroom. Regrettably or not, households consisting of two parents and two small (grown up children have quite different demands) children have nearly died out in Western Germany, and where they still exist, daily family life and spatial demands of individual household members have changed so that the above-mentioned standard design no longer meets any demand whatsoever. Proponents of market supply conclude that supplies of social housing have not been sufficiently under market pressure to adapt themselves to changes in demand. Anyway, emancipated women and children, who are now perhaps also under stronger performance pressure from employers and schools than some decades ago, have developed demand patterns to which suppliers react insufficiently.

Another point to make in this context is the need for housing estate management to provide a stronger role for tenants in the management, not only to be able to better meet the particular demand patterns, including the organisation and quality of the housing environment, but also because a stronger emphasis on the subsidiarity principle in this field contributes to the development of self-responsibility, self-esteem and creativity among the inhabitants.[1]

Over and above the design question it may or may not be a typical German neurosis to insist upon environmental issues, but it must be stated that the over-consumption of energy in industrialised countries must be stopped in the near future and that, as more than a third of all primary energy goes into the heating of buildings, the high potential to reduce energy consumption in dwellings must be better utilised. This means a strong investment requirement into heat insulation of existing social dwellings and a great challenge to housing management in the decades to come. This may lead to a further increase in the rent burden, even though heating charges may be reduced in parallel. Or, if policies go in the direction of drastically increasing energy prices, the dwellings of the poor may remain the least insulated ones, and thus the poor may suffer most from such environmental policies. Already it can be observed that the heating charges in the bad quality stock by far exceed the average and put an extra burden upon the inhabitants.

A particular problem relates to the future of large housing estates built in the 1950s and 1960s. The catalogue of measures recommended to improve the attractiveness of these estates need not be repeated here. It extends from minor improvements in the entrances and staircases via an improvement of private and social infrastructure facilities to a reduction of densities by demolition. Two major issues remain largely unreflected in this context: the first is who will in the end benefit and who will lose from all these measures; and the second - which is related to estates with considerable vacancy rates - does the problem of these estates not lie simply in their bad location and only to a much lesser extent in low standards and aesthetic qualities? Nevertheless, in all instances a greater participation of inhabitants in management, a better functional mix of uses, and a better relation between housing and social services will, apart from all the necessary investments in most cases, contribute considerably to improving the situation. Which leads us to the conclusion: re-humanising housing[2] is not a simple task.

3. The Role of Housing Quality in the Process of Social and Labour Market Integration

Economists very often do not like housing investments, and particularly subsidies in housing. They argue that the capital output ratio of housing investments is extremely high, so that economic growth is less stimulating here than in any other sectoral policy alternative. Or, housing is considered to be purely consumable merchandise which people will be better able to afford after their incomes have grown, and government money should not be wasted on consumption subsidies but rather stimulate investment and the creation of jobs. It is not simple to argue against that and to claim that housing is an intrinsic right as the Dutch do. According to some investigations in this field, it is unfortunately rather evident that an improvement in housing without any other policy measure improves neither labour productivity nor school performance nor health (except for tuberculosis), nor does it reduce the crime rate (except for sexual crimes committed outside the dwelling). At best it reduces stress which is of importance for the development perspectives of children. Beyond that, one can observe that better housing makes people more conservative.

The more suitable approach therefore is to see housing as the core of living conditions, of the existence as one of the main, if not the main expression of how human beings demonstrate that they are and how they are.

Nevertheless, better housing can quite well contribute to better productivity if not considered as an isolated factor but as a part of a long equation of factors which condition a better future, particularly of

RECONCEPTUALISING HOUSING QUALITY

by

Philip Potter
Klaus Novy Institut e.V.
Cologne

1. Introduction

There is general agreement in many European countries that at some stage in the 1960s and 1970s something went radically wrong with social housing; settlements were built at that time which have less acceptability among residents than social housing of earlier periods.

This paper is only implicitly concerned with the question of what went wrong; it is rather aimed at considering, on an abstract plane, what reorientations in housing policy might contribute towards the planning and building of more acceptable and successful environments in the future.

My first argument is that the deficits of housing policies in the 1960s and 1970s have largely been recognised, the policy response has been to remedy deficits in an incremental way, while leaving the basic structure of housing policy instruments intact, rather than by reformulating housing policy in a fundamental way.

My second argument consists in the thesis that one way to come towards a fundamental reformulation of housing policy is to rethink the notion of 'housing quality' to create a holistic category which we can then use as a tool towards the reform of housing policy. I use, in this context, the term 'housing quality' as a synonym for 'quality of the urban environment', since I see no theoretical need - at least in the context of my argument here - to distinguish between space inside and outside one's front door.

In conclusion, I make some observations on the consequences for housing research of such a reconceptualisation of the notion of 'housing quality'.

2. The Legacy of the Past

Mass social housing has acquired a bad name. This is not altogether fair, since the deficiencies we associate with the social housing construction booms of the 1960s and 1970s do not apply to social housing built earlier: indeed, the social housing settlements of the beginning of this century and of the 1920s have in many countries proved themselves as environments which conform to acceptable and desirable standards even today. They have stood the test of time well.

What went wrong in the course of the post-war period is the subject of much debate, which I do not propose to review here. Part of the answer may lie in the fact that ever more was expected of social housing, while with time the resources allocated to it were reduced.

Mass social housing in the period of 'failure' in the 1960s and 1970s had common characteristics in a number of European countries. These mass social housing programmes were aimed at large volume production, normative physical standards and the needs of nuclear families.

Social housing consisted principally in new building in large volume production on green field (though also large scale slum clearance) sites. Social housing at this time had little concern for issues of urban renewal and neighbourhood revitalisation. Urban renewal functions were added to state housing policies in the 1960s and 1970s as a kind of afterthought, without reforming existing new-build policies to incorporate greater sensitivity towards existing urban areas and communities.

Social housing of this period was the task of large-scale public and NGO organisations which had little sensitivity towards the interests of local communities and residents. There has been little movement towards democratising the structures of these organisations, though some have instituted models of tenant participation in limited respects. Perhaps the most radical drive for reform in this respect has been the sale of social housing to the occupants in Britain, though this should rather be termed an individualisation rather than a democratisation of control over social housing.

Of central importance in this period was the securing of prescribed minimum physical standards of dwelling space and dwelling amenities - floor space, sanitary facilities, heating, open space, and so on. These objectives, laudable in themselves in a time when much of the housing stock still lacked basic physical amenities, neglected more subjective elements of housing quality - what makes a dwelling a home and what makes a settlement a neighbourhood - and had little regard for the ecological issues which are becoming such urgent issues in the present day.

A further physical characteristic of the settlements built at this time was the construction of modernist urban forms. Or rather, since these settlements did not have much resemblance to the high modernism of the 1920s, a debased version of modernism. The deficiencies in the large housing estates of the 1960s and 1970s have often been ascribed to the built form associated with these settlements; and it is clear that different fashions in building prevail now, though whether these will prove more durable than those before remains to be seen. How one should theorise the relation between built form and social behaviour without lapsing into simplistic environmental determinism is an issue I shall consider below.

Finally, mass social housing of the 1960s and 1970s was built for one client group: the nuclear family. Policy neglected other household groups and produced standardised units with a very clear preconception of the nature and behaviour of the households to be accommodated. Again in this respect, this deficit in the housing programmes of this time has been recognised and a plethora of supplementary building programmes formulated for all kind of 'special needs groups'.

3. Reorienting Housing Policy

As already indicated above, the deficiencies of these monolithic housing programmes have been recognised. Where before the family was the central client group, there has developed increasing attention to the need of so-called 'special groups': that is, household types not catered for in traditional programmes or traditionally the central beneficiaries of social housing: old people, young people, people with disabilities, groups suffering from social exclusion, households in poverty, the homeless. The consequence was the formulation of special programmes for such special needs groups.

However, the adding-on of supplementary housing policy initiatives for special needs groups is not an appropriate strategy. More effective must be the refashioning of mainstream housing policy instruments in order that they be sensitive to all the various household groups in society who, normatively speaking, should benefit from housing policies.

Put in a different way, the 'special housing needs' of 'special' needs groups are not immanently 'special': these special needs are produced by the areas of ineffectiveness of mainstream housing policy instruments. Effective reform should involve the decomposition and recomposition of housing policies in order to form a series of policy tools which are responsive to the needs of all groups in society.

How is this to be done? A first rethinking involves rethinking the objectives of housing policy at the most abstract level. Housing policy then becomes not concerned with physical standards of construction per se, nor space standards for households, nor bedrooms, nor even low rents: rather, the basic principle needs to be formulated in terms of securing an acceptable quality of life for individuals, households and communities.

There is a growing awareness that mass social housing, while conforming to prescribed standards of space and amenities (physical, quantitative objectives), frequently failed in the task of creating urban environments which people like to live in, and resulted in housing settlements which needs large scale subsequent intervention to rectify social deficits - at great cost.

We need to return to issues of 'housing quality', putting to one side (though not rejecting completely) the traditional measures of physical standards (which are quantitative measures of housing quality), and reformulating quality in terms of 'softer' variables which correspond more closely to people's lived experience: the qualities which residents themselves value.

What notion of housing quality is needed in order to assess and plan good urban environments? 'Quality' becomes a processual notion, of how people live in environments, rather than in terms of static quantitative measures of floor space or central heating. It involves the assessment of environments in terms of the way in which communities can establish themselves, and how they can evolve, in terms of the chances people have in producing and reproducing their local environments: in short, real chances of participation and control in the appropriation of the environment.

This requires a reconceptualisation of what constitutes the 'materiality' of the living environment: material are those elements which are determinant of people's life chances. Thus rethought, materiality has little to do with physical attributes of an environment but a lot to do with economic (the setting of rent levels) and social (the conditions of tenancies) relations.

The question 'what is housing quality' then can be reformulated as 'what real chances do individuals, households and communities have in appropriating their environments and fashioning them to meet their own needs and aspirations?'

4. Housing Quality

4.1 Housing cost as a housing quality

I argue here that one of the primary determinants of housing quality is affordable housing costs. One frequently gains the impression in discussions on housing quality that somehow simple economic issues are not, or no longer relevant. Yet probably the most elementary aspect of 'quality of life' is economic security and freedom from poverty.

Housing quality in economic terms means, for tenants, affordable rents. And it means rents whose levels can be predicted in the future. That is, people need to know how their rent levels will develop and thereby have a perspective over their environment into the future. What exactly constitutes an affordable rent is, of course, a political issue which I do not propose to embark upon: there are no technical solutions to such issues.

For owners the securing of (economic, or financial) quality in the urban environment means stable house prices and stable repayment rates. Variability in house prices can - in cases of slumps in house prices - lead to massive financial losses for those households who buy at a peak and wish to sell through. Households are not speculators who buy and sell on the basis of specialist knowledge of the market, as with securities traders. Their decisions to buy and sell are determined by changes in their family size, by job changes which involve relocation and so on. Consequently, most people cannot speculate and are at the mercy of market fluctuations.

The same applies in the case of interest rates. A slight rise in interest rates can lead to rises in mortgage repayments which completely overturn household budgets. And when high interest rates coincide with high unemployment rates the problems, for some households, become insoluble. I think it is clear from the experience of those countries with variable mortgage rates and high variations in the level of interest rates that home owners value, as a quality of their housing, stability and predictability in their repayments.

4.2 Housing quality and housing rights

The slogan of a 'right to the city' opens up a series of issues which are not restricted to questions of legal protection: these issues include the right to access to the urban environment, right of use of the environment, right to security.

Certainly, the legal protection of citizens in the urban environment is a quality not to be undervalued: in terms of housing quality this means at the first level a clear and workable tenancy law for those renting accommodation. That is, clarity as to the security of tenure of renters, the conditions under which landlords can terminate tenancies, and rent increases. And it means clear and understandable relations between lenders and borrowers in the owner occupied household market.

But a variety of other elements are involved: for renters (at least in the public sector, but arguably in the private sector also) the administration of housing needs to be conducted in a way that is transparent to the parties concerned and not subject to wide-ranging administrative discretion on the part of housing managers: for example, the allocation of social housing should be subject to formal criteria which can be understood and verified by lay people.

Still at a legal level, the right to the city also involves people's security in urban environment: freedom from discrimination, and freedom from crime. That is, the right of enjoyment of the environment, which corresponds closely with the right of use of the environment and the right of access.

The right of access and use also concerns issues of competing interests in the city: the right of the motorist contrasted with the right of the elderly person to cross the road, for example. Here the quality of the environment for social groups with less bargaining power needs to be taken into account: mechanisms of social exclusion through institutional discrimination have to be countered.

4.3 Quality through power, participation and control

Closely allied to issues of rights to the city are opportunities of participation and control: the right to be consulted, the right to intervene.

In the urban environment the quality of life in local communities can be substantially improved by ensuring that communities have control over decisions affecting their local environments. This is particularly important for planning authorities and housing departments. It involves access to decision-making institutions, in particular local political institutions and planning decisions.

In practice, ensuring real participation requires a rethinking of urban planning procedures, which need to be de-technocratised in order to allow lay people to participate without specialist knowledge - and specialist vocabulary - in urban development procedures.

4.4 Quality through diversity

I now wish to consider the growing diversity of needs generated by the pluralisation of different household types. Housing quality, I argue, should be also achieved through diversity in provision, through sensitivity to the needs of different household groups.

Social housing policy was traditionally associated with the needs of the family. But the needs of households have changed. In particular, there has been a diversification in the nature and needs of different households. This has been particularly associated with the growth of one-person households. There has already been for some time a growth in concern with people at different stages of the life cycle than that of family formation.

The types of households referred to here are elderly people (often widowed), young people and so on. Housing policy - at least in Britain - has a tendency to call the needs of these groups 'special needs' - in Germany these groups have often been classified as 'Randgruppen' - marginal groups - a dubious term to apply to quite large sections of the population.

This definition of special needs groups needs to be questioned: in fact one can argue that the needs of such groups are not really special at all - they have quite normal requirements of housing and have quite unexceptional expectations of housing quality. The needs of such groups are therefore not immanently special but are produced by a housing policy which is, because of internal deficiencies, unable to meet the needs of these groups and therefore because of its deficiencies defines the needs of normal groups as special.

What is needed to achieve housing quality for all different expectations of the different types of household, is a housing policy which is flexible enough to meet the needs of special groups without having to define them as 'special'. How this is to be achieved in practice can only be formulated in dialogue with the users and potential users of the housing in question.

4.5 Quality through small scale forms of social organisation

This concern with the diverse needs of social groups has, at the level of housing provision for the individual households, implications for our conception of housing quality.

It has, however, implications for urban quality over and above the individual dwelling. The diversification of household types does not simply result, at a social level, in the redistribution of households into ever more atomised insularity. New forms of social organisation, at this micro level, do develop and there is a need for the development of strategies in housing and infrastructure provision which recognise this variety of informal and semi-formal networks between households.

These may consist of informal networks of social care, of links between people who live together, or live in proximity to each other, or who would like the opportunity to live in close contact with each other but who because of the existing housing supply and the allocation policies of the housing managers are not able to do so. This situation concerns single person households in particular: currently sought for solutions include shared housing for young people, housing communities for elderly people, housing co-operatives, for example. But the question of achieving quality through promoting small scale forms of social organisation is also relevant for groups of households with common interests or social situations: groups who wish to combine living and working, for example, single parent families who wish to share their tasks in childminding, groups who wish to offer social services from their living quarters.

These are all issues which require flexibility on the part of housing authorities, who need to be open to the ideas and demands of these different social groups in order to achieve housing qualities appropriate to the needs of different groups. Through building for diversity one can make steps towards the facilitation of a sense of community.

4.6 Community as an environmental quality

The need to establish what is loosely termed a sense of community in social housing settlements is uncontroversial and generally accepted. The need for a material base to a sense of community is not always acknowledged. I would argue that a sense of community springs from the rights people have in their environment and the opportunities people have of intervening in and shaping their environments. Community therefore needs a basis in rights, participation and control, and it needs to be supplemented by the recognition of the different interests of different household groups and their needs for micro-level links with each other. If these primary conditions do not apply then one cannot expect community to develop in spite of contrary circumstances.

This definition does not disregard the need for traditional social and community facilities as are now generally provided in new settlements, but it does stress the prior determinants of social cohesion for whose absence no number of community centres can compensate.

4.7 Environmental quality: Cognitive mapping

Much debate has been devoted to the urban form of the settlements of the 1960s and 1970s and the supposedly disintegrative qualities of modernist urban morphology. I have no intention of getting side-tracked into a review of the debate on whether, and in what ways, physical space determines social behaviour. For my argument, it suffices to propose that issues of the perception and cognition of urban space are significant issues: people need to be able to recognise and understand the structure of their urban environments. Many forms of modernism - in its debased form in the 1960s and 1970s - precisely broke down people's perception and cognition of space. As Jameson puts it, the built form exceeded the capacities of the individual to locate itself, to organise its immediate surroundings perceptually, and cognitively to map its position in a mappable external world.

I do not propose here a postmodernist critique of modernism, because the postmodernist critique also poses the invalidity of all metanarratives and in particular the aspiration of modernism to social reform through the built environment. My argument is that one historical variant of modernism resulted in forms which were incomprehensible to the inhabitants: this critique does not imply the need to discard the project of social reform which was one part of the modernist project. There was never a correspondence between built form and metanarrative - for the architecture of social reform often resorted to vernacular forms.

4.8 Housing quality: Ontological security

The ability of people to map, in their mind, their position and the urban totality in which they find themselves can be argued to be an element of ontological security.

The term 'ontological security' is a category generated in urban theory originally to explain housing users' preference for ownership over rental. In that context it remains controversial and not widely accepted, but in my view it can profitably be applied to all forms of housing to indicate the quality of understanding, control and security which people require in their environments.

The term may be considered by some a terminologically inflated way of describing the feeling of 'home': but it points to the issues raised above of rights, control, participation, community and cognition of the environment. Even if the term generated in debates on home ownership it can be applied equally to social housing, to generate a series of requirements to be met in order that tenants of social housing - and of private housing - have the opportunity to experience their home as 'their home' in a qualitative sense if not in a legal sense of private property. But even if the distinction of ownership and rental remains, one returns to issues of legal rights, if not of disposal, of use and enjoyment and control - in short, of appropriation of one's environment.

4.9 Ecological qualities

Until now I have purposely restricted the focus to social elements which need considering in a new conceptualisation of housing quality. There is no longer, in the present day, a sufficient and adequate perspective. It is now recognised that the preservation of the environment is a new task for society which goes beyond the interests of society: nature has interests prior to those of society.

The ecological challenge poses new tasks: tasks which can be compared to the public health interventions of the latter part of the last century, when the natural basis of urban life was brought into question by disease. The threats posed at that time to urban life led to massive interventions in the field of public health.

Tasks of greater magnitude face us today. They involve, on the one hand, a series of interventions in detailed issues: healthy building materials, preserving groundwater levels, increasing the area and variety of planted areas, reducing energy needs in housing, banning the use of tropical woods and so on. All these are incremental goals which can be achieved by legislation and regulation.

Yet laudable as each step may be, they do not in isolation guarantee the outcome striven after. Ecological qualities in housing and urban environment can, ultimately, only be secured through holistic approaches which recognise, and respond to, the interrelation between, and the contradictory nature of, the various demands to be made on housing and building in order to secure an ecologically sound environment.

To give an example, a winter garden attached to a dwelling can provide a thermal insulation buffer and provide an extension to the living space of a dwelling. But if it is heated in winter then the ecological outcome may be negative: it then consumes more energy than it saves. Similarly, an ecological settlement built in a peripheral location may include all ecological aspects imaginable (organic gardening, energy conservation, healthy building materials and so on), but the benefits of all these positive ecological elements may be outweighed by the fact that the residents have to commute long distances by car to reach their employment from a geographically isolated area.

That is, a kind of balance sheet of ecological impact has to be drawn up in order to arrive at a measure of ecological quality. One qualification should be made: this balance sheet of ecological impact may all too readily become a highly technical procedure. There is a danger that these issues become technocratised and removed from the area of decision-making by lay people. This has to be avoided, for a number of reasons. For one, as I argue above, urban qualities can only be secured if there are mechanisms of participation and decision-making which enable members of local communities without expert knowledge to be involved in the relevant decisions. But equally, ecological qualities in the urban environment cannot be achieved purely through legislation and regulation: the implementation and further pursuit of environmentally acceptable housing and urban qualities requires the conviction and commitment of lay people and local communities.

In this sense the achievement of ecological objectives becomes bound up with the achievement of qualities in the other fields mentioned earlier - power, participation, community... These all become prerequisites for the achievement of housing quality and urban quality and remain interdependent.

5. The Consequences for Housing Research: Processual Research Strategies

How can the notion of housing quality outlined above be applied to the reformulation of housing policy overall? What are the tasks for housing research?

An attempt to answer these questions involves a new type of strategy. It may involve researching into 'housing needs', though this is an inadequate approach, because it is unidirectional and non-processual. It involves a classical research paradigm which sees populations as objects of study to investigate in order to achieve expert knowledge, which is then applied by experts. The investigated populations have no clear active role in the process and there is no clear way by which they can gain knowledge of their own needs during this process. There is a large body of literature in social research concerned with the merits and demerits of classical investigative research paradigms and action-research models.

Action-research models attempt to break down the dichotomy between researcher and researched, between investigator and investigated. They posit an approach in which research enquiry yields real knowledge both for experts and for lay communities. This real knowledge can take the form of identifiable products (research reports, recommendations, policy instruments), but it can also take the form of 'immaterial' products in the form of knowledge, experience and skills for the immediate participants (whether experts or communities).

In other terms, this involves generating participation processes in which lay people (local communities), in dialogue with experts, gain the opportunity to recognise and understand the nature of their needs and the potential and constraints involved in meeting those needs. This requires an interactive process between local communities and experts in which both groups gain new skills and reach new knowledge. A precondition of such a process is the redefinition of urban planning decisions as political rather than technical decisions, and a de-technocratisation (laicisation?) of urban planning instruments and procedures. This applies both to new urban developments and to interventions in existing settlements.

We can draw an analogy with the procedures of Environmental Impact Assessments. There is an irony in the fact that Environmental Impact Assessments have become formalised into planning procedures, but Social Impact Assessments have not. The assessment of the social impact of urban planning interventions can be the vehicle to use for elaborating a new concept of 'housing quality' - or more generally 'the quality of the urban environment'.

HOUSING SOLUTIONS/ENVIRONMENTAL PROBLEMS

by

Thomas Maloutas
National Centre of Social Research
Athens

1. Housing and the Environment

Improving the urban environment and improving housing conditions seem to be parallel objectives in the context of policies aiming at the improvement of the quality of life. However, housing solutions may be detrimental to the environment and preserving the environment may obstruct the social diffusion of housing conditions improvement. How serious can this contradiction be?

Housing can contribute to environmental degradation in several, direct or indirect, ways, that is either as a polluting agent or through the paramount importance of forms of housing production to the shape and size of problems created by other agents, e.g. cars, through urban form and organisation.

This paper will discuss mainly the indirect forms of pressure that post-war housing in Athens has exerted on the environment as well as its impact on the social prerequisites for access to improved environmental conditions in residential areas. Ensuing socio-political implications will be briefly pointed at.

2. Patterns of Housing Production

Housing conditions improved during the post-war period with unprecedented impetus. Houses have become bigger and better equipped while households were becoming smaller[1]. The working classes were not excluded from these improvements. On the contrary, the improvement of their housing conditions has, comparatively, proceeded at a more rapid pace[2].

Owing to the very large increase in construction volume - during the 1960s mainly - this period is referred to as the 'building miracle'. What seems miraculous, in fact, is that this improvement in housing conditions has apparently occurred without direct state intervention. During the same period housing conditions improved all over Europe, but this was mainly the outcome of state intervention in a context of developing welfare policies. In Greece, the role of the state as a direct housing constructor or as a financing/subsidising agent has been minimal (Kotzamanis, Maloutas, 1985, Economou, 1987).

Individual savings, family aid, inheritance and often participation in construction work were the basic means that fuelled housing construction. Moreover, the merchant banks were excluded from the housing sector until recently, meaning that borrowing was not the usual route to home ownership. The lack of institutional financing was an impediment to the development of the housing market in classic terms, i.e. the consumer meeting the finished product on the market. Alternative ways of housing provision - self-build and build-to-order - have been dominant for a long time[3].

The possibility of these alternative forms of housing provision is related to certain features of Greek society and mainly to the low degree of social polarisation[4], the social diffusion of urban land being part and parcel of the absence of intense proletarianisation tendencies. Nevertheless, the boosting of housing construction would not have been possible without the specific policies affecting housing. Three aspects of these policies are interesting in this case:

a. leniency in peri-urban landed property break-up enabling the social diffusion of urban landed property;

b. leniency in observing/controlling regulations allowing a considerable reduction in construction costs, and

c. increase in construction coefficients enabling the enhanced yield of urban land exploitation.

These policies should not be referred to as housing policies because their scope and their objectives were far broader than the housing sector (Economou, 1987). They were deployed in the post-civil war political climate when political exclusion was paradoxically coupled with social integration through populist measures and clientalist practices, as well as under the beneficial effects of the favourable economic conjuncture. The fact that these policies had no immediate cost increased their attractiveness, since the financial effort of the state was directed to the reluctantly developing industry.

The first two aspects of the above policies are related to the dominant pattern of housing production during the first part of the post-war period, i.e. to self-build and build-to-order, while the third is related to the belated development of the housing market through a new housing production system. Self-build and, especially, build-to-order embraced, during their dominant period, the whole society. It was only when their decay began - since the 1970s - that they were increasingly marginalised to the social poles.

The housing market has begun to develop rapidly since the early 1960s. Its development has progressively broadened its social physiognomy, as until then it was confined to the upper middle classes (Maloutas, 1990). The impetus to housing market development has been given by a new production system. This system - 'antiparochi' - was deeply embedded in Greek tradition, i.e. small urban land ownership and small size building enterprises, and contributed to the reproduction of both. Housing production started to be more and more destined to the market. Nevertheless, the main components of the new house production system determined/preserved a significant role for the landowner. His role was secure in the new process as he received, at the end of the work, part of the product in exchange for his landed property. This system, obstructing the transfer of rent from landowners to capital, impeded the concentration of capital in the building sector, and thus permitted the development and survival of numerous small house building enterprises. The outlet this new system presented for exploiting property's potential by landowners was enhanced by a substantial increase in construction coefficients. A Hausmanian rage (with a family size, middle class rationale) swept individual housing from the city centre and, later, from the main suburban centres. Most of the neoclassical architectural heritage quickly perished in the process, as demolition decisions for individual houses are relatively easy to take compared to multi-owner apartment buildings. A reconstruction of Athens with higher densities and less character was the main spatial outcome.

3. Housing and the Environment

The extensive housing production pattern of the first post-war period has enlarged the urban tissue in every direction swallowing every bit of free space. Agricultural land and forests perished in the process. The grow of every city means inevitably that land uses will change. What is not inevitable is the way and the extent of the process. Leniency regarding landed property break-up and land use change, coupled with individualised initiative in the housing production process, rendered all planning and control procedures obsolete as they were contradictory to the spirit of the policies followed. Nature as social capital was not the only one to suffer. The urban tissue developed in unplanned ways as the aggregate result of unco-ordinated individual actions. Its structure is bearing the mark in its problematic street layout and the absence of public space impeding the development of collective consumption facilities (schools, nurseries, hospitals, transport infrastructure).

The consequences of these policies and housing practices were not alarming from the start. It was their continued reproduction in increasing intensity that produced a very problematic situation. Moreover, if in the beginning planning and control measures were not implemented as they were out of context, such measures were increasingly difficult to take as this housing pattern kept on reproducing itself. Forming one of the principal axes in the web of populist policies and representing a manifestation of the dominant political culture, it became increasingly politically suicidal for any government to proceed otherwise. On the other hand, the tolerance in the destruction of the natural, as well as the built, environment as an incentive for house production continued for a long time to have the attraction of a low (immediate) cost policy. It was not until congestion problems, coupled with air pollution, became manifestly acute that alternative policies could become socially substantiated and politically present.

The housing pattern of the first post-war period was socially diffuse, but its imprint was deeper in working classes and the areas where they were - and still are - residentially over-represented. Leniency was in fact necessary especially for working class housing and it was mainly in this case that advantage was taken with illegal construction. The working class suburbs in the western periphery of Athens were the ones that 'suffered' the most during this period.

The new dominant housing pattern since the late 1960s is based on the aforementioned production system of 'antiparochi'. Changes in the social structure of big cities, and especially Athens, had rendered the traditional housing production patterns inappropriate. Middle classes increased as tertiary occupations developed with great impetus, stimulated by considerable increases in public employment. The new non-manual tertiary occupations created a demand for housing that was increasingly met in the growing housing market where supply grew under the effect of the new housing production system. The traditional housing solutions were more and more relegated to traditional manual workers, the only ones with an appropriate skills profile to engage in self-build practices. On the other hand, build-to-order became increasingly out of reach for the working and middle classes as construction costs were climbing.

As a policy, the institution of this new housing system was again overriding the housing sector. Broader economic and political objectives were usually followed (Economou, 1987). Politically, this system was appealing to the small urban landowner and to almost every profession related to house building, that is to a very large number of voters. Moreover, the new state-related middle classes were substantially subsidised to face the output of this new system on the market (Kotzamanis and Maloutas, 1985, Economou, 1988, Maloutas, 1990). The populist essence of housing-related policies did not change with the new system. On the contrary it was exacerbated by favourable construction regulations and especially by the increase in construction coefficients.

Congestion has been the major spatial impact of the new housing production system. Problems developed incrementally and as before, they were tolerable in the beginning and politically impossible when they became serious. The centre of the city was mainly acquired in this case followed by areas near the centre and then the peripheral centres, that is all the areas where building by the new system could be profitable (higher land prices and higher construction coefficients). Congestion resulted in many practical problems: traffic, garbage collection, collective transport, parking, lack of public services, etc. But, it is air pollution, forcefully appearing in the late 1970s, that has been the main axis for the change in attitude towards the urban environment.

4. New Attitudes towards the City: The Social Inequality Issue

Attitudes towards the urban environment are changing. Its practical effects, as well as the growing literature and the increasingly important place it occupies in the media, have shaped new attitudes concerning the importance of a sound urban environment.

The change in attitude towards the environment is clear when the environment is considered as a parameter in residential location choice. According to a housing survey, environmental considerations were mentioned by households in a proportion slowly growing from 15% in the early 1950s to 17.5% in the mid 1970s; then, this proportion suddenly climbed to 25% in the late 1970s and approached 30% in the mid 1980s (Maloutas, 1990:323).

A social analysis of the environmentally sensitised households reveals that they belong almost entirely to the upper socio-professional categories. Their environmental sensitisation is practically expressed by their tendency to locate or relocate their residence in the less degraded northern and southern suburbs or in certain peri-urban areas. This tendency being far from negligible, has shaped new segregation patterns in Athens. In former periods segregation was less pronounced and more horizontal or niched. Environmental degradation has led to vertical segregation through its catalytic influence on the developing mechanisms of the housing market. As a result the northern and southern suburbs have increased the proportions of upper socio-professional categories among their residents, while the traditionally working class western suburbs have proportionally lost less salaried manual workers than the other suburbs. But the most dramatic changes occurred in the centre, i.e. the Municipality of Athens, that lost in upper and upper middle socio-professional categories more than any other area and preserved its salaried manual workers while they were declining everywhere else (Maloutas, forthcoming).

The environment is not of course the only segregative axis. Still, it appears stronger since the late 1970s. From the above-mentioned housing survey it appears that all the other reasons for residential location choice (location near parents or relatives, near work, near public or market services, because of already existing - inherited or otherwise - home or lot, because of familiarity with the area, because of land prices or rent) were socially less discriminating.

New attitudes, however, are seldom independent of old ones. The individualised family size, solutions to social problems, inherent in the Greek political culture, apply to environmental problems as well. The problems change, the approach remains the same. The deteriorating urban environment is a collective problem and the state is held responsible for it. Solutions are, nevertheless, not really expected from the state or from any other form of collective action. Individualised solutions are once more the answer.

The drive for a better environment through private means has had relative success for those who could afford it. The limits in this case are posited by the gradual reappearance of the roots of environmental degradation in the suburbs by the reproduction of the same housing patterns in suburban areas. Only time is gained in better environmental conditions until congestion reaches new spatial frontiers. Some middle class suburbs are already seriously congested and the same applies to the main peripheral centres. Still, the urban environment is far from indivisible as its social structure can be changed in parallel with environmental degradation or any other spatially determined nuisance.

5. Housing or the Environment: A Politically Uneasy Dilemma

What are the prospects, then, concerning this apparently contradictory relationship between housing and the environment? If we consider this relationship on the local level we can distinguish six major types of situation depending on geographic location and social profile.

5.1 Upper class central areas: the urban environment has been constantly deteriorating in this case due to increased construction, congestion and air pollution. Residents tend to move to environmentally sound suburbs and housing is replaced to a great extent by offices and commerce. Tension between housing and the environment here is relieved because residents choose to confront it elsewhere. Urban renovation (very limited in extent), on the other hand, has contributed to the improvement of the urban environment and either to the preservation of social exclusion or to the creation of gentrification processes in the renovated areas.

5.2 Upper class suburban areas: niche locations in the northern and southern suburbs some of which were explicitly designed as socially exclusive suburbs, while others were former upper class leisure housing areas converted to classic residential areas during the last 15 years. The urban environment is preserved by local authorities, central administration and consenting residents as it represents the main pole of attraction as well as the key feature valorising landed property. Housing is regulated in the strictest possible terms and low construction coefficients are favoured both by residents and authorities. The environment is preserved in this case at the expense of rising housing costs and intense social segregation.

5.3 Middle class central areas: environmentally degraded central areas progressively abandoned by the more affluent former inhabitants. Extremely dense housing has led to congestion, loss of character and comparative devaluation of land prices. A social restructuring of these areas occurs through the creation of affordable house prices and rent for working classes that can no longer, as a whole, use the traditional housing solutions in the city's periphery. The tension between housing and the environment is relieved, in this case, because of the departure of those environmentally sensitised and because of the recent settlement/compromise of popular strata realising that the affordability of housing in these areas is related to poor environmental conditions.

5.4 Middle class suburban areas: seeking a sound urban environment at half (middle class) price. Suburban areas with a 'date limit' as they are constructed on the model of central areas. Those having reached 'maturity' present many problems similar to those of middle class central areas. An improved urban environment is difficult to preserve in this case: (a) because of the price for individual housing that improved environment means: (b) because of the continuing demand for housing and better environmental conditions than those of the centre, but at an affordable price and (c) because of the middle class drive to exploit land - on the basis of (b) - even if it turns out to be detrimental to living conditions in the long run. A frustrating tension is created between the degrading urban environment and the drive for a better urban environment that propels middle class relocation to the suburbs. Preserving the environment, in this case, for those that are already residents is obstructing the continuation of the process that they themselves used to become residents. Local authorities would be in an uneasy position if construction regulation and planning were under their control: on the one hand, there would be pressure from apartment owners and people living in rented houses to limit further construction but, on the other hand, there would be pressure from landowners to continue on the same model so that they could also have the chance to exploit their land's potential. These areas present the politically strongest environment/housing tensions.

5.5 Working class central areas: these areas are environmentally deteriorating and socially segregated. The environment here is not only affected directly by congestion but also by industrial activities located almost exclusively in the western part of the city. Local authorities' environmental action is centred almost exclusively on the second source of nuisance. Alternative housing opportunities cannot be considered feasible in this social context, especially since there is no tradition of urban rehabilitation social programmes. In this case, there is no real tension between housing and the environment as more apparent causes of environmental degradation are mainly valued and attacked.

5.6 Popular suburban areas: a broadly similar situation with that of the lower class central areas. Moreover, social and housing patterns are more rigid here: home owners (established during the period when self-build and illegal construction were feasible as massive phenomena with broad family self-help networks) remain with what they possess since their model of access to home ownership has declined and since their situation is far better than any alternative. A defensive stance for the preservation of what already exists is characteristic in this case, following on the defensive tradition (against threats concerning illegal construction) by opposing any attempt at urban rehabilitation threatening the established equilibria. Environmental degradation, as a consequence of housing, cannot be a local political issue here.

We see then that tensions between housing production and the urban environment are variable and can, in fact, be of three main types:

- **Upper Class:** external and valued, that is produced by middle class and working class housing and is perceived as a serious threat to living conditions.

- **Middle Class:** internal and valued, resulting from the conflicting drive for better environmental conditions and the insufficient means of achievement that, moreover, depend highly on further exploitation of considerable amounts of urban land possessed by these classes.

- **Working class:** internal and non-valued, resulting from the priority given to housing problem solution and masked by other sources of environmental nuisance.

In this context, a global policy for the improvement of the urban environment is highly unlikely to survive politically. The perturbations it would produce on middle class and working class housing patterns - extremely important in a context of weak development of the welfare state - would destabilise any government. The most probable scenario would be that the upper classes will continue to buy better environmental conditions, the middle classes will continue the contradictory process of deteriorating environmental conditions by the individualised effort of their members to access better urban environment, and for the working classes securing their housing solutions will prevail and environmental improvement will be related only to other forms of environmental degradation (i.e. industrial pollution) that carry less generalised forms of social tension (environment versus employment).

6. Conclusions

Housing production patterns in Athens have contributed to environmental degradation by enhancing the effects of polluting agents via the poor organisation of urban space, as well as by producing congestion, the ensuing problems being aggravated by the absence of planning. Better environmental conditions became an issue and at the same time acquired a price. Scarcity led to social segregation through housing mechanisms. Working and middle class households seem less sensitised to environmental issues either because other problems prevail or because they are practically unable to change their situation in the traditional individualised way. The environment becomes socially divisible through market mechanisms with the sensitised social classes opting for practical remedies, even if in the long run those remedies have relative value. Becoming socially segmented, the environment becomes politically divisible as well. The political will to improve the urban environment is then far from sufficient.

Notes:

1. The average new house had 3.06 rooms in 1966, 3.37 in 1975 and 3.62 in 1984 (KEPE, 1976:12, NSSG, 1986:284). In 1982 almost the entire housing stock was equipped with electricity, bathroom, toilet and kitchen while in 1961 a considerable part of the stock was lacking in these respects (Kouveli, Sakellaropoulos, 1984:97). The size of the average Greek household was 4.11 in 1951 and progressively diminished to 3.12 in 1981 (NSSG, 1986:33).
2. The increase in the ratio rooms per person was 4.3% yearly between 1961 and 1971 for the working classes while on average it did not exceed 2.4% (Emmanuel, 1977:57).
3. Among the houses acquired between 1949 and 1969 23% were bought as finished products and 47% were either self-built or built-to-order, while between 1970 and 1986 these percentages changed respectively to 51% and 20% (Maloutas, 1990).
4. Greek society is poorly polarised as the social structure is expanded in the middle. Salaried employment is lagging far behind all other EEC countries. The self-employed and small scale employers form a very substantial part of the active population steadily reproduced in its extent throughout the post-war period. The salaried, on the other hand, have been increasingly state-employed (Tsoukalas, 1983, 1984 and 1986).

REFERENCES

Economou, D. (1987). *Housing Policy in Post-War Greece*. The Greek Review of Social Research, 64, 57-130.

Economou, D. (1988), Land and Housing System in Post-War Greece, in Maloutas T., Economou, D., *The Development of The Welfare State in Greece*. Athens, Exantas, 57-114.

Emmanuel, D. *Three Studies about Popular Housing*. Athens, TEE.

KEPE, (1976). *Housing*. Athens, KEPE.

Kotzamanis, V., Maloutas T., (1985). *Public Policy in Social Housing*. The Greek Review of Social Research, 56, 129-54.

Kouveli, A. and Sakellaropoulos, K. (1984). *Housing Conditions in Greece*. Athens, EKKE.

Maloutas, T. (1990). *Housing and Family in Athens*. An Analysis of Post-War Housing Practices. Athens, Exantas.

Maloutas, T. (forthcoming). Social Segregation in Athens, in Maloutas T., Economou, D., *The Social Organisation of Athens*. Athens.

NSSG, (1986). *Statistical Year Book of Greece 1985*. Athens, NSSG.

Tsoukalas, K. (1983). *Social Consequence of Public Employment in Post-War Greece*. The Greek Review of Social Research, 50, 20-52.

Tsoukalas, K. (1984). *Employment Structure and the Middle Classes*. Anti, 260.

Tsoukalas, K. (1986). *Labour and Labour Force in Athens*. The Greek Review of Social Research 60, 3-71.

PARTNERSHIP WITH PEOPLE?
A QUASI-BUSINESS DESIGN MODEL FOR REGENERATION IN URBAN COMMUNITIES

John Bell[*]
Community Development Foundation
London

The paper discusses a model of urban regeneration implemented in the UK which brought together the public, private and voluntary sectors, and the local community in a unique combination. The creation of a private sector PLC (SA) company with board members elected from the local community was intended to be a model for the entrepreneurial regeneration of a deeply depressed estate of social housing, and a vehicle for sensitive development. The model sought ways to rehabilitate the existing built environment and turn areas of derelict land into a mix of new housing types and tenures.

The paper describes the intentions of the model, the structural constraints on its development, and the ways in which it has performed. It discusses whether the concept of community involvement used has enabled local people genuinely to participate in significant decisions for their area, and examines the contradiction of private sector development alongside severe social problems.

By considering this model in practice, the paper is able to draw conclusions for attempts to introduce multisectoral development more widely, particularly in relation to partnership with the community.

OBSERVATOIRE OF STRUCTURED ACTIONS IN FAVOUR OF THE HOMELESS: AIMS AND PROSPECTS

Francine Boudru[*]
European Federation of National Organisations
Working with the Homeless (FEANTSA)
Brussels

FEANTSA has been instructed by the Commission to set up an observatoire of actions and services in favour of the homeless.

The first part of this communication will be devoted to presenting the approach which has been adopted, and the objectives which it sets out to attain.

In the second part of the paper, we will look at the hypotheses underlying the analysis of the type of service which is most widespread in the Community countries: hostels. We will argue for a rehabilitation of this type of facility, and we will look at the conditions which such services should fulfil if they are really to serve as a launching-pad for reintegration into society.

CHALLENGING CITIES: A NEW APPROACH TO URBAN REGENERATION?

Paul Burton[*]
School for Advanced Urban Studies
University of Bristol

In May of this year, the Secretary of State for the Environment in the UK, Michael Heseltine, announced a major new urban policy initiative - City Challenge. Fifteen local authorities were invited to bid to central government for funds to regenerate key neighbourhoods within their jurisdictions, drawing together public and private sectors in the process.

On closer inspection, it became clear that the novelty of this new initiative lay mainly in the fact that local authorities were being asked to compete directly with each other for a 'new' source of funds. Moreover, it also became apparent that the money available was not new but 'top-sliced' from existing Action for Cities programmes.

This presentation/paper will explore the strengths and weaknesses of this latest approach to urban regeneration and examine the response of one city - Bristol - to the challenge. It will conclude by setting this initiative in a broader historical context in order to analyse the real contribution of urban policies to the regeneration of urban fringes, run-down city centres and other fragile urban zones.

IDENTITY AND REPRESENTATIONS AMONG THE WEAKEST MEMBERS OF SOCIETY

Claude Leroy[*]
A.I.Q.V.
'L'Homme et la Ville'
Paris

The environment can only be imagined in an anthropological setting, especially in and around the cities. It is the connective tissue - in the sense that this term is used about the human body - between specific organs, linking the different buildings of the city.

The human person is constructed over time, starting out on the basis of his or her genetic programme, by means of behaviour in relation to the constraints of reality, in individual representations of the self, of others, of his or her territory, as well as the mechanisms of biological and psychological defence adapted to the environment within which he or she lives. One must distinguish the anthropological dimension, which is common to all mankind, the cultural dimension and characteristics having to do with age, social class and handicaps.

The weakest members of society experience a reduction in their autonomy, their degrees of freedom in relation to others, including their utilisation of time and space.

The body politic is not much influenced by their low economic level, but is more influenced by their cost. In any case, it is unaware of their desires and plans. These are very limited in time and space; frequently the temporal horizon is confined to the present, while the spatial horizon in confined to a few hundred metres around one's home (or whatever serves as a home). They are aware of the gaps between themselves and the rest of society, which depresses them and inhibits their possibilities of integration.

It is useful to consider these people as good indicators of the drawbacks in the organisation of cities, particularly as we are all handicapped at one point or another. Things which are good for the weakest members of society also improve the lot of everybody living in a city, and help to cut the costs of welfare. When welfare programmes are excessive, they keep the individual in a dependent position. All learning is an active process.

One must deal at the same time with the need for a living environment which mixes different populations and the specific services needed for each age group and each class of handicap.

The concept of 'rehabilitation' is identical for handicap and for buildings which have deteriorated: it consists of restoring the potential which enhances the degree of freedom, rather than taking action on behalf of the individuals (or the residents of a building) without asking what they think.

Finally, one must think in terms of change and evolution over time for the city, seen as an ecosystem and not in a static way, ad hoc, without any plan.

To this end, it is essential to build up a knowledge of the urban setting, with the aid of an observatoire, linked to several databases which are currently unconnected, and dealing with problems in scenarios with their advantages and drawbacks out in the open.

The management of the city involves mediating between the normal conflicts about the use of time and space which emerge there.

FINANCING OWNER-OCCUPIED AND SOCIAL HOUSING, SIMILARITIES AND INTERACTIONS

John Lomax[*]
Bank of England
London

This paper examines international trends in financing owner-occupied and rented housing. As regards the latter, the focus is on private non-profit housing associations and co-operatives. In most countries, some deregulation and liberalisation of financial institutions has occurred. Accordingly, the provision of many types of housing finance has become more market oriented. Some of the factors driving these developments have been economic, such as high inflation and lower growth rates during the 1970s and early 1980s. In addition, there have been shifts in political ideology.

One consequence of liberalisation has been the enhancement of consumer choice. A much wider range of mortgage instruments has become available. In addition, loans have increasingly been allocated by price (movements in interest rates) rather than quantity. In line with this, loans for a higher percentage of property value are now available. Some adverse effects have, however, also emerged. In particular, it is likely that the behaviour of deregulated housing finance institutions has contributed to significant house price inflation in some countries. As house prices have become less affordable, the need to maintain an adequate supply of housing has increased.

SOCIAL COMMUNITY INITIATIVES FOR HOUSING
HOUSING AND SOCIAL INSERTION. THE CONTRIBUTION OF THE GROUP OF EXPERTS IN DG V

Voula Mega[*]
European Foundation for the Improvement
of Living and Working Conditions
Dublin

This contribution presents the European Community framework in matters of housing.

It gives an overview of the themes on which the group of experts in the Commission (DG V) focused its work. This group met regularly during the last two years in the wider context of 'Employment and insertion in the urban environment and reinforcement of economic and social cohesion'.

The paper constitutes an updated version of a paper presented at the European Conference 'Housing the Community 2000' (Dublin, 3-6 July 1991) where I was representing Ms Odile Quintin.

Many of the experts participating in the group set up by DG V will be participating in our conference in Berlin and will, of course, enrich this synthetic presentation with their contribution.

We all hope that this group, this network of experts, which owes a lot to Jean Alègre, will continue its work successfully.

IRISH TRAVELLERS - AN ANALYSIS OF STATE INITIATIVES TO IMPROVE SOCIAL HOUSING AND FACILITATE SOCIAL INTEGRATION

John O'Connell[*]
Dublin Travellers Education and Development Group
Dublin

This paper will outline the background to the current accommodation problems experienced by Irish Travellers and examine the State's response down through the years. It will demonstrate how urbanisation and modernisation and the growing integration of the Irish economy into the world economic system impacted on the traditional way of life of Travellers. It will show how Travellers' nomadic way of life came under systematic assault during these changing circumstances.

The paper will attempt to show how an inadequate understanding by the State of Travellers' ethnic identity gave rise to policies which were ineffective and even racist. The paper will also examine the role played by voluntary organisations and Travellers themselves in relation to the implementation of these policies.

Finally, the paper will offer some suggestions about culturally appropriate alternatives which can meet the needs of Irish Travellers.

CONCLUSIONS, RECOMMENDATIONS

by

Marie Ganier-Raymond
IFS, Berlin

The Working Group was made up of 16 people, including 12 speakers, with a wide variety of backgrounds and work levels. There was only one unifying criterion in the working group: a topic touching on one or more aspects of social housing.

It was envisaged that presentations would not exceed ten minutes, so as to leave time for discussion and reflection. Presentations varied: some were conceptual or theoretical, other were mixed - meaning that they presented an individual case as well as some general principles - while others again introduced case studies with the emphasis on a problem or a solution connected with the situation of the urban environment.

The conceptual papers ranged from the situation of men and women in the city and the time dimension, the social classes and the influence of the city, to the conditions of finance and housing, and included concepts of integrating all classes and the quality of housing.

The case studies reported local experiences, some aspects of which could be transposed to different contexts, such as a holistic approach to the renovation of urban districts, or the problem of securing real participation by city dwellers in their own housing problems, in cities as diverse as London, Lisbon, Milan, Budapest, Dublin or Bristol.

Lastly, other presentations set the topic in a European context.

The discussion phase for the working group opened with some observations about our understanding of the definition of social housing. While some participants felt that the definition should be descriptive, based on our experience of existing social housing, other people in the working group set out from the prescriptive principles of what social housing ought to mean in the urban environment.

Each member of the working group raised comments or questions which provided headings for discussion. These were as follows:

1. **The City:**

    * Criteria for making a city which would be liveable for the most vulnerable members of society.
    * Perception of the different models and concepts of the city.
    * The bonding of social classes in the urban setting.
    * The city: a place with historic tradition. Organising a renovation programme for a given public, taking account of aspects of social housing within this concept of urban development.

2. **The Social Habitat:**

    *   Improving the notion of a social habitat - better housing policy.
    *   Improving proposals for a social habitat coming from cities in need, and improving their recognition at political level.
    *   Renovating the habitable housing stock, better housing policy in favour of target groups.
    *   Implications of market liberalisation for social housing and the economy in general, implications for Europe, political and economic development.
    *   Improvement of social housing stock.

3. **The Target Groups:**

    *   Need for target groups to participate.
    *   Establishment of tenants' associations to defend their rights.
    *   Wide-ranging assistance, not only housing, for the homeless.
    *   Finding solutions for the relationship and interaction between settled people and travelling people.
    *   Relationship between the target groups on the ground and the decision-makers at public and Community level.

These questions and comments, presented here in a positive form, make it possible to set the debate in its context. One of the major issues is the way in which urban life 'overwhelms' the human dimension in the city, which individual human beings cannot control. Dealing with this situation involves a response from the human side, in terms of a demand for genuine participation in the preparation of the individual's living space, the creation of a high-quality social context which does not involve coercion to take part in subjective competition governed by political and ideological dimensions. This would also require participation by tenants in planning strategies.

Urban regeneration would imply something which is still a utopian dream today: a break with the long-established tradition whereby social classes are subdivided in a city by a well-heeled minority which decides about the new shape of the city and about the displacement of the other social classes.

Housing within the city must therefore be managed through a holistic approach which asks the following question: can a better concept of housing (of a higher quality) produce a better quality of housing policy?

Recommendations:

1. **Financial aspect:**

    *   Gross rents and housing costs acceptable to everybody.
    *   Compatibility of wages and housing costs.

2. **Legal aspect:**

    *   Right to housing, agreement not to evict tenants, even after the district or the dwelling has been renovated.

* Right to dwelling for the most disadvantaged.
* Access regulated by a transparent (objective) order of priorities.

3. Social aspect:

* Assistance measures for the most disadvantaged.
* No stigma attaching to social housing.
* Measures going beyond social housing, which is both indispensable and insufficient to ensure social integration.
* Integration into the human, social and technical texture of the city.

4. Political aspect:

* Real participation by residents.
* No negative redistribution effects of housing policy.
* European convergence on the need for a social housing policy.

5. Contextual aspect (historical and social):

* Social housing providing a common identity.
* Consideration of residents' cultural values in areas of social housing.
* Housing acceptable to the urban environment (ecology).
* Possibility of combining places of residence and work for certain populations (including travelling people).
* Renovation of old city centres without evicting people.
* Social housing which represents cultural values in public spaces.

6. Material aspect (building):

* High standards of construction for social housing.
* Practical accessibility of social housing for handicapped people.
* Social housing accompanied by social services.
* Social housing positioned in a good surrounding environment.

One member of the group advanced recommendations so different from those of all other members of the group that it seems worth noting these differences separately. This member, whose professional work involves researching the financing of social housing, felt it important to recommend that 'social housing should not adversely affect the work ethic among its tenants'. Similarly, the same member voiced some reservations about the non-eviction clause, which he felt encourages some well-heeled people to hang on to their publicly funded housing even after their income would allow them to move elsewhere. These viewpoints met with almost unanimous disagreement from the other members of the group.

By way of conclusion, one may say that a considerable degree of consensus emerged within this working group, although it was made up of very varied social actors, as regards integration through housing. The results of the discussion showed a shared recognition of needs and the expression of a certain number of values which broaden the concept of social housing. The importance of the urban environment featured strongly in the recommendations, whereas the preliminary presentations had only attached a limited degree of importance to this aspect.

Three more papers (without abstracts) were presented in the group (and are available from the Foundation) by:

Peter Fazakas, Berzsenyi, Hungary

Maria Finzi, EUROPIL, Italy

José Garcia, European Committee for Housing, Belgium

SELECTED PAPERS AND CONCLUSIONS OF

THE WORKING GROUP

ON

SOCIAL INTEGRATION AND CREATION OF NEW URBAN ACTIVITIES

COMPOSITION OF WORKING GROUP 4

SOCIAL INTEGRATION AND CREATION OF NEW URBAN ACTIVITIES

Chairman: Mr John Reid
University College Dublin

Rapporteur: Mr Philippe Morin
RACINE, Paris

Expert Introducing the Working Group: Prof. Paul Lawless
Sheffield City Polytechnic

Speakers-Participants:

1. Dr Tony Gibson
   Neighbourhood Initiatives Foundation, UK

2. Mr Alan Sinclair
   Wise Group, Glasgow

3. Dr Yelena Shomina
   USSR Academy of Sciences, Moscow

4. Mr William Roe
   CEI Consultants, Edinburgh

5. Mrs Hilde Maelstaf
   ELISE, Brussels

6. Dr Edith Brickwell
   Senate of Berlin

7. Mr Pierre-Yves Mauguen
   Ministère de Recherche et de Technologie, Paris

8. Mrs Pascale Mistiaen
   DEFIS - ASBL, Brussels

9. Mr Bernard Le Marchand
   UNICE/CLE, Brussels

10. Mrs Geneviève Lecamp
    ILE Programme/OECD, Paris

11. Mrs Margaret Sweeney
    SICA Innovation Consultants Ltd, Dublin

12. Mr Richard Welsh
    National Association for Urban Studies, UK

13. Mr Bob Catterall
    London 2000

14. Mr Michel Miller
    CES/ETUC, Brussels

15. Mr Francisco Orta
    Unión General de Trabajadores, Huelva

16. Mr Nic Van Putten
    Ministry of Social Affairs, The Hague

SOCIAL INTEGRATION AND NEW URBAN ACTIVITIES

by

Paul Lawless
School of Urban and Regional Studies
Sheffield City Polytechnic

1. Introduction

One of the major problems facing European cities is social integration. Throughout the Community we are witnessing an increasing polarisation within and between the major conurbations. In some regions and countries the problems are relatively insignificant: most groups in society appear to benefit from a general increase in the standard of living. In other regions of the Community, notably perhaps the older industrialised regions of the north and the newly urbanised centres in the south, there are increasing signs of acute social polarisation and growing evidence that some sectors and groups in society are becoming increasingly marginalised from mainstream society.

In this paper I would like primarily to provide a broad overview of the relationship between social integration on the one hand and the emergence of new urban activities on the other. This is an important area. If traditional urban activities have, at the very least not eradicated social disintegration, we need collectively to be far more aware of the opportunities and potential constraints which new forms of urban activity will throw up. Before that I intend briefly to contextualise the debate in two ways: first by providing a historical note to the question of social integration within the urban milieu; and secondly to outline some of the major factors which have tended to diminish social integration.

2. A Brief Historical Comment

The issue of social integration in cities has a long tradition. Many of the seminal figures in Twentieth Century urban philosophy prioritised issues of social integration. Indeed it could be argued that one of the key objectives of urban planning for much of the century has been a search for 'Community' (Thorns, 1976). In this, perhaps, naïve and unattainable vision of urban society many thinkers have sought to create an integrated, socially cohesive and yet at the same time diverse localised community. In the Anglo-American tradition for example, the British new towns experiment was firmly rooted in the ideas of social mix and integration originally espoused by Ebenezer Howard in the early years of the century (Howard, 1985). Unfortunately, Howard's broad vision of social change was to be more narrowly focused on new towns somewhat distanced from the major British conurbations. His global perspective which embraced the cities as well as the new towns was abandoned in the rush to construct new communities divorced from the apparent ills of the major cities. But others in the Anglo-American tradition were to sustain the idea that urban change needed to embrace society as well as economy. Figures such as Herbert Gans (1972), Jane Jacobs (1961) and Lewis Mumford (1961) remained convinced that an objective, 'scientific', rational view of cities was not sustainable: urban planning needed to invoke diversity, society and community. These ideas were not limited to the Anglo-American traditions, great European thinkers such as Soria Y Mata and Le Corbusier produced physical solutions to cities rooted in notions of community.

3. Social Integration; Emerging Constraints

It is clear that issues of society and community have figured prominently in the thinking of many key academics and practitioners for many decades. And yet we must conclude that problems associated with social alienation and dislocation remain as one of the major problems facing the larger European conurbations. Why after several decades of increasing collective and individual wealth should this be so? This question is immensely complex (Lawless, 1988). But it merits brief comment since it is against this context that new policies designed to enhance social integration will need to be assessed.

Probably the most important factors are economic in nature. There has been a substantial debate surrounding the question of 'flexible' accumulation (Harvey, 1989, Cooke, 1990). It does appear to be the case that traditional systems of economic production based on standardised products, defined skills, mass production, large plants and delineated tasks are becoming less important to the international economy. Newer modes of production characterised by limited batches, advanced design, the accumulation of flexible skills and small units of production have emerged. In some regions of the Community notably in the specialised industrial regions of Italy, Catalonia and elsewhere, this mode of production has brought substantial gains. We may be witnessing the beginnings of a sea of change in production: the replacement of one dominant mode by another. Not all observers are convinced that this has occurred or indeed is likely to do so. Nevertheless some changes which may herald the emergence of a new economic order can be identified throughout the Community: enhanced service as opposed to manufacturing or agricultural employment; rapid technological innovation; the acquisition by some in the labour market of specialised and integrated skills; the internationalisation of economic trade and so on.

Many of these trends bring in their wake positive benefits for many in society: enhanced material standards and quality of life, a more varied work experience and opportunities for travel. But there are costs too. Two groups in society have suffered more than most: traditional blue collar workers and those on the margins of society. In the case of the former, employment opportunities in the older established industries: steel, coal, vehicle production and so on has fallen dramatically in the last decade and appears certain to continue to do so. For many of these, usually male, workers alternative employment prospects appear slim. Others on the margins of society: immigrants, the young unskilled, and some female workers, have also often not benefited from economic changes. They may be employed, but often in unskilled, poorly paid, service sectors where longer term prospects are limited.

Economic forces may well have been the most dominant in defining disadvantage in the Community in the recent past. But they are not the only ones. At least two other broad sets of factors ought to be mentioned: social and demographic considerations; and political issues.

A range of what might be broadly defined as socially based factors have also impacted on social integration. One set of factors for example revolves around demographic considerations. These have been considered in detail elsewhere (Cheshire and Hay, 1989). Many of the complexities and variations in urban demographic performance must be beyond this brief review. But two trends in particular are worth identifying. Some of the older established cities in the traditional industrialised areas of north and west Europe have seen a marked decentralisation in population. This is apparent in cities such as Liverpool, Bochum and St. Etienne. Of itself loss of population may impose relatively few costs and indeed may bring positive benefits. The problem tends often to be, however, that it is the better off, the mobile, the relatively young and the economically active that move. Cities may lose population in absolute terms, but suffer a relative increase in the numbers of the disadvantaged and the marginalised. Secondly, especially in southern Europe, there has tended to be a centralisation of population due to immigration, the movement of displaced agricultural workers, and higher birth rates. In the longer term there is every reason to believe that these centralising cities will eventually go through the process of decentralisation (and indeed that older cities which have seen a loss of population will increasingly re-centralise). But in the short term cities which have gained population tend often to be characterised by a range of socio-economic ills including high unemployment and under-employment, poor housing conditions and racial tension.

Other social problems tend to interact with demographic change. Cities seeing rapid evolution in their social composition may find demand for specific welfare services subject to considerable variation. In some cases the needs of older age groups have increasingly dominated social service provision in the major conurbations; in others, especially in southern Europe, demands for educational services have been most acute in a context of a population structure skewed towards younger people. In many cities too, demand on welfare services has been accentuated by the specific needs of groups which tend to be over-represented in urban areas relative to the national picture: the mentally and physically disabled for example. The integration of these groups into society will impose very considerable costs.

A final and often neglected factor in relation to problems of social integration is the political dimension. This may operate in a number of ways. Locally, for example, one of the key constraints impacting on many disadvantaged households and communities is the question of empowerment. It seems evident that many in older urban conurbations, the young, the uneducated and immigrants are not subsumed within what might be termed orthodox political channels. Their aspirations and fears are often not assimilated into the policies and programmes of major political parties. This sense of alienation can result in the emergence of fringe extremist groupings rooted in fear and ignorance. At the broader national context political forces can impact on urban social strife too. At this level there are marked variations within and between European countries. Nevertheless there are arguments that in some instances cities have not received the support their ills justify. Too often resources have been reduced to the cities, and their burgeoning social and economic ills not given adequate consideration by central governments. Where this occurs, it may reflect political conflict between right wing national governments eager to limit the power, influence and resources available to left wing urban administrations. Developing this theme it could equally be argued that many of the policies pursued by certain governments in the 1980s have done little to enhance social cohesion in the cities. Programmes such as privatisation, a diminution in welfare services, and implicit de-industrialisation, whatever their intrinsic merits, have done little to sustain the concept of a collective urban community.

4. Social Integration and New Urban Activities

Whatever the root causes for continuing social dislocation in the cities, it is clear that opportunities exist for a much greater integration of marginalised groups into mainstream society. There are a number of reasons for this. There is probably a greater awareness throughout the Community of constraints on social integration. Issues of poverty, racism, and urban violence have received extensive international coverage. At the same time forces such as the rapid dissemination of technological innovation, an emerging environmentalism, and a generally more flexible attitude to living and working bring in their wake opportunities for enhanced community integration. There are various strands to this argument. But in this paper I would like specifically to examine the impact of new activities, strategies and attitudes might have on social integration in the cities. This is, of course, a very complex field. But one way in which we might unravel these intricacies is through an exploration of new urban activities structured around four major themes: changing societal values; the role of technology; human capital; and partnership and empowerment. It should at the outset be stressed that this classification is not intended to embrace every new activity which may in some way impact on the urban milieu. Rather this classification is intended to provide an indication of the potential attendant upon, and some of the constraints apparent within, new urban activities.

4.1 Changing societal values

At a relatively mundane level it seems clear that changing societal attitudes on the part of the better off towards work and leisure will in turn help create jobs for the more economically disadvantaged in some service industries such as catering. But at a more fundamental level a number of other more profound trends hold out the prospect of enhancing social integration. Two are worth pursuing here; attitudes to culture and environmentalism.

Culture and the arts have traditionally been regarded as relatively marginal to the economic functioning of cities. Attitudes are changing rapidly here however. At one level burgeoning demand for cultural activities has increasingly helped to sustain employment and economic activity in many of the larger conurbations (CLES, 1989). But the role of culture in enhancing social integration has not received the emphasis it deserves. Cultural developments can play a liberating role in community development by building on local skills, sustaining a common history and tradition, and using locals as artists, actors, producers and so on. Some of the most successful local trusts in the United Kingdom have cleverly integrated economic goals with appropriate cultural objectives. The Tower Hamlets Environment Trust in east London has for instance actively promoted the history and working class traditions of the area (Department of the Environment, 1988). In other cities, especially where smaller municipalities cluster within larger conurbations, a sense of community is often engendered by policies specifically designed to highlight local economic, social and political traditions. Too often the integrative potential of the local culture has been played down.

Changing societal attitudes towards the role of culture has been paralleled by a dramatic increase in concern for, and about, the environment. In recent years the issue has received attention from, amongst others, the Commission (1990), the OECD (1991) and Friends of the Earth (1991). Much of the debate has tended increasingly to concentrate on notions surrounding the sustainable city. The application of this principle is likely to be achieved through the incorporation of a number of subsidiary objectives. These include the idea that future generations should not be compromised by contemporary activities and the realisation that the full and true environmental costs of human activity should be taken into account in assessing developments. These principles are likely to play an increasing role in structuring the governance of cities. Of themselves they need not impact on social integration. But other ideas subsumed within the overall concept of sustainability will have a more positive impact: equity and participation. In the case of the former the assumption here is that sustainability is about enhancing equity within and between generations; that costs and benefits attendant upon sustainability should be shared. And in relation to participation it seems clear that progress will only emerge when individuals and communities are able to share in decisions surrounding, and developments associated with, sustainability. But how can these broader principles impact on the more immediate problems of social integration in the cities?

At one level the search for the sustainable city is about creating jobs in areas such as pollution control, energy saving, greening and recycling. The latter is of particular interest here. As much as 60% of domestic waste could be recycled. At present it is usually considerably less than 10% in most cities. Recycling requires less energy than production from raw materials; in essence it tends to substitute human resources for fuel and electricity. Canadian studies indicate that six times as many jobs can be created through recycling as by land filling. And of course many of these jobs will be attractive to those on the economic margin of society; the unskilled and the unemployed for example (Friends of the Earth, 1991). Yet there is a possible danger with environmentalism: it has the potential to become middle class, elitist and divisive. It may be relatively easy for the materially well off to accept ideas surrounding sustainability; less so for those trapped in poverty and disadvantage. Sustainability needs to embrace different sectors of society. One way in which this can occur is through community involvement and empowerment in environmental management. McLaren for example writing through the aegis of Friends of the Earth has argued that 'it is only possible to improve the urban environment by empowering all the people that live in it' (McLaren, 1989). Environmentalism must be about equity and power if it is both to embrace disadvantaged groups whilst at the same time providing them with the advantages which will otherwise accrue to better off sectors in society.

4.2 The role of technology

Mention has already been made of the role that technological change can play in accentuating social disintegration. But we should not play down the potential which technological innovation has for engendering community development and enterprise. There are a number of strands to this thinking.

At one level advances in readily accessible technology can dramatically improve communications between organisations. Traditionally this has been most obviously realised by business. But community groups can benefit too. Ready availability of FAX and E-Mail can for example provide community groups with immediate accessibility to other community groups, to regional and national governments, and to the Commission. Schemes such as the HOST initiative in Manchester can thus help to play an important function in helping to integrate community organisations into national and international informational networks. In an era when so many community initiatives are being effected throughout Europe and when there is probably more potential support available for locally based initiatives than has usually been the case, information is power.

Technology is not however simply about enhancing information to community based organisations. Innovation and adaption have the potential to instil a much greater sense of social and community integration than is often realised.

Mention has already been made of the way in which certain regions have developed specialised and successful industrial districts. Events in Emilia-Romagna and Catalonia have clearly demonstrated that substantially enhanced output can emerge from indigenous firms operating in selective market niches. The factors responsible for this transformation in local economic activity are complex and have received very considerable attention (Amin, 1989, Brusco, 1986). Not all of the impulses responsible for these developments are rooted in technological change. The availability of a dense network of sector specific skills, of sensitive and supportive financial institutions, and of an economic environment, which is both competitive and co-operative have all clearly helped. But the enmeshing impact of technological innovation on the one hand with a more flexibly organised economy on the other is nevertheless a crucial factor in the success of specialised districts. In essence what we tend to be seeing is that as mass production weakens and with it the need for intensive capital investment in one place, so opportunities arise for decentralised, small scale enterprises. And in general these kinds of firms will employ relatively skilled labour forces utilising a specialised, but not necessarily intensive, capital equipment base.

It is important that we do not drift too readily into the easy assumption that specialised industrial districts can be recreated throughout Europe. There may be very specific social, economic and political factors which have encouraged their development. Nevertheless the emergence of more such districts would prove an important mechanism for integrating different sectors into society. Communities within such districts have a heavy investment in the success of activity within specific niches. A large proportion of output emerges from indigenously controlled firms. Activity is not concentrated in externally controlled firms with little interest in the consequences their actions have for localised communities, but rather in small, local firms intimately embedded in the societies within which they are located.

It is easy to be enthusiastic about the potential role of industrial districts in enhancing social integration; much harder to suggest how this might occur. In some ways we are talking about human capital and institutional contexts, issues which are addressed below. But we are also talking about ways in which technological change and adaption can be used to stimulate the evolution of specialised districts and firms within them. In this latter context some initiatives merit wider consideration. Three might briefly be mentioned. First, some community-based product development centres operate successfully. In reality it should be stressed that here we may not be talking about high-tech innovation. Very often product development centres are dealing with relatively mundane innovations the most successful of which will be taken through to commercial production. But the more interventionist of these centres are cheap, accessible and able where necessary to assemble appropriate technological expertise from a wide range of organisations and individuals. At least some of them are fundamentally concerned with enhancing community-based innovation and enterprise. Secondly it would appear that some of the national/regional technological transfer and innovation networks have a wider potential applicability. The activities of say the TVA in Berlin in enhancing innovation in small/medium-sized enterprises through networking, transferring information, establishing innovation centres, and so on, may offer a model which other regions should look to in their efforts to instil a stronger sense of community enterprise. And thirdly, the efforts of various European-wide networks hold important lessons for those wishing to boost community-based initiatives. For example, the European Business and Innovation Centre Network, whilst relatively marginal in the wider context, can nevertheless be seen as an exemplar which may well be suitable for other cross-national initiatives. We need to know more about the ways in which some technology developments, innovation and adaption measures seem to succeed more than others.

4.3 Human capital

One of the key factors in enhancing the integration of traditionally marginalised groups into mainstream society revolves around the question of human capital; of how we can build on existing, and encourage new, skills and responses. As with other aspects of this overall debate in relation to new activities, this is a complex issue which can only be addressed here in outline. Nevertheless it is an important area and perhaps three specific issues merit comment: training; the social economy; and synergy in relation to human capital.

Education and training are crucial in engendering economic growth. Studies have consistently shown that those with higher educational qualifications are much more likely to work within, and themselves later to establish, successful firms. Technological advance, innovation and enterprise are intimately bound up with the acquisition and updating of skills. We might argue therefore that social integration could be eased if more resources were to be put into training and education. But too often the socially marginalised and disadvantaged are least able to operate effectively in training and educational markets: they often receive poorer education, less training and less updating. Resolving these constraints and dysfunctions will not be easy. But some approaches are worth investigating in greater detail. Decentralised training based on localised needs and aspirations may offer more for the disadvantaged than centrally articulated programmes.

Utilising those who have themselves emerged from disadvantaged backgrounds as trainers will help. So too will studentships or other forms of direct financial support which link technologically advanced firms to socially marginalised groups. And flexible modes of training and education based on distance learning packages backed up by mobile face to face support is more likely to succeed in integrating the disadvantaged than more rigidly organised systems.

Many of the more marginal members of society operate within what may be seen as the 'black' or 'social' economy. They may well be employed on a semi-permanent basis but have no legal or financial status within society. The whole question of the black economy raises delicate dilemmas for policy-makers. On the one hand it is clear that there are drawbacks. For example, the economically marginalised will have few of the benefits and certainties evident within more professionally organised sectors. Equally so the informal economy reduces levels of taxation and hence imposes additional costs on others. But on the other hand there are advantages too. From the point of view of the individual there may be immediate financial benefits in that taxation may be avoided. And fundamental to this debate is the role which the informal economy may play in assimilating more marginalised groups into economic activity. It may be in some societies that this is one of the most effective ways for enhancing social integration. We need to know much more about the operation of the informal economy and how it assimilates the disadvantaged. But it would probably be worth while more widely to introduce higher tax exemption limits on both enterprises and individuals. Perhaps too in selected locations it would be acceptable to follow through the implications of positively encouraging the informal economy. It may prove to be as effective a mechanism as any in stimulating activity amongst the more disadvantaged despite its undeniable costs.

Finally in relation to human capital we need to look at the ways in which synergy between different aspects of training, education and enterprise can be increased. Too often it is possible to identify perfectly good programmes, but not a collective strategy towards increasing human capital skills within traditionally marginalised groups. Genuinely collective approaches are possible to develop however, which both attain legitimate efficiency criteria but which also help sustain a strong purpose of community integration. These might be achieved in a number of ways. For instance there is enormous potential in the area of community self-help. Various projects in Britain's inner cities have been based on utilising the innate skills and entrepreneurial talent of local communities both to train individuals whilst at the same time enhancing social infrastructure and/or economic activity. For example, a number of imaginative schemes have used unemployed local construction workers to improve housing within their immediate locality whilst simultaneously helping to train apprentices. We begin here to see a synergy of effort and outcome: training for locals; jobs for the unemployed; community-based initiatives; and improved social housing. There are of course other approaches which can be adopted. But the important issue here is not so much the details inherent to particular schemes but rather the central message: training, education, employment and community entrepreneurialism can be forged into an effective force for social integration at the local level.

4.4 Partnership and empowerment

Sections of this paper have addressed some of the mechanisms through which new urban activities can hope to instil a stronger sense of social and community integration. Changing societal values, technological innovation and new approaches towards human capital have all been identified as playing an important function in helping to assimilate marginalised groups into mainstream society. We need finally to explore one other crucial dimension: partnership and empowerment. Ideas and innovations in terms of policy delivery are important: they need to be complemented by new approaches to decision-making and power.

In many European countries the concept of 'Partnership' has become one of the key areas of debate in relation to urban policy in recent years (Lawless, 1991). It is not an easy concept to define with any degree of accuracy. But fundamentally it is concerned with attempting to integrate different actors and agencies into decision-making in order to help achieve a consensual, pro-active vision of urban development. The range of actors and agencies involved will vary from country to country and partnership to partnership. But typically the most effective partnerships are those which try and tease out an agreed strategy in relation to economic and social policies from elected local authorities, central government, business, chambers of commerce, the media, trade unions, community groups and universities. Different constituencies will bring different powers and attributes. For example, local authorities will often have the necessary legal basis and, perhaps, resources. Business will bring market acumen and skills, universities technological and social expertise, and so on.

Partnerships will attempt to undertake many different activities. In Europe we are perhaps only beginning to see how coalitions of interest can play a crucial role in many aspects of urban policy; certainly American experience shows that there is very considerable potential (Parkinson, Foley and Judd, 1988). Some partnerships are best seen as 'growth coalitions' where the primary function is to improve the place marketing of the city or region concerned and hence to increase inward investment. Other partnerships may be concerned with technological advance, or the implementation of specific projects in areas such as leisure, tourism or culture. Yet others are devised to effect the construction of specific commercial, hotel, conference, or convention developments.

It is easy to see why so much effort should recently have been placed on partnerships in urban regeneration. Coalitions of interested parties bring different skills, legal powers, resources and ideas into the public domain. In some countries too it is clear that central governments have often placed a very considerable emphasis on ensuring that local authorities embrace market attitudes and aspirations. And for many local authorities wishing to fund prestigious schemes or to improve the image of their locality, bringing in the private sector is essential.

However, it is not immediately evident that all forms of partnership will necessarily enhance social integration in the major cities. There are several points which might be made here (Lawless, 1990). First, some forms of partnership are essentially about image, they are established in cities which are seeking to attract inward investment from within the host nation concerned and from abroad. These partnerships are concerned with success not with questions of poverty, race and disadvantage. These tend not to be issues stressed in many partnerships within which the private sector has an important role to play. Secondly, agenda set by most partnerships are primarily economic in nature. Other problems, relating to housing, to education, to public services and so on may not figure prominently in debate. Yet for more marginalised groups in the cities, these are important considerations often central to the lives of many. And thirdly, we should not expect too much from partnerships. Often they may be created to provide a veneer of success and activity. In reality many of them have relatively little in the way of resources and may only be able to affect issues at the margins. Other considerations such as resources available to local government or broader trends in the economy will in reality be much more important in defining the fates of many cities.

Nevertheless despite these caveats partnerships can be about social integration. Not many partnerships will identify this as a primary objective in their activities. But even if by implication their policies and programmes can assist in instilling a sense of community awareness and identity. This can occur in a number of ways. For example, coalitions of interest can prove crucial in helping to establish and sustain community and co-operative enterprises. In parts of Spain and Italy, and to a lesser extent elsewhere, networks of financial, technical and managerial organisations have been created to nurture and foster indigenous enterprise. These networks may not necessarily be labelled as partnerships. Yet often it is a coalition of mutually supportive institutions which provides the institutional framework vital for the success of small and medium-sized firms. In other partnerships we can see key actors and agencies implementing policies designed to assimilate poorer residents into partnership successes. This can happen when efforts are made through agreements with developers to ensure that a proportion of jobs and contracts should be allocated to local residents and firms. Whilst there may be legal issues at stake here because of Community law, the principle of linkage is an important one. Developments within cities should benefit local residents. Urban regeneration is about people as much as it is about property. And finally in this discussion of how partnerships might enhance social integration it is clear that the benevolent corporate sector can assist in a number of ways (Fogarty and Christie, 1990). Again American experience shows that it is possible for major corporations to play a pro-active role in community affairs. They can provide expertise, resources, property, ideas and personnel to local firms and initiatives. In Europe there is much that can be done in this area.

Nevertheless, however much partnerships may help in sustaining social integration in the cities it should be remembered that this is not why many of them have been created. Many of their programmes and policies are not centrally concerned with issues of equity and disadvantage, partnerships are likely to be perceived as, at best, relatively marginal to their needs and aspirations and, at worst, patronising irrelevances. For some groups, in some cities, much more will need to be done to provide people with a sense of ownership and power. It is vital therefore that urban communities have a direct influence over decisions which affect them. It is never possible to satisfy demands from each and every community. But many in the major conurbations have a perfectly legitimate grievance: their opinions appear irrelevant to the governance of the city in which they reside. There is a crying need for a greater sense of empowerment, pride and self-esteem amongst disadvantaged.

However, it is much easier to restate what has been widely perceived as a problem central to many of the conurbations than to suggest appropriate remedies. But some ideas are worth pursuing. There is an overwhelming case for the decentralisation of many services to local areas in cities. This need not be a purely administrative process. Structures can be established which allow for locally elected community-based institutions with power over appropriate services and resources. Different electoral systems need to be assessed to establish the extent to which contrasting approaches provide greater sensitivity to local issues. And when decisions are made affecting local communities these should be made in association with local people using their attitudes and expertise. This is not to say local communities can inevitably overturn every decision likely to impinge on them. But what it does mean is that communities are empowered to consider, debate and evaluate relevant projects. It means too that social audits embracing community views are undertaken by proposed developers which then are subsequently made available to the community, its elected representatives, and those ultimately taking key decisions.

5. Social Integration and New Urban Activities: Some Concluding Observations

This paper has attempted to explore some of the mechanisms through which a greater sense of community and social integration within the major cities might be achieved. It has not attempted to provide a comprehensive coverage of potential avenues for development; rather it has tried to develop some ideas whilst pointing out associated constraints and difficulties. In this brief final section a number of broad integrative issues are highlighted.

Four issues merit comment. First, it is clear that social integration in cities needs to be addressed at the regional or city/regional level. Experience constantly tells us that top-down initiatives emerging from central governments are often not flexible enough to deal with local circumstances and opportunities. We must be looking to pursue more bottom-up strategies which emerge from local communities and local governments. Of course in reality successful regeneration requires both top-down and bottom-up approaches. But if problems of social integration are perceived as a central dilemma facing the cities and many within them, progress will be crucially dependent on local innovation, commitment and people. A second issue here is that of resources. Many of the initiatives developed in this paper may require relatively little new funding as opposed to the reorientation of existing programmes. But equally some innovation and experimentation will necessitate additional public sector investment. Many programmes directed at social integration are unlikely, at least at the outset to attract much in the way of market investment. It will be the public sector which bears much of the initial investment. And although this will attract criticism in some quarters, it needs to be stressed that so much urban regeneration has been predicated on buildings and relatively prestigious developments. Far less has gone into community-based initiatives. Thirdly, many of these initiatives have shown how important it is for organisations and/or individuals to articulate complex programmes at this local level. Many community-based schemes require inputs from a range of actors and agencies. One of the most important, and often neglected, skills is that of the local arbitrator, able to assemble and articulate complex local programmes by synthesising the power and resources available to a range of local actors and agencies. And finally we simply need to know more about community-based initiatives. There is a wealth of experience and activity in Europe. Some of this is reasonably well known; but not all. Much more can be learned from our common experience.

REFERENCES

Amin, A. (1991). *Flexible Specialisation and Small Firms in Italy: Myths and Realities*. Antipode 21, 1, 13-34.

Brusco, S. (1986). Small Firms and Industrial Districts: The Experience of Italy in D. Keeble and E. Wiener (eds) *New Firms and Regional Development in Europe*. Aldershot, Croom Helm.

Cheshire, P. and Hay, D. (1989) *Urban Problems in Western Europe: An Economic Analysis*. London, Unwin Hyman.

CLES, (1989). *Arts and Cultural Industries*. Centre for Local Economic Strategies, Manchester.

Commission of the European Communities, (1990). *Green Paper on the Urban Environment*. Brussels.

Cooke, P. (ed), (1989). *Localities*. London, Unwin Hyman

Department of the Environment, (1988). *Creating Development Trusts*. London, HMSO.

Fogarty, M. and Christie, I. (1990). *Companies and Communities*. London, Policy Studies Institute.

Friends of the Earth, (1991). *Reviving the Cities*. London, Friends of the Earth.

Gans, H.J. (1972). *People and Plans*. Harmondsworth, Penguin.

Harvey, D. (1989). *Post Modernism and the City*. Oxford, Blackwell.

Howard, E. (1985). *Garden Cities of Tomorrow*. Eastbourne, Attic Books.

Jacobs, J. (1972). *The Death and Life of Great American Cities*. Harmondworth, Pengiun.

Lawless, P. (1988). *Britain's Inner Cities*. London, Paul Chapman Publishing.

Lawless, P. (1990). Regeneration in Sheffield: From Radical Intervention to Partnership, in D. Judd and M. Parkinson (eds), *Leadership and Urban Regeneration*, Newbury Park, Sage.

Lawless, P. (1991). *Public-Private Sector Partnerships in the United Kingdom: Analysis and Critique*; DIFU. Köln, Germany.

McLaren, D. (1989). *Action for People: A Critical Appraisal of Government Inner City Policy*. London, Friends of the Earth.

Mumford, L. (1961). *The City in History*. Harmondsworth, Penguin.

OECD, (1990). <u>Environmental Policies for Cities in the 1990s</u>. OECD, Paris

Parkinson, M. and Foley, B. and Judd, D. (eds), (1988). <u>Regeneration the Cities: The UK Crisis and the UK Experience</u>. Manchester, Manchester University Press.

Thorns, D. (1976). <u>The Quest for Community</u>. London, George Allen and Unwin.

SOCIAL INTEGRATION AND CREATION OF NEW URBAN ACTIVITIES

by

Alan Sinclair
The Wise Group
Glasgow

1. Introduction

Waste is offensive; not just the waste when bread goes mouldy or tomatoes become bruised and spoiled, but waste of human potential. Glasgow is the city where I take pleasure in living and working. I live in a warm apartment that is 100 years old and next to a leafy park. A short walk away are ugly, grey parts of the city where six out of ten adults are unemployed and live in cold and damp houses.

Scotland is famous for kilts, whisky, haggis and the cold and rain. Whisky helps us put up with jokes that foreigners make about kilts. Unfortunately, decades of poor building standards and practices have given us houses that do not keep out the cold and rain. As a Danish friend once said to me, 'The energy standards of a Scottish house would be illegal in a Danish garage'. Haggis, we just do not talk about.

Here I would like to tell a short story about the Wise Group, and how we have taken unemployed people, trained them, paid a wage, supervised and put them to work improving housing and the environment. Our model has worked for eight years. We have made mistakes but fortunately our progress has outstripped our errors. Lessons can be drawn from our experience that are relevant beyond Glasgow.

2. What is the Wise Group?

Very simply it is a charitable company with three operating subsidiaries. Heatwise specialises in energy conservation and home security. Landwise concentrates on improving the environment and Enterprises is a commercial merchandising company which gives its profits to the Group.

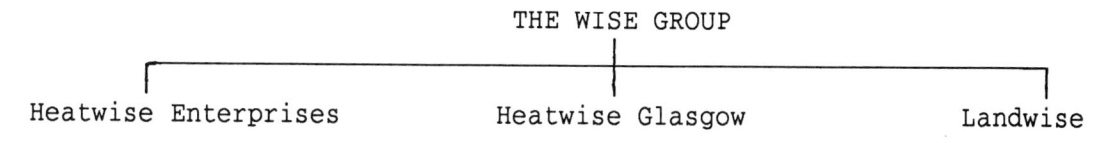

```
                    THE WISE GROUP
        ┌───────────────────┼───────────────────┐
Heatwise Enterprises   Heatwise Glasgow      Landwise
```

We give people training and work experience and at the same time provide socially useful goods and services. At the moment we have 400 trainees and 150 permanent staff with an income of £7.3 million last year (21.5 million DM). Our main funders are the City Council, the European Social Fund and central government, though we raise 14% of our own income.

Remember that Glasgow has a population of 732,000 and that 160,000 houses (60% of the total) are owned by the Council. Unemployment averages 12% but in the worst areas can be as high as 30% to 50%.

3. Heatwise Glasgow

In Heatwise Glasgow we recruit long-term unemployed people from the worst part of the city. Our average employee is male, 26 years old, has been unemployed for two years and has no qualifications or recognisable work record. We offer a one year contract, pay the union rate for the job, provide work experience for 40% of the time and on the job and workshop and classroom training for the other 60% of the time. As an installer, he will draughtproof doors and windows in sub-standard houses and insulate the loft.

During the year with us he will most likely gain, through examinations, two nationally approved certificates. More importantly, he will gain in confidence, self-respect, good work habits, hope and a track record that will make him more attractive to a potential employer. Five out of ten of our employees who finish their training find a job.

In 1991, we have 280 trainee workers in Heatwise and 90 permanent members of staff involved in management, training, finance and marketing. Apart from carrying out insulation, trainees also work in administration, advice work and other types of training. In our work we strive to produce a good quality loft insulation job, a survey form properly filled in, leaflets well laid out and written in plain English.

Over the last seven years we have achieved a scale of operation that has helped many different people and had an effect across the city. Over 85,000 homes (45% of the Council's stock) have been draughtproofed, security devices fitted to 12,000 houses, 4,000 lofts insulated and thousands of home visits carried out while giving energy advice. Over 1,600 trainee workers have been on our payroll.

4. Landwise

Three years into Heatwise's life, and because of its success, the City Council asked if we could repeat our formula of training, work experience, multi-funding and now improve the outside of the houses. Today, Landwise has remodelled and improved the backcourt areas for 354 families and employs 35 staff and 110 trainees. Once we select a housing area, intensive house-by-house interviewing takes place, we form a local committee and work up designs suitable for that locality and as far as is possible recruit people from that area to work on the scheme. From consultation to design, earth shifting, pathlaying, binstore construction, grass and shrub planting to fence construction, takes a total of 24 months. Areas that were previously unloved, full of puddles, old mattresses and coarse overgrown grass are turned into gardens lifting the previous gloom. When we move on, some of the gardens remain loved and used, other falter and some would deteriorate beyond an acceptable level if we did not go back to do maintenance.

A third company, Heatwise Enterprises, has the objective of making money and does this through merchandising insulation materials and glazing contracts for developers and property managers. It employs 15 people and has a turnover of £1.5 million.

What's important is that we have been able to construct and grow more than one company that delivers good quality services through a combination of work experience and training. With a combined wage roll of 550 people, the group of companies is now within the top 100 employers in the City.

5. Take the Model and Replicate

Other new ventures are at present being researched, methods of funding found, and effective managers being recruited. This winter we will employ 30 new people and start planting trees on 5 sites of 5 hectares each as a pilot demonstration scheme for urban forestry.

We aim to prove that this pilot could be the forerunner for an urban forest stretching from the City's green belt into the heart of the urban setting through vehicle routes, wasteland, land purchased for development but not used, and industrial estates. Then there is recycling. Can we, through public drop off sites and through schools, collect and sell enough glass and aluminium, which along with grant support, will pay for a new business unit? We will soon find out. Can the model we have developed targeted on the long-term unemployed combining work experience and training related to energy conservation and landscape improvement, be replicated in other parts of Britain and Europe?

6. Recognising a Solution when you See One

We are in a period of recession. Even if that were not the case and we were in a period of rapid economic growth, the growth in wealth may not produce a corresponding increase in employment. From automated petrol stations to numerical control machines in engineering, increased business activity and the number of people employed are inversely related.

People in secure jobs find their income rising annually. If you are out of work, you are likely to find yourself in that state for an increasingly long period of time. In Glasgow today, there are 51,431 registered unemployed. Of that number, 12,025 have been unemployed for more than two years (23.4%). The world of work and the world of unemployment are moving further apart.

What we need is a platform or bridge that binds together, what we are at present, two separate worlds. This link will help people with training and with work experience, it will be regarded as being a worthwhile period in its own right, but will also assist with transition into the labour market.

UNEMPLOYMENT		EMPLOYMENT
Sitting at home doing nothing, contributing nothing, and getting more and more depressed.	Quasi-Job Market that provides a wage, training, and produces a social product or service.	In the job market and on a steady or increasing income.

In my judgement British and USA programmes aimed at getting people into work have been based on a major conceptual flaw; what the unemployed need is training to get a job. This fails for two reasons. First, there are not sufficient jobs to absorb the newly trained unemployed people. Second, most long-term unemployed people have had a bad educational experience; to then offer training as the way ahead is to offer what is seen as school for grown-ups. What we need is not more training, but the creation of a quasi-job market which produces useful goods and services.

In this market, people will be recruited to do a job and will receive training and supervision to enable them to do the job properly. Unemployed people will want to join because they will be better motivated by a wage higher than their benefit level, companionship, the possibility of qualifications for self-respect and the need to feel worthwhile - to have a purpose.

Training in this context makes more sense because it has a direct application. For example, in the Wise Group we had problems picking out from a group of ten trainees those who have literacy and numeracy problems and even more trouble getting that group to turn up for extra tuition. However, now that we have extended training sessions in how to fill up survey forms with extra support when needed, we have made more progress.

Politically, the quasi-job market makes sense. It is good for the unemployed. A product or service (energy conservation or environmental improvement or care programmes) is produced that meets a community need and adds to the quality of life. Society benefits as the potential workforce has better training and an attitude that is more shaped to the demands of the working world. Financing is easier as you are combining monies for work experience, training as well as money that may be spent on products and services. This is further strengthened by institutional decision-makers who recognise the sense in tackling more than one policy objective. And by the tax payer, who recognises the need for benefit payments as a safety net for the unemployed but recognises that it would make more sense for the unemployed to be paid to do something useful rather than to remain economically idle and to spiritually deteriorate.

7. It Cannot Work

Last week, I had the latest in a long line of meetings where three well-paid professionals gathered for two hours to think one way and then think another, how a new proposal would just not work. They may be right. A fraction more thought into how to make something happen would result in a lot more progress in meeting job and social needs.

For people, like myself, trying to put ventures together and make sure they run properly, there are often a number of self-imposed handicaps. Take emotional fervour. Anger, and a display of righteousness about bad social conditions and unemployment, are often substituted for the steps of practical management that lead to sound and definite achievement and progress. Too often the leaders and supposed managers of employment and social initiatives have been more concerned with the intensity of feeling than setting objectives, monitoring progress, line management, making decisions about people who are not performing and technical familiarity. We are right to feel emotional about unemployment but if we are to do justice to our feelings then we must become, or hire, very good managers.

8. Conclusion

From my practical experience in Glasgow, with the Wise Group, we have demonstrated that it is possible to train, supervise and employ long-term unemployed people to provide a socially useful service. An idea has been combined with grants and earnings led by professional managers and competent supervisors. What has been learned at City level could be used on a wider stage. If that is to happen it needs institutional backing combined with good management. The moral is, don't just criticise, organise.

URBAN FORESTRY

by

**Margaret Sweeney
SICA Innovation Consultants Ltd
Dublin**

1. New Lives - New Landscapes

In her seminal book 'New Lives - New Landscapes' first published in 1970, Nan Fairbrother drew attention to the dynamics of landscape. 'Landscape is not a static background which we inhabit, but the interaction of a society and the habitat it lives in, and if either man or the habitat changes then so inevitably must the resulting landscape. Landscape = Habitat + Man.' Survival had depended on change. If the equation has seemed stable in the past it is because the pace of change has been slow in comparison with our brief human generations. Democratic planning of change demands intervention by consensus and these principles should be very much to the fore in planning environmental changes in or around our urban centres.

In the concept of Urban Forestry we have the possibility of bringing together many actions which are now recognised as being required for the well-being, even survival, of our cities and towns and for enhancing the prospects for peripheral spaces where scattered development has left populations marginalised and the landscape without identity.

The environmental and psychological benefits of trees planted in urban locations have been well documented during the last few decades. Environmental benefits such as dust filtration, oxygen-enrichment, improved aesthetics and landscape quality as well as the mental well-being of city inhabitants are being attributed more and more to city trees.

2. Common Public Space

The scope of common public space in our urban areas needs to be expanded. Old European cities, despite or because of their cramped conditions attached great importance to well-designed squares and public areas and street space where people came together to participate, agitate or celebrate or simply just to be 'outside'. Modern land-absorbing cities dispensed with the luxury of city squares for a long time and many town spaces have become parking lots and the victim of the motor car. Nowadays, the restricted amount of space available and the precarious financial situation make major town planning changes in favour of creating space and further large scale projects difficult. But not all projects to regain forgotten concepts of urban quality of life need to be big and expensive and not all projects need to follow the well understood ways of the past.

3. Environmental Needs

The behavioural sciences tell us that man needs not merely to observe but to interact with his surroundings and thus acquire a sense of place or territorial identity. An important form of environmental perception is exploring, an innate desire to discover, which is modified by the experience of the observer. Exploring is the most important single link between behaviour and environment and lends itself to many kinds of application in all urban functions not least in our concepts and design of space and landscape.

This need to participate with our environment finds little expression in the biological sterility of our city centres, the treeless and geometric layout of modern housing estates and apartment complexes and the sprawling periphery which make up the landscape for modern urban man. This is one of the reasons, amongst others, for the growing dissatisfaction with urban life. Nature must be part of our everyday surroundings. Children especially must be allowed to touch, to learn and to interact with natural systems as part of man's basic animal response to his surroundings. We are more and more divorced from nature owing to the organisation of our society, in the way we build our cities and in the new networks of ordinary lives. Often the resulting attempts at interaction are expressed in rejection and vandalism.

A highly cost effective way of achieving this contact with nature, with a sense of place and landscape identity, combined with a community's requirement for public space which satisfies many complex needs is being worked out in the concept of urban forestry.

4. Urban and Community Forests - An Explanation

Arboriculture is the term used to cover the management of trees and their needs in street and park environments. However, important as tree welfare is, it is only part of the systemic concept that urban forestry seeks to embrace. It has become the description current amongst urban and suburban landscape managers as well as those in traditional silvicultural and forestry practice for the hinterland where these two disciplines work together, not only with the local authority or land owner but in partnership with the local community. The confluence of interests can be seen in the objectives set out for urban forestry in Ireland for example:

- to establish and maintain tree and woodland environments (common social space) in urban areas through the medium of community initiatives;

- to optimise the aesthetic, conservation, recreational and wood production potential within the urban environments;

- to provide an educational and training facility for community involvement;

- to dedicate urban woodlands to the concept of sustained yield and ultimate production of wood e.g. for furniture, craft, etc.

Urban forestry is then an amalgam of the various aspects of tree usage within the conurbations of modern society. It is the preparation, planting, after-care and final usage of trees, either singly or collectively, within urban environments. However, for urban forestry to fulfil its real objective, it must afforest the hearts and minds of people. It must be community-driven but professionally-led. It must have the unfettered support of all community elements and the participation of most (Mulloy, 1991).

Until now parks, gardens and other public space have been provided by public authorities, developers or benefactors for the benefit of the urban population and as a relief to the hard landscape which makes up our urban environment. In many cities and towns of Europe we have magnificent parks, gardens, street trees and perhaps individual mature trees set in tiny spaces which reflect the cycle of the seasons in our daily lives and provide a satisfying sense of context and proportion to the urban scene. Even before World War II 'Unter den Linden' gave a special ring to the meaning of Berlin and the role that lime trees played in this city.

In many European countries, the traditional division between town and country is increasingly fudged both in economic activity and the social and building patterns with which they were previously identified. In urban and community forestry we have examples of intervention in the landscape orchestrated by groups of partners that would not previously have been involved together in either planning or execution of the project. And the objectives of the project and the strategy used are quite a new phenomenon in urban activity.

Let us look at the strictly urban forest approach which differs from community forests and then look at some specific examples.

We have established that for thousands of years in cities throughout the world human communities have been planting and caring for trees. However the growth of our urban settlements has expanded and accelerated without the parallel planning, planting and management schemes to bring urban tree management into the twentieth century.

5. Urban Forestry - How it is Done

Urban forestry is a planned, systemic and integrated approach to the design, planting, maintenance and management of the urban forest resource, i.e. all the trees a town has in the boundaries. This is a multi-purpose resource that needs to be managed by a complex multi-disciplinary team to bring a wide range of benefits to urban communities (Miller, 1989). Planning, in the sense of thinking out a course of action in anticipation of the future is central to the urban forestry approach. This is precisely what has been lacking in the recent past where, in spite of recognised evaluation systems showing the value to the local community of the public tree stock, the fluctuations of the local authorities budgetary resources can leave the planting and maintenance programme the first casualty of cutbacks. In some cities, where the tree population has been surveyed attempts have also been made to give a financial value for the urban forest. These financial values are developed from a range of criteria using recognised systems such as the International Society of Agriculture (ISA) Tree Valuation Formula. These systems may have their limitations but nevertheless can be very useful in making comparisons with the value of other public assets such as roads, indoor sports facilities or the city sewerage system. The results of these valuations can be quite staggering and have often revealed the urban forest as a multi-million pound resource. The city of Huntsville, Alabama, which has one of the most advanced urban forestry departments in the United States, recently valued its street tree population, using the ISA formula, at a massive US$27.2 million. With some 22,300 trees under its care that is an average value for each tree of almost $1,220 (ACRT, 1989). Armed with this information the city felt justified in granting the necessary funds to effectively manage such a valuable community asset.

The first step in establishing urban forestry with serious intent is to find what is already there. A wide range of information, continually updated, needs to be gathered. Surveys of the existing tree population need to be supplemented by ecological, land use, sociological and other data if an accurate picture of the urban forest and the conditions in which it grows is to be developed.

Here I can give you some examples of what is happening in the United Kingdom, where although hardly any local authorities have an accurate idea of the nature and extent of their urban forest, currently about 25 out of over 1,000 separate authorities have a computerised inventory of their street trees (Hort. Week 1991a), some recognition that five words in local authority planning documents are not enough is taking place.

Detailed survey work has provided the basis for comprehensive urban forestry management plans now being developed in Edinburgh, Belfast, London and some other major cities. It is particularly encouraging that London with its thirty-two individual local authorities, is now trying to develop a London wide urban forestry strategy developed from a database of the capital's entire resource (Hort. Week 1991b). Perhaps an even more significant development has been the decision by the Department of the Environment to commission a survey of urban trees and their management for the whole of England and Wales. Although the overall picture will be developed from sample and aerial surveys, this is still a huge undertaking that will take some time to complete. The Community Forests Programme of the Countryside Commission and Forestry Commission, developed within the context of urban forestry, will conduct detailed surveys within the urban fringe to provide the essential data to formulate the plans for these exciting new forests that are to be established on the edge of many of the major cities.

Having gained an accurate picture of the existing urban forest, its potential and the conditions in which it grows, one can begin to decide on management objectives for the kind of urban forest we want in the future.

All levels of the community should be involved in this crucial aspect of the planning process. One of the fundamental principles of the urban forestry approach is its emphasis on meeting the needs of urban communities. Community involvement in the planning and management of urban forests can deliver a wide range of social and psychological benefits to urban residents and should therefore be a major objective of urban forest policy.

To find out what the community wants we have to ask them. We cannot assume that we know. That means regular consultation, on a wide range of issues that affect the whole urban forest (Kirby 1991).

One crucial factor affecting the nature and extent of the future urban forest is the amount of money that is spent on it now. It is a sad fact that the recent dramatic growth in the public's interest and concern for trees and the environment has usually not been matched by a similar increase in local authority spending on the urban forest. Public concern for the world's forests has not been reflected in the way we look after the forest that most of us live in. Professionals need to communicate to both the public and politicians a vision of the kind of healthy and vibrant urban forest that is possible and then spell out the level of funding required to achieve it and maintain it with good husbandry over the long-term.

The urban forest is a growing resource that develops over time. The conditions under which urban trees grow can change rapidly both locally and city-wide. Managing the urban forest also changes the nature and extent of the resource. To keep up to date with conditions in the urban forest, and to understand what is likely to happen to it, requires adjusting the management plan accordingly. Any urban forest management plan should be under constant revision, assessing the impact of ecological, climatic, economic, sociological and other changes, and revising the plan to meet new and clearly defined objectives (Johnston 1991).

6. Community Forests

The concept of community forests can be essentially the creation of forests around some of our major conurbations by using the existing tree stock and land available to engage in the establishment of well-wooded landscapes on the edges of towns and cities for timber production, wild-life, work, recreation and education.

The land available for the community forests can come from a variety of sources and their design will depend on the terrain, land use and the hectares available. Community forests will not be wall to wall trees, they will link the conservation of some of the habitats and landscapes, created by agricultural practice and still being farmed, with forestry in the countryside. They will add an extra dimension to the multiple objectives of the standard national forest policy which is currently expressed as follows:

- to produce a national supply of timber;

- to offer an alternative to agricultural use of land;

- contribute to rural employment;

- create attractive sites for public enjoyment;

- enhance the natural beauty of the countryside;

- create wild life habitats.

Apart from the linkages here with the rural and urban communities and the accessibility policies that will have to be worked out, community forests open up new opportunities for management agreements, funding sources and work and training schemes.

In the UK 12 community forests of approx. 1,500 hectares will be established from 1991. These are dependent on the Countryside Commission, the local authority, the Forestry Commission, farmers and landowners and representatives from the local community coming together in 12 project teams. Funds will be made available through the European Community for afforestation, rural development, diversified farm activity, landscape management and training schemes. The land bank required will be built upon partnership agreements rather than compulsory purchase.

This is essential planning for what is seen as joint urban-rural needs in peri-urban situations in the next century. Urban dwellers need recreation space - rural dwellers need alternatives to agriculture. There is a vision of well-wooded landscapes containing a variety of woodland trees, commercial and amenity, some planted and some by natural regeneration. The woodlands will be the framework for environmentally friendly farming. The woods and forests will contain a wide range of wildlife habitats. Throughout, public access and informal recreation will be important. These community woodlands will form a link between town and country.

7. Design and Composition

Urban and community forests' composition and structure are very different from those of commercial forests where silviculture leading to timber production is the main aim. However, both urban and community forests are distinctly forests and not parks. It is not accepted that forests become so adapted to the public that they lose their identity and begin to resemble parks. To this end very great importance is attached to variation and range in how the forest is experienced. The forest should be given such a dimension that it can accommodate degrees of utilisation from intensively busy areas to less used areas for people seeking the peace and quiet of the forest.

Designing community forests on urban fringes will differ from country to country and one of the most important challenges to the designers will be the different objectives of private and public land owners. They need to be working side by side with a project team/manager whose creative, catalytic and co-ordinating skills can bring together the people, policies and resources that are essential to manage the forest from concept to fulfilment, which can be a very long time.

The layout of individual woodland areas needs to take account of the overall landscape character of the area as well as accommodating the objectives. As one of the chief objectives of community and urban forests is accessibility and recreation it is interesting to look at the limitations that experience suggests should be placed on the recreational potential and carrying capacity, both visual and physical, of different sizes of woodland:

- \> 75 hectares - woodland capable of handling large numbers of people. Open spaces and a sense of seclusion possible with over 100,000 visitors per year. Woods over 300 hectares are capable of absorbing large numbers of visitors.

- 50 - 75 hectares - lower size range for significant level of use. Open space and secluded wild areas possible. Variety of woodland structure and quite wide range of recreation possible.

- 25 - 50 hectares - good path network possible and some open space, but visual carrying capacity lower due to intervisibility of paths. More difficult to feel alone. A range of informal recreation possible, but not noisy types.

- 10 - 25 hectares - informal recreation possible, mainly with small open spaces. Disturbance to wildlife likely to be much greater and intensive use may make it feel crowded.

- 1 - 10 hectares - low visual carrying capacity; small number of uses per wood. Wildlife very disturbed, wear and tear high.

- < 1 hectare - very limited recreation use, mainly limited to paths through woods. Some informal play. Valuable as landscape elements.

Some time must elapse between planting a wood and being able to use it fully for recreation, though there is some educational value in seeing a young wood develop, especially to those who helped to plant it. This time can be shortened by using a proportion of fast growing pioneer species, both broad leaves and conifers, which can get above head height in four to five years (Bell, 1991).

Areas under consideration for urban forestry and community woodland may include areas of derelict or disused industrial sites, storage areas, railway lines and sidings, open cast coal workings and deep mine spoil heaps, sand and gravel pits and quarries. The appearance of these, especially when restored to woodland, depends on the quality of their restoration. The implications for woodland design of these sites is to ensure a good growth medium.

In Mediterranean countries there is a continuing urgent need for afforestation because of accelerating tree loss caused by forest fires, mostly as a result of incendiaries or carelessness. There is a long tradition of multi-purpose use of forests and grazing lands in southern countries where silvi-agricultural practices have been common over the centuries. The concept of community forestry is not new - but the need for trees here is to stabilise the soil, protect the water table, build up the depleting forest cover and reinstate the linkage between the local community and their forests.

8. An Irish Example

In the Irish context the establishment of urban and community forests is quite a recent phenomenon and they have an additional objective which deserves attention. Over the past ten years since the formal establishment of The Tree Council of Ireland (Comhairle Crann Na hEireann) all the different organisations working with trees and promoting an increase in tree planting have found an enthusiastic response from the urban population and many rural dwellers to conserve the trees that Ireland has and to increase our tree stock. We have not as much tree cover as the rest of Europe for many historical reasons although trees grow very well in the temperate climate. At the beginning of this century we had a tree cover of less than 1%, at the moment it is 6%. As a nation we have become urban people, mostly with a rural background, but with no tradition of forestry or trees. We have neither a great woodland tradition nor many old woodlands.

In the national context, trees, their growing and their harvesting is now part of our economy in a way that it never was before. More agricultural land is being put under trees, decisions about changing land use into timber have become everyday debates. Because of the upheaval in the Common Agricultural Policy it is probable that more and more farmland will have trees as part of their crops. As a nation we need to know more about trees, now, to help us make the right choices for the future. Thus the support of urban and community forests in the Irish context are as much about attitude changes and establishing a tree culture in all the population where growth, maturity and harvest are accepted elements of the forestry process. By improving the level of involvement by communities in the care and maintenance of trees and in understanding their value as ecosystems, all age groups in a community can become partners in the challenges associated with tree and woodland management.

The first urban forest in Ireland was launched this year in Limerick, a city with 70,000 inhabitants on the west coast of Ireland, to coincide with the 300th anniversary of the Treaty of Limerick. It was launched in the Maternity Hospital and the new forest will grow alongside Limerick's new citizens. The first draft of the design for two areas of Limerick to become part of the Forest of Limerick are now on display in local shops, libraries, health centres, etc. for everyone to see and say what they think. Many people have already said a lot in the first few days of appraising how this new Forest could come about, especially communities in the neighbourhoods. The prospect of planning for thousands of trees is exciting to most, fearful and oppressive to some. On this occasion, which is a pilot project in Ireland, the local authorities identified the space that could be available from their existing land bank. The local communities have been invited to take part in the planning and planting which will be under supervision of local Forestry inspectors. The advisory group for the Limerick Project covers a broad spectrum balancing the professionals and the local community. Some interesting new funding is available in that because the production of timber is an equal objective with that of access to the community for recreational and educational purposes, the Department of Energy Forest service are able to include Limerick Forest under their Grant schemes funded from Europe as part of our Forestry Operational Programme (CSF). In addition training courses for the community to enable them to be involved in the planting and maintenance can receive European Community funding.

Urban and Community forests are first and foremost for people. The very nature of Europe is expressly seen in the diversity of its people, diversity of the landscapes and ecosystems. Because the design, management and use of these forests will be specific to each location there is the prospect of seeing an enrichment of the landscape and natural resource that reflects our differences as people if we have enough confidence in the future and imagination now to make it happen.

REFERENCES

ACRT, (1989). <u>City of Huntsville, Alabama, Urban Forestry Survey and Management Plan</u>. ACRT. INC. Urban Forestry Specialists, Kent, Ohio, USA.

Bell, (1991). <u>Landscape Design</u>. Urban Forestry Conference, Dublin, Tree Council of Ireland.

Fairbrother, N. (1970). <u>New Lives, New Landscapes</u>. London, Architectural Press.

Forestry Commission, (1989). <u>Urban Forestry Practice</u>. Handbook No.5, HMSO, London.

Horticultural Weekly, (1991a). <u>Keeping Track of Council Trees</u>. Horticultural Weekly 209 (20), 25-26.

Horticultural Weekly, (1991b). <u>Making the Most of London's Trees</u>. Horticultural Weekly (20), 25-26.

Johnston, M. (1991). <u>Planning the Urban Forest</u>. Urban Forestry Conference, Dublin, Tree Council of Ireland.

Kirby, M. (1991). <u>Community Forests</u>. Urban Forestry Conference, Dublin, Tree Council of Ireland.

Miller, R. W. (1989). <u>Urban Forestry, Planning and Managing Urban Greenspaces</u>. N.Y. Prentice Hall.

Mulloy, F. (1990). <u>Urban Forestry - The Concept</u>.

Urban Forestry Conference, Dublin, Tree Council of Ireland.

SOCIAL INTEGRATION AND URBAN REGENERATION - A HOLISTIC APPROACH INVOLVING COMMUNITY-BASED EMPOWERMENT AND LOCAL, URBAN AND INTER-URBAN PARTNERSHIPS

Bob Catterall
London 2000

---

1. a) We argue that dominant approaches to urban regeneration are, analytically, lacking in comprehensiveness, and, practically, socially divisive.

   b) The approach of London 2000 to urban regeneration, in general, is holistic. In our analysis of social change and of the potential for social regeneration, we do, however, emphasise the role of culture - particularly the arts, the ethical and psychosocial dimensions of social behaviour and action, and a wide notion of education (of which schooling is a contradictory part) - in relation to economic trends and possibilities.

2. Our approach to action-research is both pluralist and committed. Our current work:

   a) considers the main developmental trends and proposals for London (including party policies);

   b) proposes a particular course of action, i.e. to further the development of a cross-London and European network committed to 'partnerships' and community-based empowerment with specific reference to particular areas (notably Kings Cross, Spitalfields and Docklands) and boroughs (e.g. Islington and Camden) in London and in some other European cities (see 2e below) as well;

   c) explores the role of transport and of technology within such an approach to social regeneration;

   d) considers both the evidence for acute social polarisation (notably marginalisation and racism, on one hand, and, on the other, the nature of 'the organisational landscape') and ways of overcoming this polarisation;

   e) clarifies and exemplifies this analysis and our approach by drawing on our own experience and that of other urban initiatives - in Barcelona, Berlin, Birmingham, Leeds and Paris;

   f) sets out strategies for regeneration that interrelate the main trends and proposals (2a above) to our proposed course of action (2b to 2e above).

The paper/presentation will develop these points.

SOCIAL INTEGRATION AND THE CREATION OF NEW URBAN ACTIVITIES

Brigitte Gaiffe
ELISE/AEIDL
Brussels

Creation of educational, social and cultural services improving the environment and facilitating social integration in cities.

Focusing on: culture (and education)

> 'Arts and culture, cultural industries are playing a key role in the regeneration of the cities, creating jobs, training facilities, improving the image of the city and the neighbourhoods, stimulating economic growth, improving communication, variety and richness to local life'.

The following items will be treated:

* What is culture?

    * Culture, cultural industries and local (economic) developments: the creation of jobs/employment ... which type and for whom?
    * Restoration of cultural heritage, theatres, concert halls, galleries and revitalisation of poor neighbourhoods ... what about the local inhabitants?
    * Culture/cultural services as a tool for social integration.
    * Culture as a tool for the revitalisation of a neighbourhood in decline and culture as a tool for social integration; contradiction or complimentarity?

    * Local cultural identity; myth or reality?

    * Lessons from different cases:
      (Marseille, Sociale Vernieuwing in The Netherlands, Bremen, Avignon, Sheffield, Antwerp, Dublin and others).

THE NEIGHBOURHOOD AS A HIDDEN RESOURCE

Tony Gibson
Neighbourhood Initiatives Foundation
Telford, Shropshire

Hitherto, the well-being and economic prosperity of our societies has usually been seen as the result of a working alliance between government and industry, varying for its effectiveness according to the changing powers of the unions and the private sector.

There has always been a missing component - the capacity of ordinary people to do things for themselves. To have a 'do' as well as a 'say' in shaping their surroundings and their future.

We are gradually realising the defects of the 'top-down' philosophy. In European terms we are favouring the idea of 'subsidiarity'. But as yet that notion has only percolated to the upper reaches of government. The idea of the neighbourhood as the crucible within which the different ingredients of society and the economy come together, is still a long way from reality.

Yet the neighbourhood is the common ground where the effects of market forces and government intervention can be seen and felt. It is a patch on the map - it could be as wide as a valley or as narrow as a tower block - and it is also a living organism, made up of everyone who lives and works in it, black and white, old and young, male and female, the lot. It is a package of human and material resources, 'up for grabs'.

Some of the most important resources are virtually untapped. Youngsters with zest and initiative denied the opportunity to show their mettle and achieve status - except by resorting to vandalism and petty crime. Middle-aged, redundant before their time. Elderly, with a lifetime of experience, left on the shelf.

Alongside these human resources there may be derelict land, disused premises, buildings which could be converted to new uses, a worn-out, uninspiring environment badly needing a face lift.

Wasted resources. Wasted partly because there is a communication gap between the local residents, especially the young, and the professionals they come up against in local government, central government, the private sector, charities and voluntary agencies. Neither side fully understands what the other is about, and this is mainly because the circumstances in which they meet put a premium on verbal fluency.

The talkers nearly always win, and these tend to be the professionals, or those few activists who speak on the community's behalf without necessarily having the community's real backing. So this is a pyrrhic victory. The local knowledge, intuitive understanding and the potential commitment of the bulk of the community is largely ignored; people feel marginalised and become alienated. The communication gap creates a confidence gap. Neither side has much reason for confidence in the other. The professionals say 'Leave it with us' and when their efforts fail, residents bitterly reply 'It's all your fault'.

The conflict between Us and Them underlies most of the problems we face. The continuing war of attrition, the distrust and the unwanted dependency which exist in many deprived areas, are the worst kind of deterrents to outside investment. Hard-nosed financial managers look for growth and security, and this is true of public funders, commercial investors and charities alike. Investing in communities where everyone keeps themselves to themselves for fear of each other seems like throwing good money after bad.

So we all agree, no doubt, on the necessity for 'partnership'. This is a Boardroom word easily used in public relations brochures, but not so easily applied at ground level. If we really want people to have a 'do' as well as a 'say', we have to create working relationships which are immediately rewarding, which are even fun. Within these working relationships many functions can come together - information gathering, training, crime prevention, livelihoods, environmental improvement, better housing and care.

The word 'synergy' has been used to indicate the interdependence of government, the private sector and the community. I prefer the word 'compound'. These different elements are like the ingredients in a mixture. Whilst they retain their identities, each simply has its own properties and nothing more. When a chemical reaction occurs and they become a compound, the new product has new properties. It is an alloy, with greater strength and a sharper cutting edge, as our Bronze Age forebears discovered.

Put another way, from the residents' viewpoint, they see things whole, as department officials seldom do. So our strategy should be built on this basic understanding of the way things fit together.

In my Foundation, we are working alongside community groups and local authorities in order to promote this strategy.

We are seeking to involve youngsters at risk with other older residents in working relationships with the local authorities both in planning and in implementing neighbourhood regeneration. The neighbourhood provides the terms of reference - how to match all its needs with all its resources. People need to see what can be done, here and now, with what is immediately available. They need to be able to take a hand in improving the environment, adapting premises to set up home-based small enterprises which might become half-way stages to full-time employment; making better provision for children, the handicapped, the homeless and the elderly. Helping to plan these improvements, helping to make them happen, sharing the credit, and as a result being determined to safeguard what they have achieved together.

None of this gets done simply by talking about it. This is why over the years we have developed and field-tested techniques and materials which enable residents and professionals to show each other what they mean. We publish kits to make crude 3-D models, and charts with moveable elements which everyone can join in re-arranging, so that gradually, and visibly, people can explore possibilities, sort out options, rank priorities and share responsibilities.

Methods such as Planning for Real are proving increasingly popular, with the authorities as well as with the community groups, because they begin with what is literally common ground. They bring people together, literally on a level footing: working around models and charts rather than ranged in rows with a 'platform party' confronting an angry audience. Neither side feels intimidated or threatened, and the process of coming together in these novel circumstances is actually fun. As one old lady said 'It's better than Bingo!'.

Alongside this exploration of problems and opportunities go house-to-house enquiries conducted usually by residents themselves with 'user-friendly' questionnaires they have helped to draft. This reveals, to everyone's surprise, the extent of the buried talent and experience which lies, hitherto unnoticed, within every community. So it is in itself a confidence-builder and the follow-up can bring together the residents and the professionals working out together how these buried talents could be fuelled with outside resources. Also, how they could be reinforced by training, purpose-built to suit neighbourhood needs and priorities; custom-built to enhance latent capacities and to deploy the skills already within the community in training others.

Information gathered from within the neighbourhood needs to be supplemented by technical, legal and financial information from outside. But this has to be distilled and made accessible in a form which everyone can grasp. So we have developed a series of Fact Banks, totalling about a thousand information cards, each one complete in itself and, hopefully, cleansed of jargon and officialese. Now we are seeking to take these publications a stage further by promoting the idea of modem terminals accessible to ordinary members of every community, sited in libraries or community centres, and linked to a data base designed to match the way residents themselves identify the information they need.

No element in this strategy is easily achieved in the early stages. We have all to overcome bad habits of blinkered departmental thinking, top-down decision-making, obsession with words at the expense of deeds. But there are reasons for hope, and one of these is the fact of our coming together here.

REVITALISATION THROUGH INTEGRATED SOCIO-ECONOMIC APPROACHES

Geneviève Lecamp
OECD, ILE Programme
Paris

---

1. Disadvantaged young people, especially those living in city centres or other impoverished urban areas of OECD countries have, for more than 25 years, been the target of many policies in the social area, for teaching, training and employment.

2. In fact, as shown by many studies and especially by the report prepared on the basis of an analysis of the situation in the cities of Barcelona, Glasgow, Hamburg and Metz, this population group, in spite of many efforts made by the central authorities, local government and the voluntary sector, is still faced with the problem of segregation and marginalisation in its quest for social and occupational integration.

3. While the overall unemployment rate for young people has shown a relative decline in most OECD countries, as compared with the record rates between 1982 and 1985, for reasons which include demographic development and the number of public policies aimed at containing unemployment within acceptable boundaries, it still remains extremely worrying, in the light of its principal features and new characteristics, in relation to our topic of study:

    -   Thus, in Spain, despite a slight drop, young people represented 64% of the long-term unemployed between 1983 and 1987 (young women made up a large part of the total numbers during this period).

        At the moment the city of Barcelona is having difficulty in coping with the problem among young adults (21-22 years of age) and especially young women.

    -   Unemployment tends to be concentrated both from a geographical and a social point of view in impoverished urban areas, victimised by the economic changes which have affected, and are continuing to affect, the texture of urban life.

        Pockets of poverty lie cheek by jowl with areas of wealth, even in cities which have shown economic dynamism. But unemployment is compounded by further ills (housing of substandard quality; inadequate social facilities; difficulties in access to the centre of the city or, more generally, to transport, social and family problems created or at least exacerbated by the high level of unemployment; and an inadequate and frequently irregular family or personal income). It is the cumulative effect of these factors on young people which makes their problems difficult to resolve.

- The growth in unemployment connected with the slow-down of economic activity in impoverished urban areas, or linked to structural mutations which have occurred in the labour market (a demand for qualified young workers in booming sectors or new areas of activity, and an excessively high grading for certain jobs) is striking very sharply at young people who live in marginalised districts, far from centres of innovation, both on a social, educational and economic level.

    Victims from the start of an inadequate level or quality of education and training, they meet a labour market, when they move from school to active life, which is increasingly segmented and selective, and moreover often fails to include the geographical area in which they live.

    Their low (or non-existent) degree of mobility - for obvious reasons - constrains them to suffer the consequences of their handicaps, which combine and reinforce each other.

4. From the study undertaken by the secretariat of the OECD and the contacts recently established, especially with the cities of Barcelona, Glasgow, Hamburg and the French authorities, it is clear that the International Seminar organised in 1992 in Birmingham (UK) by the OECD and the Community Development Foundation should try to build its research projects around the following guidelines of analysis:

    - Any measure or policy concerned with disadvantaged young people from impoverished urban areas cannot confine itself purely to corrective action. It must anticipate the future and take a long-term view, in a detailed relationship to a plan for a town or an urban area, based on a participatory approach.

    - The acute nature of the problems experienced by these young people, and the increasing impoverishment of certain districts in urban settings, require that public authorities should undertake a massive intervention with the difficult aim of seeking to analyse the short and the long term, in order to restore, first of all confidence, especially among young people at risk, to encourage a climate favourable to the emergence of new economic activities and innovation and to respond specifically to emergency situations, while progressively structuring the economic, social and cultural context of urban life with the aid of the private and voluntary sectors, and trying, with this in view, to 'fortify' the possible partners from the impoverished areas and enhance their solidarity.

    It is also the responsibility of the public authorities to co-ordinate their different policies and adapt them to local settings, in a framework of action which gives priority to partnership at local or regional level, with a lever effect which makes it possible to integrate local initiatives which are numerous but scattered, or may be badly capitalised (financial insecurity deriving from short-term funding and limited resources), into the sphere of lasting controlled development.

- The growing increase in the number of marginalised young people makes it imperative to renew policies of employment promotion and assistance with entry to the labour market, as recalled in the latest contribution from Simon Wuhl ('Du chômage à l'exclusion'): 'exclusion appears as a by-product of the way in which the economy works...action must be taken on the mechanisms of producing, maintaining and developing jobs...'.

It is important to place the enterprise at the centre of the arrangements to labour market entry, and to attack the underlying causes of exclusion: the insufficient creation of jobs in certain areas and the attitudes of employers towards recruitment and human resource management.

This implies the study, at an early age, of arrangements for bringing together schools and enterprises. In the light of the activities pursued by companies today, the restructuring of economies and growing internationalisation, fresh thought must be given to study programmes, diversified and subdivided into cycles, which are capable of building bridges with the world of work through occupational training and in-service training.

It also seems essential to break through the ghettoisation of these districts, offering their residents, and the most disadvantaged young people, possibilities of access to local and regional labour markets.

OBSERVATIONS ON THE MEANS OF SOCIAL AND ECONOMIC INTEGRATION IN DISADVANTAGED URBAN AREAS IN DIFFICULTIES

Pierre-Yves Mauguen[*]
Centre de Prospective
Ministry of Research and Technology
Paris

Actions aiming at integrating fragile populations in urban areas in difficulties come from very different horizons.

The involvement of the population and the recognition of exclusion factors play an essential part in any one of these methods of integration.

In France, the means used for achieving the goal of social integration include:

- the understanding of situations of individual and collective exclusion;

- the support of the creation of local micro-activities;

- integrated activities for the reinforcement of cultural, economic, social and ideological links within a community;

- general tools of 'town planning' (State-City agreement, Development Plan).

Is it necessary that all these methods converge constantly?

The paper formulates a set of observations on the specific instruments used in France for the enhancement of urban areas in crisis.

NEW ARRANGEMENTS FOR SOCIAL INTEGRATION IN DISADVANTAGED DISTRICTS OF BRUSSELS

Pascale Mistiaen[*]
DEFIS - ASBL
Brussels

A series of new projects has been developed in recent years in Brussels. They are new as regards their objective - the social occupational integration of poorly qualified young people - and by the approach which they adopt - they combine economic, social, cultural and even town-planning elements, and are run on a 'partnership' basis.

Thus, the arrangements for local missions and priority education zones, or more precisely, the projects for enterprise nurseries or enterprise centres, as well as certain renovation programmes, are all examples illustrating the new trends in the 'social' area. These arrangements have numerous points in common: they set out on the basis of campaigns or associations seeking new funding, they form the subject of agreements with public authorities, undergo quantitative evaluation by them and are multi-functional.

But the most specific feature of their organisation is their local connections. Problems are thus dealt with on a territorial basis, corresponding to the geographical scale of the organisation of power.

THE SOCIAL ECONOMY SECTOR IN ITS RELATIONSHIP TO THE ENVIRONMENT AND TRAINING SCHEMES FOR THE INTEGRATION OF THE DEPRIVED

William Roe
CEI Consultants Ltd
Edinburgh
and EC ERGO Programme on Long-term Unemployment

Throughout the 1980s, in many European countries, a wide range of new actions have been taken to improve the quality of life in urban areas and to try to integrate the most disadvantaged members of the community into the mainstream of society. One of the most innovatory, and often successful trends, has been the growth of practical action by local community organisations and other non-statutory bodies to improve their urban environment. In the most imaginative cases, initiatives of this kind have brought multiple benefits:

- the creation of employment and income for disadvantaged people;

- the development of skills and qualifications;

- the improvement of living and environmental conditions;

- the empowerment of local communities;

- the development of leadership skills and organisational capacity.

This presentation will **describe** recent trends and innovations in different EC countries, illustrated by a number of practical examples. It will **identify** some lessons of good practice that can be drawn from past experience. It will **propose** some key issues for attention by public policy-makers, the social economy sector and the private sector. And finally, it will **look ahead** to the possible impact of trends in the urban environment and in employment and training, particularly as they affect disadvantaged communities and deprived groups in society.

NEW RESIDENTS' ORGANISATIONS IN MOSCOW

Yelena Shomina
Centre for Comparative Analysis
Institute of Labour Studies
Academy of Sciences
Moscow

Over the past few years the economic, social and political life of Russia has been transformed. Not surprisingly, these changes have included unprecedented developments in the area of city management. Urban administrators are being forced, for example, to adapt themselves to the totally new phenomenon of privatisation. The process of democratisation has led to the rise of numerous local organisations and initiatives. Environmental issues have featured among the most prominent areas of activity for such groups.

In this contribution I would like to describe two important new popular organisations which have been formed recently in Moscow. These are the Moscow Ecological Federation and the Association of Moscow Self-Management Committees.

The Moscow Ecological Federation was founded in 1989 as a result of joint efforts by a number of small ecological groups in various areas of Moscow. Each group focused on particular local issues, such as saving small parks, limiting traffic flow through residential neighbourhoods or blocking inappropriate construction activity.

The main form of popular action during the initial stages was the organisation of protests - meetings, pickets, and blockades. Before long, activists in various groups decided to unite their efforts, reasoning that it was impossible to solve legal problems without addressing the major issues of the economic development of the city. If at first these environmental groups had not participated in political struggle, they discovered after a series of defeats that local problems could not be solved unless they participated in political life at the level of the city as a whole. If the environmental movement was to have a meaningful impact on city politics, it needed to act in a united way. The Moscow Ecological Federation thus came into being.

Today, the Federation unites some 60 local groups, and has contacts with a further 30. Several dozen environmental scientists have volunteered their skills to help the Federation's work.

In recent times the Federation has concentrated on working through the established political structures in order to influence the activity of the city administration. A considerable number of Federation members have been elected as local deputies. The Federation is also trying to co-ordinate the work of experts in elaborating a general plan for the environmentally sound development of Moscow. The local environmental groups meanwhile continue to address the problems of the local environment.

The upsurge of activity by environmentalists has also led to the appearance of grass-roots residents' organisations. The first example of such a body is the residents' association in the 'micro-region' of Brateyevo. Located on the outskirts of Moscow to the south-east of the city centre, Brateyevo is a dormitory suburb flanked on three sides by heavy industrial areas and on the fourth by vacant land.

Brateyevo residents had long hoped that this area of vacant land would be turned over to them for use as garden plots. But in 1989 they discovered abruptly that construction activity was about to begin there. For the first time in the history of Moscow, local residents united in order to block the construction site. After the residents had occupied the site for three days the city authorities backed down and construction work was suspended. The initiative group that had organised the blockade subsequently formed itself into the first local self-management committee.

At present in Moscow there are 220 such committees, which have set out to take control of various aspects of everyday life in the micro-regions or urban neighbourhoods. They are exerting an active influence on urban policy, elaborating alternative projects for the development of urban districts. The self-management committees are also active in electoral work, seeking to secure the election as deputies of people sympathetic to environmental values.

In July 1991 many of these local groups united to form the Association of Committees of Self-Management. The statutes of the Association state that the organisation's main aim is to 'assist the organs of self-management to solve local problems, including shaping the living environment, providing local amenities, securing employment for the local population, developing social infrastructure, and crime prevention'.

One of the first tasks undertaken by the Association was to attempt to influence the resolutions to be adopted in the forthcoming Document on the Status of Moscow. The Association has drawn up its own draft of this document.

At present, a new and highly centralised system of city administration is being set in place, with 'prefects' appointed to control urban regions and with the recently elected Mayor substantially outside the control of the City Soviet Deputies. Within this context, the Association is fighting a battle to assert the right of the population to democratic self-management.

Despite the powerful trend towards the restoration of hierarchical authority, the growth of local organisations devoted to the defence of the environment and of residents' rights is an encouraging sign that civil society, including the active involvement of the population in deciding their own destinies, may at last be arising in Russia.

AWARENESS INTO ACTION: LOCAL INITIATIVES IN URBAN STUDIES

Richard Welsh
National Association for Urban Studies,
Lewis Cohen Urban Studies Centre, Brighton Polytechnic, Brighton

---

Urban Studies in Britain encompasses a variety of education and community development work based on a commitment to the values of issue-based active learning and participation in urban environmental decision-making.

This paper looks briefly at some examples of urban studies work which illustrate the awareness into action process. It attempts to show how Urban Studies Centres and other local environment resource centres can help to raise awareness of issues among different groups and encourage wider participation in improving the environment. Examples cited include:

* oral history and reminiscence groups;

* cultural gardens, playground and school ground improvement projects;

* environmental audits and action planning;

* publishing and the development of local information resources;

* local environment fora and local or regional networks;

* Sustainable City Forum and Network.

The paper concludes with some questions about how the role of Urban Studies Centres and other local environment resource centres could be developed, especially in relation to the model of 'urban local initiative centres', referred to in the European Commission's Green Paper on the Urban Environment (Chapter 2, §5.10):

* How could such centres facilitate wider consultation and involvement in the planning process and in environmental decision making?

* What kinds of activity in the centres could contribute to the improvement of the built environment, while involving and empowering people of all ages and from all sections of the community as citizens?

* Where should the funding for such centres come from, taking into account the fact that the source of funding determines the kind of work centres are able/permitted to undertake?

CONCLUSIONS, RECOMMENDATIONS

by

Philippe Morin
RACINE, Paris

In order to provide a better context for understanding the work carried out in this group, some preliminary remarks are necessary. There were 13 papers - probably too numerous to facilitate a really productive exchange of views. And the relatively heterogeneous nature of these contributions, although it greatly enriched the debate, did not facilitate the task which was assigned to us. In particular, it proved impossible, for lack of time, to hold the final summing-up discussion which was to lead to recommendations. Hence, the present text can only aim to provide a partial summary of the very interesting exchanges which took place within the working group following the various presentations.

1. The Points in Common between the Different Contributions

Despite the diversity of approaches and logical bases in the various experiences which were described, it is worth trying to read across their whole range and identify common denominators.

The list of themes proposed by the different contributors may give a more concrete notion of the nature of the exchanges:

- The neighbourhood as a hidden resource (Tony Gibson);
- Social integration and the creation of new urban activities: the experience of the Wise Group in Glasgow (Alan Sinclair);
- Observations on the means of economic and social integration in neighbourhoods in difficulties in France (Pierre-Yves Mauguen);
- Social integration and urban regeneration: a holistic approach involving the emergence of community power and partnerships at local, urban and inter-urban levels (Bob Catterall);
- The hazards of freedom for culture in Romania (Maria Octavia Treistar);
- The creation of services in the cultural field in the service of improving the environment and social integration in cities (Hilda Maelstaf);
- New residents' organisations in Moscow (Yelena Shomina);
- Observations arising from a number of innovative actions carried out in Europe for the improvement of urban life and the integration of people in difficulties (William Roe);
- Account of an experiment carried out by the employees of a company in East Berlin facing closure (Edith Brickwell);
- Awareness through action: local initiatives and studies of the city: the experience of Urban Studies Centres (Richard Welsh);
- Urban forestry interventions in the urban environment and community initiatives in Ireland and the United Kingdom (Margaret Sweeney);

- Reflections on urban development policies: the necessary developments (Geneviève Lecamp);
- New arrangements for social integration in the disadvantaged areas of Brussels (Pascale Mistiaen).

On reflection, three major points emerged which were common to the different presentations. These were linked to three key words: appropriation, project, complexity.

All papers emphasised the fundamental importance of the appropriation of actions and initiatives, whatever their form, by the local populations. Nothing can be imposed from above, exchanges must move from lower to higher, the horizontal must take precedence over the vertical ('bottom-up', not 'top-down').

In keeping with the previous point, all experiences are built on projects which were meaningful for the people concerned - they were connected with day-to-day experience, whatever the area of action (whether this involved work and action in the area of the environment and town planning, the cultural field, or questions of employment, training or education).

Interventions on the problems of integration and the creation of new activities in cities, once they are planned on a substantial scale, become more and more complex. This complexity has to do with, among other things, the range of parameters to be borne in mind (cf. the idea of a holistic approach), the different nature of the actors involved, who operate according to principles and interests which are not always consistent, and may even be contradictory, and, lastly the fact that one is dealing with problems of change which are subject to uncertainty and where simple cause and effect relationships do not apply.

2. The Key Points Emphasised by the Participants

To take up an image suggested by one of the participants, it is possible to relate these key points to the image of a table, equipped with the usual four legs. These legs are the key parameters, the elements underpinning the action, and they form the support for the flat surface (the table in its functional character) which represents the strategy, a condition which is felt to be essential in handling operations or initiatives affecting the creation of new urban activities in a perspective of social integration.

The first leg is self-esteem, or self-confidence in one's ability to change the situation (whether the 'self' is individual or collective). This idea is obviously closely linked to the previously mentioned idea of appropriation. It brings us back to the importance of changing the image which people have of themselves and their capacity for action. It underlines the importance of those initiatives methods, and instruments which draw on people's resources, which exist but are not clearly visible (hidden resources), which draw on people's potential creativity, and which also draw on manifestations which can give tangible expression to their power to change things (including certain symbolic manifestations which reveal this potential).

The second leg of the table is the transfer of power which is implicit in the establishment of new power relationships between decision-makers and the social groups (who are at the same time clients, consumers, users and actors). This requires a search for more integrated and participatory forms of interaction, leading to real forms of balanced partnership. This idea implies other notions such as responsibility, agreement on aims, and accountability. Depending on the context, it presupposes radical changes in the habits, representations and practices both of the political and administrative decision-makers, and of the social groups concerned.

The third leg is management. This function appears essential in so far as it constitutes the function which links and articulates the various parameters, which orders the complexity previously described. It is the quality of this management that determines the identification of resources and the synergy between them, whether one is dealing with human, technical or financial resources, whether the activity falls within the framework of private initiatives or territorial or national policies.

The fourth leg is training and education. These must be addressed to two kinds of target: the professionals and the population (of clients, of users, etc.). As regards the professionals, the task is to transform their practices (methods of decision and management), while for the population the goal is to increase their resources and competence in relation to the problems which they have to face (urban planning, creation of services, employment problems, environmental questions, etc.) and to stabilise the projects and forms of organisation over time (ensuring that they survive beyond the initial mobilisation phase). The accent must be placed both on the active and concrete character and on the qualitative dimension of these processes of training, so that the people involved can appropriate them for themselves.

We thus find four key points supporting a strategy, the overall framework in which the project is organised.

Moving beyond our somewhat simplistic and static image of the table, three important notions must be taken on board. All action implies a dynamic of exchanges, negotiations, even conflicts of interest, so this table must be round, or have a variable geometry. This does not arise in a vacuum, but fits in - or should fit in - to a political context in a broader local, regional or national perspective of social integration. Finally, it fits into a material, natural and cultural environment which absolutely has to be taken into account.

3. Some Concluding Remarks

On examination, the diversity of the different contributions and interventions within this working group could be characterised by distributing the contributions along a continuous line. At one end of this continuum, one finds 'spontaneous' initiatives carried out by groups or communities at a given moment, on issues which they felt crucial enough to justify a major mobilisation. An extreme example of this would be the experience described by our participant from Moscow, where residents' associations were set up in the absence of urban, environmental and other policies. At the other end of the line one finds national or local policies which are sometimes very elaborate, but where the main interested parties, the social groups concerned, seem to disappear as actors. Certain arrangements put in place by some Community countries give that impression. Between the two extremes, there are a number of experiences which, depending on the individual case, manage more or less to combine the two aspects. It would obviously be impossible to give an exact location on the continuum for each experience described - it is merely an image which tries to account for an overall trend.

In this idea of compromise between community initiative and political decision imposed from the top down, which seems to be a central issue in the problem of social integration, one comes back to the difficulty of combining long-term and short-term perspectives. This can be expressed in terms of three questions:

- How can one conduct operations and experiments, based on the mobilisation of the groups concerned, over a long enough duration to allow them to achieve enough social significance and effectiveness to deal with the problems encountered?

- How can one implement effective policies - ones which hold up in the medium or the longer term - that are credible in the short term and allow the populations concerned to take them over?

- In other words, how can one handle this mutual dependence between decision-makers on the one hand, and the populations concerned as local actors on the other?

When one moves into a European perspective of discussion and exchange, one has to consider the questions of transferability and reproducibility of experiences. Today, therefore, we have to ask about the question of modelling.

The elements contributed and discussed within the working group tend to show that we must try to build models or scenarios which combine two aspects, moving beyond their contradictory character. On the one hand these have to be formalised and structured so as to be effective and coherent - that is to say, they must mean something in political terms (in relation to the surrounding society); on the other hand they must leave enough freedom and autonomy for the direct actors to be able to take them over and get involved.

In practice, the construction of such scenarios is not without its difficulties or risks: conflicts arising from the non-convergence of the interests which are present; the contradiction between participatory democracy and elective democracy; the contradiction between what is said and the real practices (talk about partnership may very well mask autocratic practices); the weight of habit; resistance to change, etc.

SELECTED PAPERS AND CONCLUSIONS OF

THE WORKING GROUP

ON

THE CO-EXISTENCE OF URBAN FUNCTIONS AS A MEANS TO ENSURING
ENVIRONMENTAL PROTECTION AND SOCIAL INTEGRATION

COMPOSITION OF WORKING GROUP 5

THE CO-EXISTENCE OF URBAN FUNCTIONS AS A MEANS TO ENSURING ENVIRONMENTAL PROTECTION AND SOCIAL INTEGRATION

Chairman: Mr René Schoonbrodt
Commission of the EC, DG XI

Rapporteur: Prof. Sten Engelstoft
University of Copenhagen/Commission of the EC, DG XII

Expert Introducing the Working Group: Prof. Yannis Tsiomis
Ecole d'Architecture de Paris - La Villette

Speakers-Participants:

1. Prof. Panayiotis Getimis
   Pantion University of Social and Political Sciences, Athens

2. Prof. Richard V. Knight
   Urbinno Network

3. Prof. Tjeerd Deelstra
   International Institute of the Urban Environment, Delft

4. Dr Ekhart Hahn
   Wissenschaftszentrum Berlin

5. Prof. André Loeckx
   Catholic University of Leuven

6. Mrs Cristina Paula de Jésus Garrett
   Ministry of Environment, Lisbon

7. Mr Hermann Seiberth
   Senate of Berlin

8. Mr Alexander S. Matrosov
   Moscow City Government

9. Mrs Maria Octavia Treistar
   'FEMEIA' Magazine, Bucharest

10. Mr Nuno Portas
    University of Oporto

11. Mr Xenophon Constantinidis
    Employers Group, Administrative Board, European Foundation

12. Mrs Klara Szabó
    Ministry of Environment Protection, Budapest

LIVING SPACES IN THE EUROPE OF TWELVE
URBAN CULTURES IN MUTATION

by

Yannis Tsiomis
School of Architecture
Paris - La Villette

The 1980s were marked by the emergence of themes which were common to the various European countries: urban 'reconquest' and 'restoration'. People were concerned with 'experiencing the city' and 'living together'.

These fashionable phrases were the consequence of a new awareness: Britain and France were experiencing urban riots marking a 'living disorder' which had been long established in suburban areas, if not in city centres. Athens and Naples (but also Fos-sur-Mer and Milan) were declared pollution disaster areas. Everywhere in Germany, there was a rejection of environmental destruction due to conglomerations.

In this continent which had been celebrating the merits of the **city** since the Greeks, questions were now being asked about the 'urban adventure'.

1. Urban Mutations

More than changes, we were dealing here with far-reaching mutations. Urban Europe was in a state of mutation which had become unmanageable through normal administrative, legal and sometimes even technical and aesthetic instruments. The situation can be summed up as follows: the city and its habitat are no longer fulfilling their role as places of culture and socialisation. Rather than the problems of excessive density, overloaded networks and dysfunction, one was finding visible ruptures both of the spatial and of the social texture.

Centres were 'on the move', traditional city living spaces were becoming volatile, and faced with the signals launched sometimes violently by the young people in the 'peripheral areas' (in France and in Britain), it was admitted that there was now a need to 'start all over again' and devote some thought to the two textures (spatial and social) and their organisation.

The question of urban areas in Europe in the 1990s no longer involved nostalgically seeking to 'restore past history', but rather to create and win through to a new history in the territories not only of the twelve Member States, but in the whole of Europe.

For European cities, the end of the century will involve handling not only the legacy of Renaissance or nineteenth century cities, but the legacy of the 'modern city' of the twentieth century, built on an 'instant' formula. This will be the dominant model, and a problematic one.

Indeed, the urban crisis which the European Community has faced during the 1980s has finally ended the illusion of the 1960s, shared by politicians and urban specialists, according to which post-war reconstruction and the 'rational' planning of national territories would be sufficient to defuse the 'crises' of the city. There was a housing crisis, in the first place, but there were also crises regarding work space, offices, industry, etc. At the time, there was no talk of economic crisis, still less of social crisis, but only of a housing crisis. Building was going on more or less everywhere in the European countries, whether industrialised or not; there was an attempt to gain control over space and the post-war city through nationally based bodies (the Ministry of Town and Country Planning in the United Kingdom) or regionally based bodies (Cassa per il Mezzogiorno in Italy).

Under the aegis of the State or local communities, laws were promulgated and planning projects flourished everywhere; in Italy where, between 1950 and 1961, Intercommunal Plans and Regional Plans were created; Denmark, where rural character of the country persisted up to the beginning of the 1980s, saw the early establishment (in 1949) of a growth threshold for urban areas, and certain zones were identified and declared ineligible for building; in the Federal Republic of Germany, regional directorates of town planning were set up and, in 1971, the Federal Law on Urban Renewal under the control of each Land was adopted; lastly, in the 1960s a policy of New Towns and Major Conurbations was established in France, in the Netherlands, in England, etc.

Thus a gap opened up between the industrialised countries of Northern Europe and the southern countries (such as Spain, Greece or Portugal).

The so-called 'Southern European' countries abandoned themselves with an unprecedented enthusiasm to what became known as 'tourist development' without any proper planning at either national or regional level. Industrial development was left to north-western Europe, with the south and south-east of the continent becoming a holiday space for this northern area.

Thirty years later, this dream of subdividing functions and spaces has produced results which belied the initial intentions, and disproved the plans which had been made by town planners, economists and politicians.

2. Noisy and Chaotic Urban Europe
   Silent and Diminished Rural Europe

Not only had there been a failure to 'control' space in Europe (this was true of the whole continent, including Eastern Europe), but in addition, one was now dealing with something which had better be called by its proper name: a generalised environmental disaster, both rural and urban.

In fact, if one leaves aside the 'hard kernels', the centres of historic cities (Paris, London), or whole cities which are difficult to 'dismantle' (Florence, Evora), the whole of Europe has seen two decades of the breaking down of cities, their suburbs and rural space. In short, there has been a de-structuring of long-established textures, through a widespread and ill-considered urbanisation process.

Official statistics (Eurostat 1985 and 1987) indicating that the European population, with the exception of Portugal, is overwhelmingly urban (86% in West Germany, 78% in France, 72% in Italy, 92% in the United Kingdom, 88% in the Netherlands, 67% in Greece, etc.), all confirm a new reality.

The **scattering** of urban space has thus led to a dislocation of the relationship between town and country (a relationship which had been seen as based on conflict just half a century previously), with complex consequences. We may point out one paradox for a start: the difference between the countries of northern Europe and the countries of southern Europe, which is quite sharp when one defines it in terms of industrial development, becomes blurred when one considers urban development and all that flows from it.

But a corollary to this consistency in destructive tendencies is a far-reaching modification in living spaces. With spatial and social textures being modified, lifestyles involved with urban culture were the ones which became transformed and - a second paradox - despite the differences between each town and each country, the same phenomenon appeared everywhere. Urban cultures, these multiple ways of living in one's city on a daily basis, appropriating its private places at its special times, experiencing its memories while creating new ones, in short, everything which had given city dwellers a feeling of belonging and identity, had, through their transformation, led to the emergence of a different sentiment; a feeling of indifference and abandonment.

3. Definitions of Planning Techniques and Varying Types of Legislation

One could draw a distinction between one Europe (northern Europe) where urban planning is explicit and planned (the provision and installation of infrastructures), and another Europe, where town planning takes place on a de facto basis (an almost complete lack of forward planning). The difference here is accentuated when one comes to planning techniques: the legislative framework, the laws which pre-empt decisions, the varying infrastructure technologies (sewerage, motorways, drainage), techniques for controlling urban space (town planning regulations, density controls, land use coefficients, prospects, etc.), but also the application of specialist skills which involve architectural quality.

Thus, alongside a trend towards uniformity in ways of life, one finds a disparity in methods of intervention and action on urban questions.

The urban crisis is not experienced in the same way in every country. At the beginning of the 1990s, it is still difficult to make a serious comparative analysis of towns and agglomerations in the Europe of the Twelve.

While generally speaking suburban areas contain more and more population as compared to 'traditional' centres - the ancient cities are stabilising - on the other hand this 'plus' factor shows a qualitative difference from one country to another. The disparity in instruments (for example, the absence of statistics in certain countries), the differences in definition and approach to the urban phenomenon (various definitions of a megalopolis, which vary from country to country) and the differences as regards administrative and territorial boundaries; all of this would suggest the need for prudence.

One fact is certain, the very different economic position of urbanised areas surrounding cities did not make it possible, other than through an abuse of language, to include all European suburbia under the heading of a social crisis or an industrial wasteland.

In this connection, the Neapolitan hinterland, and the surroundings of Oporto, have shown great dynamism, unlike the dislocated suburbs of Manchester or the organised dormitory suburbs around Amsterdam.

4. Affinity rather than Resemblance or Opposition

Despite all this, towards the end of the 1980s and the beginning of the 1990s, the increase in 'urban scourges' (minor crime, drug abuse, educational problems, etc.) took on a general character. Beyond all differences, what seemed to be unravelling was the European city itself, the **complexity** of urban textures in an area of communication given articulacy and solidarity, despite everything, by centuries of shared history of aggression and mutual understanding. And in this sense, the ways of life, their modification and even the urban crises found in the conglomerations of Paris, Berlin, Madrid or Athens, more than resemblances or contrasts, involve relationships of **affinity** - European cultural affinity is made up of detailed differences which spring, apart from national and dominant models, into ways of life which are permeable.

5. A New Awareness, in Spite of Everything

The new awareness of this general crisis has meant that the European Community, despite the fact that habitat and urban development are not covered by the Treaty of Rome, has been persuaded to launch a series of studies, starting at the end of the 1980s, dealing with reintegration through social and urban development, and with the relationship between 'employment and integration for the strengthening of economic and social cohesion within the urban setting'.

Europe has long been working under the burden of urgent pressures and 'quantitative' needs, neglecting the linkage between social and spatial textures; the habitat was 'classified' into categories (collective, semi-collective and individual), and no longer necessarily corresponded to realities and people's imaginative patterns; it did not match the neglected and dislocated communities any more than the scattered and disorientated individuals lost in the 'peri-urban' ocean.

The 1980s reminded us that the city is made up of mixed and differentiated functions; urban culture depends on this mix. One of the most important steps still remains to be taken: moving to global urban action in what might be called a European urban plan, not in order to impose a single set of models or functions, but with a view to sharing ways of thinking and approaches; a spatial and social plan, as far removed from constraint as from mere embellishment or appeasement, made up of a multiplicity of approaches maintaining the central principle of not dissociating the citizen from the city-dweller.

INTEGRATION AND PARTNERSHIP
IN THE REVITALISATION OF URBAN AREAS

by

Nuno Portas
University of Oporto

1. For a number of years, most European cities have been striving to overcome very serious problems of physical and/or social deterioration in their urban areas. The new factor is that we are no longer dealing solely with older districts, with the classic processes of an ageing population and dilapidated buildings, but also with more recently built districts on the outskirts of cities, which provide accommodation - especially public housing - for young and relatively disadvantaged populations: people who have arrived either from the countryside, or from the older parts of the city, or as immigrants from foreign countries.

    Even in the case of conglomerations where demographic growth has slowed, the suburban crisis has become more threatening to social cohesion than the crisis in the centre of town; moreover, the solutions to deal with these new problems are much less clear-cut.

2. In the case of older urban areas, the restoration of buildings and the rehabilitation of public spaces are no longer considered as activities unconnected with the development of local productive and cultural activities, and with the creation of new jobs and better occupational training. The situation is different in suburban working-class areas: separated from the city centre and zones of economic activity, and handicapped by their exclusively 'dormitory' function, their condition merely serves to aggravate the problems of coexistence which can be found among different groups, whether divided by age, origins or race.

    Whereas in the rehabilitation of an existing town, whether mediaeval or bourgeois, the space containing the problems coincides (more or less) with the space where actions have to be undertaken, in the case of recently built dormitory suburbs this coincidence does not apply, given the scattered nature of working activities and locations, in relation to the place of residence. This explains the small number of recent attempts at suburban renewal which have taken on the aim of providing compatible production structures in mono-functional (residential) districts.

    The two situations which have been summarised above also lead to different institutional solutions, even though the overall objective is the same. This is true, first of all, because in traditional urban areas, the resources to be mobilised, the synergies to be built up, can largely be seen as 'internal'. Things are different in the 'new' areas, where one has to bring in 'external' resources (particularly for productive investment) and consequently one has to make changes to a greater or lesser extent in the physical setting, especially in the area of collective space, in order to create new opportunities for social life affected by the present context.

3. Undoubtedly, the two (extreme) types of urban situation - like the different intermediate situations which can be found in each conglomeration - have one essential characteristic in common: the timely solution of problems always involves a **strategy** of mobilising resources - public and private, internal and external - while integrating diversified activities, organised in a way which is made clear in time and space, as a condition for arriving at solutions which can 'be made

to stick' because they go beyond surface features to tackle the deepest causes of both environmental deterioration and social exclusion.

An intervention in urban areas experiencing crisis must be not only 'inter-sectoral and interdisciplinary' in its technical design (a condition which is already well established), but must also be 'inter-organisational' - a condition which is much harder to achieve in material terms on the ground. The **system of organisation with variable complexity**, according to the nature of the concrete problems to be resolved, cannot confine itself purely to the bodies involved in conventional public administration (central/regional and/or local), given the strategic importance of revitalising economic and cultural activities which depend on initiatives from private sources.

4. 'Institutional design' thus becomes a key factor in the success of operations aimed at revitalisation.

Naturally, the diversity of political and administrative contexts, and the specific features of the cases to be resolved, do not allow us to recommend any one universal model. Nevertheless, there are some criteria which can be identified from fairly recent experiences, and a discussion of these criteria should be helpful in identifying a new, more broadly based form of intervention.

    4.1 In the first place, as regards the State's responsibility, the **operational centre** must be **'displaced'** from sectoral authorities, which tend to reflect a vertical/bureaucratic type of organisation, **towards the area of operations.** This rule cannot be limited merely to the central or regional departments of the State, but must also be applied at local level, especially in the case of large communes or urban communities.

    The main difficulty which arises stems from the fact that certain keys to revitalisation (transport, health and social security, occupational training, aids to rehabilitation and economic activity from Community funds, etc.) still come directly from budgets and areas controlled by ministers, and there is resistance to the idea of mixing these in with 'mission' orientated bodies, where leadership tends to have a more local character. Moreover, the fact that a mission team includes a representative from a ministerial department does not mean that it has a real decision-making autonomy (a right to enter into commitments) going beyond the technical level and the immediate timescale.

    The second implication, which is well known, of opting for administrative bodies based on missions or problems to be solved, is the alienation of some parts of the sectoral administration, even on a local level, which are very sensitive when it comes to settling accounts or carrying out sectoral works through conventional services.

    The greatest asset of a mission team anchored on the ground is not only its ability to perceive the interdependence of problems - and thus the synergies between different measures to be adopted - but also its ability to ensure that solutions are **monitored** in direct contact with the people involved. This feedback is essential in order to get practical programmes adjusted as they run, given a timely realisation of their results and drawbacks. The weakness in this formula, due to its temporary character, comes at the moment of withdrawal from the area, once the initial objective has been attained, leaving the ground to a standard form of administration which, in most cases, has remained outside the process and held on to its old ways.

My personal experience, after various attempts which always led to problematic results, has recently led me to transform the conventional administration - within an individual commune, that of Gaia (Oporto) - into a mission-orientated administrative body, by regrouping various professional bodies and certain departments into decentralised territorial units, co-ordinated by team leaders who have been given a sufficient degree of responsibility. It must be said that this experiment is very recent and that, in the initial phase, the responsibilities of the decentralised teams are confined to rather physical domains: planning, public spaces, active negotiation with the promoters, mobilisation of local forces and resources. The social and cultural action modules will come after this attempt at reform has gone through a period of consolidation.

What is at stake in this experiment therefore goes beyond the motivation of 'special' teams for local development, and involves the whole issue of motivation in the public services in general, its capacity to take on multi-sectoral actions, to learn from experience, to make contact with players on the ground - in short, to attain a greater legitimacy for formal local democracy.

4.2 In the second place, as regards the broader mobilisation of resources and solidarity, effective formulae must be found to achieve results on a local level, where public projects and private investments cannot be dissociated from each other.

A recent trend among 'poverty' programmes, especially in Portugal, has led the authorities to bring together all the possible institutions concerned in 'special' councils, made up of more or less qualified representatives. The formula of these councils only guarantees co-operation at the level of intention, and remains strictly under government control, while the so-called representatives of civil society represent neither the populations concerned nor the private agencies which it is hoped to involve in the operations. At the same time, on the ground, fragile teams with a limited lifespan are at work, and they oscillate continually between promises which cannot guarantee results and counter-authoritarian practices which end up in honourable resignations.

To overcome the weaknesses in this formula, which have already become clear, a strongly associative solution has been tried. In this case, a Foundation has been set up which brings together, in the case under review, the following founding members: the Commune, an autonomous public authority (a port authority) and an association of private companies operating in the project zone. In the case of Gaia - to which I am still referring - the aim is to revitalise and rehabilitate a river port area which has fallen into disuse, an old working-class quarter which is on the verge of ruin and marginalisation, and also the majority of the port wine cellars in Oporto, which today play a major role as a tourist attraction from which the district is hardly benefiting at all. What the Foundation is expected to do is to provide integrated management for all the efforts to reclaim the 'docklands' in economic and cultural terms, and the application of the benefits from different concessions for the use of resources in the public domain for the rehabilitation of the historic area nearby, as well as the occupational training and recycling of the workforce required by the renewal of activities (tourism, leisure, craftwork, etc.).

It must be said that in Portugal there is no significant system for public aid for the rehabilitation of old housing. The Foundation - in which the local population is represented only by the Commune - brings together in a second line of associates the institutions of social solidarity concerned, popular and sporting associations from the area, and other private or public enterprises which it is hoped can be brought into the project. As regards the resources set aside for launching the renewal process, these comprise the riverbank areas - which are in local authority ownership, and can be leased out as commercial concessions - together with a proportion of the profits from port wine companies, under a sponsorship scheme. Later, the Foundation will submit sectoral projects to Community funds and State funds (the 'poverty' programme) which so far have been confined to the opposite side of the river (the town of Oporto).

It is possible that the Foundation formula may evolve into a more autonomous partnership structure (mixed enterprise) while safeguarding, in this case, the municipal responsibilities of a legal nature which, for the time being, the Commune has delegated to the Foundation for the local development of the Ribeira de Gaia, where it holds a majority at management level.

4.3 Thirdly and finally, as regards the process of intervention it is important to ensure, right from the start of operations, that legal and administrative instruments are used as flexibly as possible, whether they are of a budgetary nature or are concerned with town planning. In fact, the success of operations run over a long period and on a multi-sectoral basis, for the revival of ancient or recently built areas, is highly sensitive to the creation and practical implementation of opportunities, and hence to the timing of the various measures adopted. Frequently, technical teams tend to make the launching of actions conditional on the previous preparation of conventional planning instruments, forgetting the more interactive methodologies along the following lines: 'strategies - priority actions - plan or programme - generalisation of actions'. These replace the analytical and forecasting studies from the initial stages, as the later phases involved in the intervention processes are activated. There is a double advantage here: actions involving the mobilisation of resources are speeded up, while on the other hand there is an orientation of studies towards situations – and solutions – which arise as time goes by, and which would probably not be foreseeable. This calls into question the traditional method of starting out by commissioning a plan from a consultancy office which is external to the process.

It is not a question here of denying the validity of plans or projects for intervention – on the contrary, we have seen cases where a visualisation of the results which are sought has proved to be an important instrument in motivating the different actors, especially when one is dealing with plans for public spaces. Rather, it is a matter of bringing these technical instruments of synthesis and formalisation to bear at the most appropriate moments, in accordance with a strategy arising from the participation process – not before that process, still less as an alternative to that process.

FROM DE-URBANISATION TO RE-URBANISATION?
SPATIAL CHALLENGES FOR A CONTEMPORARY URBAN CULTURE

by

André Loeckx
Catholic University of Leuven

1. The City: Masterpiece of European Culture

In a recent paper discussing the creation of a European centre for education, recreation and culture in Belgium, the Belgian historian and theorist Geert Bekaert elaborated upon the essence of European culture. Europe is alive in many countries, regions, landscapes, cities and villages. It manifests itself in multiple, relatively autonomous activities such as art, science, politics, economy, technology. The consciousness of a century-old history still defines Europe's self-image. 'European' is a qualification one recognises but which can never be strictly contained or delimited. It is a fleeting reality, endlessly in search of itself. European culture defines an identity that doesn't cherish itself but develops in a process of continuous negation. It is a project one keeps working on never reaching an end. Such an open, dynamic and critical attitude distinguishes the European culture from many other cultures in the world. One cannot isolate such a culture as a separate entity of human life nor concentrate it in one privileged place. Its continuous striving for renewal, its rejection of dogmatism and its critical attitude precisely originate from a blend of all possible factors and influences relativising and fertilising each other.

The place where such confrontation occurs is the city. A city is not defined in its form and size but by its mental and spatial capability to let the most heterogeneous fragments live together autonomously with and next to one another (1).

The city however is not only a place where culture happens, the packaging that envelops cultural contents ready for consumption. The city on the contrary illustrates a basic principle of European culture, namely that form cannot be dissociated from content. The city is not a collection of sign vehicles each transporting their identifiable message, but rather a matrix of signifiers whose interplay endlessly generates multiple meanings which in turn redefine the matrix itself. The European city is at the same time generated by and generator of, European culture. Such viewpoints complete the generic image of urbanity Aldo Rossi develops in his 'Architettura della Città' (1966).

In Rossi's view the city is architecture, a man-made object built over time and giving form to society. The city and its component parts are artefacts which take shape during a complex process of transformation and permanence comparable to language. Such a city cannot be reduced to a single basic idea; its processes of formation are many and varied. The city, although it constitutes a totality, must be examined in terms of parts '... a unity, a system, made solely of reassembled fragments'. The relationship between parts, artefacts and fragments composing the city is one of analogy. Urban design becomes a combination and transformation, a 'collage' of pre-established elements whereby the significance that springs forth at the end is authentic, unforeseen and original but nevertheless referring to the historical continuity of urban morpho-typology. Such an 'analogous city' is a human artefact with gives form to reality, not only the place of the human condition but itself a part of that condition. The concept of analogy, displaying homogeneity and heterogeneity, defines the European city as a mediating space '..attesting to the tastes and attitudes of generations, to public events and private tragedies, to new and old facts, ...the fixed stage for human events. The collective and the private, society and the individual, balance and confront one another in the city' (2).

2. Urban Space as Counter-Form and Mediating Scale

In this city social and built space constitute dimensions that never define each other completely but which are continuously entangled in an unstable complementarity. Architectural theory repeatedly searched for concepts and metaphors that would make it possible to describe the mutual interaction of people and built spaces without denying the relative autonomy of social life and spatial articulation. The very principle of functionalist thinking, the one-way relationship between form and function, quickly lost ground when not only elementary activities but also more complex social functions had to be taken into account. What Baudvillard announced as 'the beginning of a political economy of signs in architecture' - one signifier (space) tightly corresponding to one signified (function) - seldom achieved more than a simplistic, poor, not even cheap but quite brutal living space (3).

The pattern language by Christopher Alexander presented a much more human neofunctionalist method aiming at a 'timeless quality'. Patterns try to grasp particular parts of the built environment, both in the public and private realm, which were supposed to solve identifiable social, psychological or cultural problems. Multi-disciplinary research has to define a vocabulary of patterns: design involves selection and combination of patterns into a built environment. 'The subculture cell' for instance provides a delimited area for an identifiable group large enough to allow a scale of personal contacts; 'the front door recess' is supposed to regulate the house-street relationship, an important component of the public-private gradient (4).

Already ten years before Alexander's first pattern ideas, the Dutch Team Ten architect Aldo Van Eyck moved away from the deterministic form-function, space-people relationship. Using his 'Otterlo circles', presented at the special CIAM congress in Otterlo 1959, Van Eyck reflected upon the relative autonomy of architecture on the one hand, and social life on the other hand. The ever changing social reality is represented in one circle by the continuously widening and closing spiral movement of a traditional dance performed by Kayapo Indians in Venezuela. The architectural abilities of defining space are illustrated in the other circle by the complementarity of three traditions: modern architecture's capacity of giving form to change and movement, immutability and rest expressed by the great historical tradition and finally the wisdom of settlement ecology brought by the best of vernacular architecture. Both circles do not determine each other; there exists no confusion or collision. Architecture is not 'the three dimensional expression of human behaviour' as expressed by Van Eyck's CIAM colleague Bakema. The relationship between the two circles is one of reciprocity, of interaction, of analogy. Architecture has to provide 'counter-forms' to social life, forms originating from its own plastic and aesthetic means that structurally support the logics of society (5).

The idea of material 'supports' enabling but not determining, modes of inhabitation constitutes the main component of John Habraken's double scale theory. 'Supports' refer to the long-term, durable, non-individual core of a dwelling environment, asking for considerable investment, large-scale technology, formal planning. Supports are completed by 'infills' i.e. the short-term, changing, individual alterations involving current costs, small-scale technology, even informal planning. A living environment necessarily contains both support structures and infill components. The 'Stichting Architecten Research' (SAR) elaborated Habraken's vision into a design methodology for open prefabrication. Later on, applying the idea on an urban scale, the SAR presented its tissue models based on the interweaving of permanent zones and flexible margins (6).

The concept of complementary scales also forms the basis of Donlyn Lyndon's viewpoints. Good urban life occurs where architectural forms act as 'mediating scales' supporting 'powers of inhabitation' - opportunities to make alterations, to invest care, to choose conditions of enclosure and gathering. Such forms relate unforeseen, spontaneous, particular inhabitation to a collective identity, to a more enduring order. Lyndon preferably identifies mediating scales in European historical urban centres: piazzas, arches, facades, courtyards. The author agrees with warnings by Richard Sennett and Alexander Tzonis who pointed to the impoverishment brought about by the absence within contemporary urban design of public forms which can be appropriated (7).

Whatever the concepts and metaphors might be - patterns, counter-forms, supports, tissues, mediating scales - the synergism and symbols of people, forms, functions and activities are obvious but fundamental characteristics of European urbanity as far as the historical city is concerned.

The city at the same time forms and is formed by society. Hence transforming conditions of society can always be identified in the built space either as cause or as consequence. Until recently, the European city seemed to be capable of absorbing societal shock waves such as industrialisation, rural-urban migration, world war, recession, emigration. The interplay between society and city certainly did not occur without radical ruptures and through transformations but however without questioning its very urbanity as locus and focus of 'public events and private tragedies'. Periods of urban degradation, even decomposition, are followed by urbanistical 'retour à l'ordre' movements. In the middle of the 19th century, Haussmann equipped the obsolete tissue of Paris, affected by overcrowding, insalubrity and political turmoil, with a new spatial order, a higher technology and a more efficient management defining in this way the outline of the prestigious 19th century bourgeois 'Grosstadt'. Team Ten texts of the 1950s, populist participatory and advocacy planning in the 1960s and the 'Reconstruction of the City' movements in the 1980s - such as IBA 1984 in Berlin - heavily criticised the modernist decomposition of the city into mono-functional repetitive schemes. The city was restored as a place of multiple interaction between public and private events taking place in neighbourhoods, on boulevards and in squares.

More recently modern architecture rediscovered it role to catch the contradictory forces of the modern city so as to 'increase the potential energy of modern urban places', to quote Zaha Hadid. Through all its stages of formation the urban space seems to enhance complexity and contradiction. However, historical selection and the power of urban morphology help the European city to contain disruptive forces. A contradictory urban space still acts as counter-form of a contradictory society. The architecture of the city still mediates the city dwellers' inscription in modern society.

In scarcely twenty-five years however, a number of phenomena, originating from the 19th century and gradually developed during the 20th century, seemed to accelerate, turning the city inside-out as a social and built space and as a medium fostering modern culture. Two phenomena will be highlighted.

3. Challenging Urbanity: The Sprawling Peripheries

The traditional bipolarity between city and rural areas was for centuries one of the fundamental characteristics of European settlement history. Although many interactions and combinations existed, urbanity and rurality defined two spheres of existence encompassing their particular culture, behaviour, world view, economy, power relations and their particular built environment. Such bipolarity, however, is increasingly disappearing because of the generalisation of a third type of built space covering a continuously expanding area between the historical urban centre and the traditional rural landscape and village. The third sphere moreover affects the remaining pure ends of the bipolar system: the intramural city centre, the remaining rural enclaves and nature reserves. This in-between space bears no name and is vaguely designated as 'periphery' although it spreads far beyond the actual urban fringes. It does not refer to a particular type of environment but comprises different kinds of constellations without apparent common characteristics. Some of these do not even appear as constellations. Often terms of reference are missing. Geography, regional planning and architecture have something of a blind spot where the periphery is concerned.

The 19th century industrial suburbs are probably the best known part of the periphery. Factories and infrastructures were located in the city outskirts and working-class communities grew up around them. This near-by periphery - the urban quarters on the other side of the canal or railway line - is now characterised by a dense mixture of old housing stock, largely abandoned factories, warehouses and worn-out infrastructures. Social cohesion and identity of the area were in many cases based on a once dominating factory, now subdivided or abandoned. The area offers a reserve of cheap housing inhabited by an ageing native or a growing immigrant population.

Many of the late 19th and early 20th century middle class suburbs are still attractive residential areas. In fact, the residential suburb continuously expanded, particularly owing to almost general car ownership since the golden sixties. Extensive residential areas, varying in social status from lower-middle to upper class, exist around most European cities. Recent instant subdivisions lack the style and care of former residential suburbs such as the open garden estates of the twenties. The styleless small villa, endlessly duplicated in monotonous streets and mono-functional neighbourhoods, nevertheless represents the most popular dwelling ideal.

Satellite settlements are disconnected from the urban fabric - city centre and immediate suburbs - but are linked to it by rail and road and are functionally highly dependent on the centre. Planned satellite towns were designed by public authorities as large-scale, low-rent housing projects during the post-war period. The drawbacks are well-known but unsolved: inadequate amenities, high maintenance costs, monotonous living environments, lack of identity, marginality. Small towns and villages situated along major traffic arteries to a central city developed from relatively self-contained communities into dependent commuter towns, another type of satellite.

Ribbon developments along main trunk roads are no recent phenomenon. They consist of irregular strips of various house types mixed with small business of all kinds. The extension of strip formations along secondary and even rural roads, however, became much more general in past decades especially in areas with a poorly defined planning tradition. A recent development is the commercial strip. Booming commercial enterprises mainly involved in mass consumption (hypermarkets, furniture stores, garden centres, textile stores, shoe shops, car dealers, garages, etc.) are setting up alongside major road connections, avoiding the land prices and access problems of the city centre. Industrial and administrative complexes are following this trend. The road no longer has the sole function of linking urban centres but is increasingly attracting urban activities. However, such strip developments are geared purely to the requirements of accessibility, visibility and expansion. No real public place is emerging. Strips are disconnected from their immediate surroundings; their exclusive orientation towards a motorised clientele reduces the open space to parking lots and transit corridors. The sign of the most visible hypermarket replaces the former local landmarks.

Urban functions, both dwelling and non-dwelling, are spreading over the former rural areas attracted by availability of land, access and mobility and the absence of regulations. Villages and landscapes are gradually being eroded by suburban sprawl: privately built houses, residential services, craft industries, small industrial estates, mass commercial centres and leisure centres. They sprawl on an ad hoc basis in enclaves, along strips, in hasty subdivisions. The resulting nebulae are fragmented areas, disjointed, indefinable conglomerates where the most diverse land use elements exist side-by-side without any relation to one another to or a greater whole. A coherent spatial structure is lacking. Quick replacement of names and shapes makes even a visual identification quite difficult.

However, such developments can also give rise to network configurations: poly-nuclear structures with activities concentrated at well-defined points, connected by quick roads forming constellations which again start to lend a structure to their surroundings. Some major infrastructure nodal points - motorway junctions, airports, rail terminals - may attract the development of specific amenities: hotels, congress centres, exhibition halls, care hire firms, etc. A real new centre may arise, fulfilling a number of functions which have become impossible in the inner city, but which can also enter into competition with it.

In general, the phenomenon of de-urbanisation of the inner city and sub-urbanisation of the former countryside generates all kinds of superpositions and juxtapositions without achieving true urban symbiosis. This historical European city is a conglomerate of interacting fragments within a constraining morphological framework resulting in a complexity which confers a marked added value to the whole. The city forms a whole which is more than the sum of its constituent parts. In this part-whole relationship, monuments and public places acting as mediating scales, play a primary role. In the periphery, the divergent fragments do not interact but co-exist independently. A strong morphological structure, formed by history, loaded with memory and identity, is missing. In the periphery, the whole is therefore less than the sum of its parts. The fragment is not a reminder of a specific history, quotation of a general text, but an alien body, dropped in an unknown space, seeking its own survival. Vagueness due to careless random combination of heterogeneous components, isotropy due to the lack of structure and the shapeless gathering of ever similar elements and pure fragmentation are the characteristics of the new periphery.

Related to these phenomena, the concepts of 'centre' are changing. Centrality includes concentration, availability in one place, accessibility. Electronic communication, mechanical traffic and traffic congestion have disrupted the traditional correspondence between proximity - availability near one place - and accessibility. Peripheral nodal points may be more accessible than central ones; distant points connected by free flowing traffic arteries can be 'closer' than neighbouring points separated by traffic jams. Fax machines and computers are unaffected by distance.

Where centrality and geometric centre are no longer synonymous, a distinction has to be made between 'peripheral location' and 'peripheral condition'. A peripheral location means distance from the urban centre as a geometric middle point. A peripheral condition is characterised by the absence of centrality. This can be the result of different factors such as decline of an existing centre or disconnection with regard to emerging centralities. Peripheral condition means marginalisation. In any case the shifting centrality related to de-urbanisation and sub-urbanisation involves the increase of a peripheral condition in the inner city, the old suburb and the new periphery. Within the urban realm this leads to impoverishment of the functional fabric, characterised by the synergy of multiple functions, to physical degradation of both public and private places, to social marginalisation and to loss of cultural pride and identity. In the new periphery, this peripheral condition is expressed by the spread of a chaotic built space and the absence of public places as mediating scales, by insufficient connections and facilities and by socio-cultural marginalisation of a new kind. This new marginalisation particularly affects those already less mobile and less informed sections of the population unable to mobilise the physical, financial and intellectual means necessary to make use of commercial and public service networks spread over a large area.

However, this paper does not wish to present an apocalyptic doomsday vision. Shifting centrality is an irreversible and unstable phenomenon which certainly entails negative implications. But rejection of sterile stability and incorporation of societal changes into creative transformations have always been the basis of European culture. The periphery at the same time is a dumping ground of the broken city and the laboratory of a new, non-dogmatic and as yet unknown urbanity (8).

4. Challenging Urbanity: From Space to Network

A second phenomenon of societal transformation affecting urbanity itself has to do with the impact of a new kind of spacio-functional organisation: the network. The young Belgian philosopher Bart Verschaffel discusses the generalisation of a common type of experience related to a new kind of space in modern daily life. In traditional world view, man dwells in the world. The act of dwelling, based on defining and appropriating a centre and a familiar circle, becomes the root metaphor of living in the world. The house - and by extension the cathedral, the village square, the intramural city - offers a tangible archetype representing man's being in the world. Society and its spatial counter-forms are made up of centres and circles. Figures of such a 'topical' appropriation of the world as inhabitable space always found counterbalance in figures of 'a-topical' experiences: the desert, the forest, the drifter where man's destiny is not one of home-making or home-coming but one of wandering. In early modern culture, the 'Großstadt' and the 'flaneur' became figures representing man's incapacity to dwell in the modern alienating and contradictory world. In Verschaffel's opinion networks constitute a recent, less mythical and much more general version of a-topical experience. It is almost impossible to imagine modern life without networks of all kinds: road networks, metro, bus, water supply, postal services, telephone and fax, chain stores and fast food outlets, mail order firms, TV, computer... all of them are constituted by circuits and terminals. A network is a system of connections between points aiming at the transfer or diffusion of people, objects or signs. Networks try to offer goods, services and information as quickly as possible at any place using fast connections and reproductions. They aim for the immediate and complete accessibility and availability of everything, everywhere, and thus try to dissolve time, distance, space, scarcity and waiting. In the perfect network principle, even the modernist sensation of speed - moving quickly through different spaces - disappears. The immediate availability of everything, everywhere allows the network user to reduce his mobility i.e. the necessity of moving to many places in order to fulfil his needs.

Networks replace centres and circles. Networks take no account of streets and houses, they only consider trajectories and addresses. Networks don't recognise residents, house-mates, neighbours, fellow townspeople or colleagues, but deal with large numbers of individual subscribers, clients and customers. Verschaffel furthermore distinguishes on the one hand 'imperfect Networks' which transfer people and matter, and therefore are somehow linked to places (stores, metro stations, post offices) and, on the other hand, 'perfect networks' such as telephone, computer, TV, which carry signs, images, hard information. Perfect networks to a large extent are a-topical. Locations required by imperfect networks become very common in modern cityscape. However, they do not form circles, enclosures or rooms in which one dwells. They offer the minimal equipment needed to enter and use the network. They are passageways to destination, utility space, not places to stay. Most perfect networks (TV, computer) on the other hand are not even accessible by the human body. Programs and channels define only a space in abstract and imaginary terms. When the network operates, the place where the terminal stands disappears and the user mentally enters the spaceless channel. Subscribers are not supposed to enter headquarters, exchanges or studios which command the network, but are however not present in it. Verschaffel analyses how networks at the same time connect and isolate the individual addresses. The fact that most Networks address large numbers of individual users who can use them simultaneously does not mean the networks define a real public realm. However, the imaginary public realm created by networks increasingly replaces real public culture (9).

The urban culture of public space is based on physical meeting, gathering, presence. Markets and fora concentrate ideas, messages, goods, services and experiences in one important place to which people go and participate in one way or another. Galleries, boulevards and facades mediate with varying intensity between the individual experience and the enduring order. Powers of inhabitation allow residents to alter within certain margins, the boundaries between the public and private realm, between absence and presence on the public scene.

The network culture breaks up the urban mass, guaranteeing the powers of inhabitation, into individual subscribers. The network defines strict rules of use; otherwise one has to keep out. Mediation is not relevant, altering boundaries is impossible. Transitory network places have to attract and service people (and urge them to leave quickly afterwards), not support them in any form of inhabitation or participation. Networks are not counter-forms supporting social life. They induce pre-programmed take-it-or-leave-it actions by customers who do not want to take part in the establishment of the network. The most perfect example, the multichannel TV, replaces the urban forum of streets, squares, cafés and theatres with an imaginary public scene.

Networks spread over both city and periphery. Business districts combine network places in which thousands of people may be served without creating one public place of event. Large distances and dispersal of facilities in sprawling nebular peripheries offer another suitable terrain for a-topical networks. Video, TV, telephone, mail order, all introduce a culture of dispersal in the vague, isotropic and fragmented non-urban non-rural realm.

Street, square, neighbourhood, tower, factory and quay decreasingly act as supports of identity, pride and belonging. In principle, everyone is free to use public space. The spatial articulation of the European inner city offers places for every age and status. Networks on the contrary mostly operate on a commercial basis and within sets of rules that cannot be negotiated. A certain amount of knowledge and financial capacity is essential to play the game. A new threat of marginalisation comes to the fore.

5. Re-urbanisation and the Design of Public Spaces

The growth of peripheries and the development of networks are closely related to a tendency of de-urbanisation affecting urban space and culture. Urban planning, urban design and architecture have no ready-made answer to these phenomena. Return to a closed pre-industrial, urban culture and urban form made up of centres and circles is out of the question. As both phenomena, periphery and networks, seem irreversible, at least to a considerable degree, it is preferable not to consider them as absolute obstacles but to examine carefully the new condition they create in order to identify starting points for appropriate intervention.

The general objective of design sounds clear enough: to induce spatial structures and components that again allow for identification; to guarantee a public realm which enables open mediation between the general and the particular, between the public and the private; to stimulate the powers of inhabitation of a large majority of residents against a passive and discriminatory consumption.

The scope of the city can no longer be limited to the former intramural centre. However vague it may look, the sprawling periphery, together with the old suburbs and the inner city (all affected by de-urbanisation), has become an integral part of the contemporary urban realm requesting our attention. Reflecting upon another scale of urban experience, upon another articulation of urban function and another morpho-typology has become essential.

It goes without saying that in the first place the deterioration or misuse of existing public spaces in the inner city should be stopped. Squares and green spots are often turned into car parks and residential streets are used as transit corridors. The issue is a very common one; solutions are, however, in many cities, still restricted to a few areas of commercial or high historical value. In some of those cases an anxious conservation attitude or an over-articulation of design reduces the capacity of public places to act as a support for a wide range of activities. Powerful mediating scales have a certain archetypical rigour capable of stimulating and surviving acts of inhabitation which inevitable alter the outward appearance.

In most inner city fabrics large underdeveloped or deteriorated areas exist as a result or by-product of major events in urban history. New public spaces can be introduced, the design of which need not imitate, in an inevitably less prestigious way, the well known 19th century typologies of boulevards, parks and squares. New public spaces should try to translate modern urban functions - traffic, publicity, office space, etc. - into inhabitable forms. Although the final outcome was not successful, several design proposals for the so-called 'Crossroad Europe' - a huge fragmented traffic node in the heart of Brussels - illustrate this issue (10).

In the old periphery - the 19th century industrial suburbs - a dense fabric of old factories, warehouses, cheap housing and worn-out infrastructures apparently leaves no room for intervention. However, the dismantling of a factory, the destruction of a dilapidated group of houses or the sale of a neglected domain may suddenly create a new opportunity in a particular spot. Moreover, the bad status of the neighbourhood keeps land values low in an area near the prestigious inner city and near the dynamic outer periphery. The spot available for intervention is often situated in the middle of a dense, irregular and functionally mixed fabric so that easy, well-known solutions are not applicable and new articulations of the public-private gradient have to be tested. Very recently several municipalities in Belgium began the preparation of pilot projects in such areas and therefore organised design competitions. The outcome of the competition in Kortrijk offers a good example of the potentials hidden in such forgotten suburban locations (11).

The necessary re-use or renewal of traffic infrastructures defines a problematic issue of much larger scale in the old periphery. Canals, railways and, later on ring roads and major penetration axes, crosscut the periphery to reach the immediate urban fringe. Along the banks and siding all kinds of equipment, workshops and warehouses emerged which, at the present, are largely under-used or even in ruins. The renewal of these infrastructures and their surroundings needs heavy investment. This could be attracted by the redevelopment of large areas of well- situated and relatively cheap urban land. Again the unusual character of the area calls for imaginative proposals. The operation addresses itself to very diverse partners with interests in different urban functions: housing, business, leisure. Redevelopment proposals have to take into account the interrelation of divergent functions as much as the structuring role of the new public domain. The study for the redevelopment of the old canal zone in Leuven, ordered by the municipality, shows the scale and the prime targets of this innovative kind of urban design (12).

Defining appropriate means for the spatial organisation of the vague and chaotic outer periphery is a complex design objective since it crosscuts the domains of architecture, urban design and regional planning. Starting from a detailed study of local conditions and from an evaluation of local opportunities, a long-term strategy of stressing existing and introducing new, structuring features has to be elaborated. Articulating secondary centralities (landmarks, public places, points of attraction), emphasising boundaries, stressing distinctive features of landscapes and dwelling tissues, and improving accessibility should by means of differentiation and mobility, add to the creation of another type of synergism of people and functions. The issue of centrality has to be reconsidered in the old city centre and in the periphery. Both inner centres deserted by a number of functions in favour of the periphery, and the emerging peripheral centres attracting mass functions but lacking public places, should gain a new role within a better structured regional network of recognisable places, accessible by improved mobility. Such networks will gradually replace the undifferentiated nebulae. The result of an international commission for the redevelopment of the southern periphery of Kortrijk, organised by the municipality and by the inter-municipal development agency, illustrates a designful way of rethinking the architecture of the contemporary urban realm (13).

Generally speaking, the revaluation of public space constitutes a key component in the struggle against de-urbanisation by defining an appropriate urbanity both for the old centre and for the periphery. At the same time it seems for the present the only way architecture can contribute to a counter-move against the generalisation of a spaceless network culture. Moreover, architecture should not avoid the often despised topical network places (bus terminals, gas stations, supermarkets), but on the contrary transform them into recognisable public areas. Considered as architectural objects even certain a-topical terminals (phone booths, banking machines) can eventually contribute to the revaluation of public places.

The issues raised by de-urbanisation and the emergence of a network culture can certainly not be solved by means of design. It would be a denial of the autonomous and relative status of architecture. Often design only performs minor corrections to societal problems, in several cases it hides or even reinforces tendencies of decultivation. However, at its best, good architecture offers a counter-form, a scale of mediation, a support for cultural acts.

We believe that in so-called post-modern times this role is still a valid one.

REFERENCES

1. Bekaert, Geert, (1990). Trefpunt Europa. De stad als metafoor voor een themapark, In: <u>Archis 8-90</u>, 47-51.
2. Rossi, Aldo, (1982). <u>The Architecture of the City</u>, MIT Press, Cambridge (1966), p. 21,22,34,86,100,169 and Rossi, Aldo, (1981), <u>A Scientific Autobiography</u>, MIT Press, Cambridge, 8.
3. Baudrillard, Jean, (1972). <u>Pour une Critique de L'èconomie Politique du Signe</u>, Gallimard, Paris, 230-233.
4. Alexander, Christopher, (1979). <u>The Timeless Way of Building</u>, Oxford University Press, New York, and Alexander, Christopher, et al (1971). <u>Houses Generated by Patterns</u>, Centre for Environmental Structure, Berkeley.
5. Strauven, Francis, (1986). <u>Aldo Van Eyck, De Gestalte Van De Relativiteit</u>, unpublished doctoral thesis, Katholieke Universitelt van Leuven (K.U. Leuven), 250-251.
6. Habraken, John, (1972). <u>Supports: An Alternative to Mass Housing</u>, The Architectural Press, London (1961) and Stichting Architecten Research, SAR-73. Het methodisch formuleren van afspraken bij het ontwerpen van weefsels, Eindhoven, 1973.
7. Lyndon, Donlyn, (1981). Mediating Scale, Middle Ground for Participation, in: J. Schreurs, M. Smets, L. Janssens, (eds.), <u>Leuven Seminar on Participatory Design</u>, Acco, Leuven, and Lyndon, Donlyn, et al, (1977). <u>Powers of Inhabitation: Observations in the Via Monserrato</u>, MIT, Department of Argiculture, Grunsfeld Program, Rome.
8. Heynen, Hilde, Loeckx, André, and Smets, Marcel, (1990). The Periphery: an exploratory study, in: <u>Green Paper on the Urban Environment</u>. Expert Contributions, Commission of the European Communities, Brussels-Luxembourg, 19-30.
9. Verschaffel, Bart, (1990). De kring en het netwerk. Over het statuut van de 'publieke rulmte', in: Masschelein, Jan, (ed.), <u>Opvoeding in de stad. Maatschappelljke ultdagingen aan de pedogogiek</u>, Acco, Leuven, 47-58.
10. Loeckx, André, (1989). 20 jaar ontwerpen voor het Europakrulspunt te Brussel, overzicht en kritiek, in: <u>Monumenten en landschappen 8/2</u>, maart-april, 29-48.
11. Dubois, Marc, (1991). Ontwerpen voor een verkrotte Kortrijkse buurt, en Vermuulen Paul, De Smet Henk, et al., Architektuur-wedstrijd Sint Denijsstraat-Zwevegemstraat Kortrijk, in: <u>Stichting Architektuur-museum 91.01</u>, 24-27, Gent.
12. Uyttenhove, Pieter, (1991). De verbeelding van de werkelijkheid. Ontwikkelingsplan voor de Vaartkom in Leuven, in: <u>Archis 5-91</u>, 24-31.
13. Bekaert, Geert, Debaere, Karel, and Jult, Herman, (eds.), (1990). <u>Hoog Kortrijk, Multiple Urban Development Commission</u>, Interkommunale Leledal, Kortrijk.

APPROACHES TOWARDS INTEGRATION OF URBAN FUNCTIONS AND SOCIAL GROUPS IN CITIES: THE SUPPORTIVE ROLE OF ENVIRONMENTAL DESIGN AND BUILDING POLICIES

Tjeerd Deelstra[*]
International Institute for the Urban Environment
Delft

A mixture of the functions (economic and cultural activities stimulating each other) and social mix (different kinds of people living and working together) is vital to cities.

Functional and social mix makes commuting less necessary (with positive impacts on the environment) and reduces vandalism and crime (social control).

In some innovative projects in European cities, a well-balanced re-division of living costs is aimed for by the creation of new organisational structures at neighbourhood level (co-operatives for instance). This makes it possible for people of different income levels to live in the same street, and increases the involvement of people with each other and with their physical living environment.

Some cities in Europe have experimented with new ideas of local economy. The principle of local economy rests on residents having maximum influence on the financial and economic business of the district. Only then can they themselves decide on how to spend their own, and government, funds. In many cases, it is very advantageous for residents to organise themselves. This can eventually lead to making environmentally sound construction affordable.

The political guideline for these activities is that from environmental, social, economic and political points of view, it makes good sense to use taxpayers' money to create new markets, jobs and training places.

The paper mentions 12 points of attention within 3 areas of response, in order to develop supportive urban design and planning systems, based on experiences in projects that serve as 'examples of good practice'.

A survey and evaluation of approaches and developments in projects of the kind referred to in cities in EC countries would be helpful in developing a further European policy on social coherence, integrated in policies to improve the urban environment.

SOCIAL CONFLICTS AND THE LIMITS OF URBAN POLICIES IN GREECE

Panayiotis Getimis[*]
Pantion University of Social and Political Science
Athens

Urban policies depend upon both the general orientation of state policy and the limitations imposed through social reality itself. In this context, and through the evolution of the forms of urban policies in Greece, it is possible to examine: i) the conditions of urban policy formation, ii) the intervention of vested interests and their cross engagement at the local and supra-local level, iii) the contradictions and limits of urban policies, concerning the 'resistances' from social groups in the urban areas in Greece, especially Athens.

These issues will be studied from the point of view of the confrontation over the possession and use of urban space between various social agents (e.g. landowners, house owners, squatters etc.). This confrontation is not directly reflected in state policies, but consists of economic and social interests intermingled at various levels of complexity.

Furthermore, it is important to stress the limits of the reform intended in the 1980s and the efforts to implement a comprehensive urban and housing development policy that includes the principles of decentralisation, democratic participation and local autonomy. The limitations of this reform mainly depended on the existing interests in building and land development which were incorporated within the new institutional agents (e.g. local councils).

ECOLOGICAL URBAN RESTRUCTURING

Ekhart Hahn
Wissenschaftszentrum Berlin

Cities are 'built thought'; they represent the most materialised form of the relation between society and environment. Thus, in a special sense, cities worldwide have become a symbol of the environmental crisis, of the transformation of valuable natural resources into waste and pollutants.

Cities, however, have also always been places of innovation. Solutions emanate from people whose living conditions are threatened. Many signs indicate that the time is ripe for basic changes in production and consumption processes, in people's attitudes and behaviour, and also in the built structures of cities.

This paper, therefore, introduces the concept of 'Ecological Urban Restructuring'. The concept was theoretically developed and empirically tested in an international comparative research project. The four main elements of the concept are:

1. The 'eight ecological orientations': these were compiled as topical guidelines, that is as a basis for discussions on concrete projects, strategies and individual measures.

2. The 'model of fields of activity and modules': this model was developed as an overview of possible activities and measures on the topic of ecological urban restructuring which are possible today. It is an aid for thought and work while dealing with the contradiction of the continued existence of sectorally oriented professional planning, political and administrative departments, on the one hand, and the necessity of new 'integrated' thought and action, on the other.

3. The 'conception of ecological neighbourhood development': neighbourhoods which are comprehensible for their inhabitants have been discovered to be the most important level of action for ecological urban restructuring. Multiple possibilities towards networking individual measures to integrated concepts with the participation of the inhabitants and other local agents are possible here. Through decentralised local networking, individual measures become ecologically effective, economically viable, socially acceptable and politically realistic.

4. The 'concept eco-station': eco-stations represent an indispensable infrastructural prerequisite for the process of ecological urban restructuring. They should be ecologically oriented communication, culture and trade centres which are funded by local authorities. The establishment of a network of decentralised eco-stations is proposed which will have an exchange at the national and international levels and thus represent the infrastructure for local and international tasks of urban ecological restructuring.

KNOWLEDGE-BASED DEVELOPMENT

Richard V. Knight*
Urbinno Network
London

This paper considers the role of knowledge-based development and how strengthening the knowledge infrastructure and improving the quality of life in cities can contribute to sustainable development. The paper draws from the author's recent experience conducting research on the nature of knowledge-based development in several European cities and focuses on creating conditions for knowledge-based development, i.e. on the needs of citizens seeking access to opportunity in the knowledge sector and of organisations seeking to position themselves in the Single European Market.

Historically, cities served as centres of civilisations; they were the primary civilising force and they evolved as civic cultures. With industrialisation, urbanisation and the creation of nation states, the role of cities changed; they grew by accommodating manufacturing and became production centres serving the national production system. In the process, they lost control over their development; power became increasingly centralised at the national level and cities became increasingly dependent on national policies and programmes. Now, with industry being globalised and restructured at a European level, cities can no longer depend on national governments for resources and leadership in creating employment opportunities in the production sector; they must find new ways to create wealth.

The processes of renewal and concentration of cities must incorporate new sources and new forms of wealth creation such as the growing role of knowledge resources and knowledge-based activities. Knowledge resources are strategic because wealth creation is becoming increasingly knowledge-intensive and knowledge tends to be deeply rooted in the local culture. In short, the knowledge-base is the new economic base of cities and needs to be recognised as such. Cities must, therefore, strengthen their knowledge-base and improve the quality of life so they can accommodate new types of work, new types of careers and new lifestyles.

Knowledge-based development is also desirable from a social welfare point of view. The knowledge-base not only has great development potentials, it can also provide continuity and stability to a city's economy. Unlike industrial production, which grows rapidly in its early stages of development but then becomes cyclical, footloose, easily relocated and consequently, an increasingly uncertain source of opportunity, knowledge-based activities evolve slowly and steadily as complex cultures which create new values which makes them difficult to replicate or to transplant. This type of development will not, however, continue accidentally; knowledge resources have to be securely anchored by the city and integrated into the mainstream culture, economy and policy of the city and its region. The merging of cultures is never easy, knowledge cultures are no exception.

The challenge for cities is to conserve their knowledge resources. The question is how? Part of the answer lies in the fact that, as knowledge-based activities develop, they become increasingly sensitive to their milieu and increasingly dependent on other actors in the city for creating conditions conducive to their development. Up to a certain point, knowledge-based activities are able to operate fairly independently of their surroundings by creating their own settings, science parks, or technopoles. As they become more advanced and more specialised, their environment becomes more important because they must be able to attract talent from other cities, they must be able to offer a quality of life which is competitive with other clients.

Moreover, the knowledge sector functions better when it is well integrated into the local culture, not just in a physical or spatial sense but integrated into the social fabric, psychologically and aesthetically. That knowledge resources are culture-based does not mean they are well integrated into the local culture; the dominant culture may even inhibit the development of new values and new mentalities. The city or region may not even be aware of their presence or of their importance. There are many different types of knowledge, some are of a formalised nature, others are informal. As knowledge advances, it tends to become increasingly specialised and , as this happens communications between different specialisations or disciplines become increasingly difficult. Consequently, knowledge-based activities can have proximity without propinquity. Different types of knowledge resources can be present in an area or region without there being any synergy between them. The milieu has to be right if synergies are to be realised. In short, a knowledge-infrastructure has to be built, investments have to be made to create new institutional linkages, to open up the city, and to improve the intellectual infrastructure and the quality of life in the city. The shift to a learning-based society oriented towards knowledge from an industrial society oriented to production requires a fundamental rethinking about the role of the city and its citizens and about the nature of city development. Cities can no longer count on national policies and programmes to protect them from technological and market forces which are becoming increasingly global in nature. Cities have to become wilful and pro-active; in short, they have to reassert their role as a civilising force.

Cities have to be transformed into innovative and intentional places. Cities have to learn how to humanise technology and to create high quality living and working environments. They must make the transition, from accidental growth based on the exploitation of locational or natural advantages and the requirements of industrial capital to intentional development based on man-made advantages, i.e. on their human and cultural resources and on their built environment.

The idea of knowledge-based development is presented as a framework for rethinking the role of cities and conceptualising city development in qualitative and non-material terms - as a way of focusing attention on the need to create new types of advantages through prudent investments in knowledge and cultural resources and by creating environments conducive to learning, innovation and creativity. Developing and valorising local knowledge resources does not mean turning cities into high-tech environments or buildings technopoles or new types of planned cities such as the multi-functionalpolis or technopolises as some nations are doing, but rather to humanise the cities and to make them more liveable and intentional so knowledge remains rooted in the city.

To become intentional, European cities must define their role in the context of the 'New Europe'. They can gain insights into the special nature of their knowledge-base and its development potentials by carefully assessing knowledge resources based in the region and identifying those attributes of their environment which are critical to the specific types of knowledge-based development which are occurring locally. Knowledge-based development is basically a collective learning process; an ongoing dialogue among all the actors in the city and region is essential. Such a process has to be open and well-orchestrated and participants have to be given the opportunity of becoming well informed about the issues. Communications between locally-based organisations, citizens and public administrators have be constructive so that collective intentions can be articulated, a civic vision created and strategic decisions made so that the city can position itself in the New Europe.

All cities have potentials for knowledge-based development and such development is sustainable but knowledge resources require careful conservations and constant renewal. Knowledge is a quality not a commodity; knowledge resources have to be carefully nurtured over time and securely anchored by integrating knowledge-based activities and knowledge workers into the city. Knowledge resources have to be continuously valorised which means that knowledge has to be diffused in order to increase its value and talent has to be attracted to the city so that the knowledge can be passed on and advanced by succeeding generations. The paper explores how a residential strategy can be used to anchor knowledge resources and make the city more intentional.

IMPROVEMENT OF THE ENVIRONMENT AND SOCIAL INTEGRATION IN URBAN AREAS

Alexander S. Matrosov[*]
Moscow City Government

---

1. Brief description of Losini Ostrov Park (Elk Island Park).

2. Brief historical outline of the position with regard to conservation of the territory situated in Losini Ostrov Park.

3. Living conditions of a major bio-geo-econosis in the highly urbanized ecosystem.

    - Living conditions of flora.
    - Living conditions of fauna.

    Fundamental principles of management of business activities.

    - Combining the interests of the city and of nature in a sensible manner.

4. Measures to restore the environment and preserve the national park.

    - Removal of companies that disrupt the environment and changing their range of activities.
    - Segregation, within the framework of the national park, of conservation zones, leisure areas and special conservation zones and the activities therein.
    - Introduction of elements of ecological monitoring.
    - Resolution of urban development problems.
    - Participation of public organisations and local residents in the restoration of the national park's ecosystem.
    - The national park's work in increasing ecological awareness in the whole city.

5. Basic conclusions.

CONCLUSIONS, RECOMMENDATIONS

by

Sten Engelstoft
Institute of Geography
University of Copenhagen

Being the last of five working groups to report, it is worthwhile noticing that none of the first four rapporteurs mentioned the word 'URBAN' or 'CITY' explicitly. The approaches to the discussions in each of the various groups has, so it seems, been predominantly sectoral. We have thus heard reports respectively on transport, housing, crime etc. One might thus be tempted to ask the question whether specific 'urban problems' actually exist or whether in fact we are really considering various problems in an urban context?

Contrary to this, the discussions in group 5 took the heterogeneity and the diversity of 'the urban space' as their starting point. David Harvey, by the example of Tompkins Square in New York, so eloquently described this diversity in his background paper for the conference. It thus seemed as if the mixity of co-existence (of functions) is a key feature of urbanity. In fact the chairman of the group, René Schoonbrodt, put it rather strongly in saying that to him the city would cease to exist if the diversity and mixity of it disappeared.

The urban mixity and heterogeneity reflected itself in the papers presented in the group. Two types of papers were presented, namely (1) a series of presentations where focus was on specific issues, i.e. to solve specific problems in an urban context, and (2) a series of presentations with a more conceptual approach.

1. Specific Approaches:

* Integration of urban functions and social groups in cities.
* The supportive role of environmental design and building policies.
* Social conflicts and the limits of social and political science.
* Ecological approaches and community actions (i.e. grass-roots or bottom-up approaches).

The general discussion revealed that even though the group felt that 'bottom-up approaches', citizen participation and community actions within urban development are important factors, these actions have a tendency to promote a 'middle class' approach. Community actions thus have a tendency to support the ambitions of 'the ruling class' and as such they do not promote a true urban social justice. Their functions are consequently more than anything to legitimise market forces.

2. Conceptual Approaches:

* Knowledge-based development.
* Spatial challenges and opportunities for a new urban culture.
* The rural-urban realm.
* From de-urbanisation to re-urbanisation, the urban space.

The general discussion concentrated on one main theme, namely the problem of urbanity i.e. what is urban? On one side the very real problems on the fragmentation of the urban space developed through de-urbanisation and creating a non-urban non-rural space. On the other side the idea of a specific and individual urban knowledge-base embedded in the heritage and history of each individual city: it was suggested that the successful future of our cities is closely related to the ability of the cities to promote, sustain and develop their knowledge-base.

3. Conclusions

The diversity of the problems discussed made it quite clear that the actual problems which emerge in an urban context are of a highly complex and thus complicated nature: no one individual problem can be solved independently of others.

If we are to develop an effective management of urban resources on the local and European scale it is essential to take a holistic perspective within an international development framework. An explicitly formulated European urban policy and institutional framework is the inevitable corollary of an integrated market. This would provide the strategic framework necessary for a coherent multi-level policy process. Otherwise the process will just mirror the inadequacies of the current sectoral approaches practised at the national level.

For example we might improve the social conditions of the population: fighting unemployment by supporting various training programmes, improving housing conditions by urban renewal programmes, strengthening social networks in low income and ethnic population etc. Or we can improve environmental conditions within the city by reducing industrial emissions, by improving public transportation, by better waste disposal handling, by use of centralised heating systems and ecological planning. We may furthermore attempt to attract investment to our cities by various economic initiatives and try to improve their image through monumental post-modern international architecture. And we may attempt to improve competitiveness of cities by investing in 'smart buildings', teleports and various other high-tech solutions designed in order to improve efficiency and communications of the city. But all of these initiatives are partial attempts treating symptoms rather than addressing the basic underlying causes. Such initiatives alone are not sufficient to sustain a viable future for our cities.

If we are to improve the living conditions and social justice of the urban population we must sustain the urban mixity i.e. the magnitude of urban functions that must co-exist. Within this framework the city can be described as a network of networks. However, to make this 'super-network' function creates immense problems but at the same time is a challenge with enormous potential for development. In this context it is vital to recognise:

* The need to sustain and develop the human capital of cities.
* The need for a holistic and European perspective on urban problems.
* The ambiguous role of new technologies as a one dimensional solution to urban problems.

Using the words of Michael Godet the working group thus concluded that cities are actors within 'an essentially conflict-ridden and inegalitarian world ....(in which).... the future is not the same for everyone ....(and that).... certain actors are more equal than others. (The future).... which actually transpires will arise out of the conflict of unequal human forces'. Several members of the group stressed however, that the individual cities can choose to act themselves, thus creating their own future.

Two more papers (without abstracts) were presented in the group (and are available from the Foundation) by:

Klára Szabó, Ministry of Environment Protection, Budapest

Maria Octavia Treistar, 'FEMEIA' Magazine, Bucharest

ANNEX

List of Participants

John Bell	Community Development Foundation 60 Highbury Grove London N5 2AG United Kingdom Tel: 71-226.53.75 Fax: 71-704.03.13
Clelia Boesi	Regione Lombardia Via Ricordi 4 I-20131 Milan Italy Tel: 2-295.126.04 Fax:
Francine Boudru	FEANTSA 1, rue Defacq (boîte 17) B-1050 Bruxelles Belgium Tel: 2-538.66.69 Fax: 2-539.41.74
Edith Brickwell	Senatsverwaltung für Stadtentwicklung und Umweltschutz Lindenstraße 20-25 D-1000 Berlin 61 Federal Republic of Germany Tel: 30-258.60 Fax: 30-258.622.11
Paul Burton	University of Bristol School for Advanced Urban Studies Rodney Lodge Grange Road Bristol BS8 4EA United Kingdom Tel: 272-741.117 Fax: 272-737.308
Enrique Calderón	ETSI Caminos Ciudad Universitaria E-28040 Madrid Spain Tel: 1-33.66.695 Fax: 1-54.92.289

William Cannell   Commission of the European Communities
                                  SAST Unit, MONITOR Programme
                                  Directorate-General on Science, Research and
                                  Development (DG XII)
                                  Rue de la Loi, 200
                                  (MO75 05/55)
                                  B-1049 Brussels
                                  Belgium
                                  Tel: 2-236.09.52
                                  Fax: 2-236.33.07

Bob Catterall   London 2000
                                  Parliament House
                                  81 Black Prince Road
                                  London SE1 7SX
                                  U.K.
                                  Tel: 071-735.42.50
                                  Fax: 071-627.96.06

Gesa Chomé   CEDEFOP
                                  Bundesallee 22
                                  D-1000 Berlin 15
                                  Federal Republic of Germany
                                  Tel: 30-88.41.20
                                  Fax: 30-88.41.22.22

Vincent-Pierre Comiti   (Representative of WHO)
                                  Ministère des Affaires Sociales
                                  1, place de Fontenoy
                                  F-75350 Paris
                                  France
                                  Tel: 1-46.62.45.68
                                  Fax: 1-46.62.47.21

Xenophon Constantinidis   Société Aluminium de Grèce
                                  Usine de Saint-Nicolas
                                  Paralia Distomou
                                  GR-32003 Beotie
                                  Greece
                                  Tel: 261-226.61
                                  Fax: 261-226.64/226.65

Tjeerd Deelstra   International Institute for
                                  the Urban Environment
                                  Nickersteeg 5
                                  NL-2611 EK Delft
                                  The Netherlands
                                  Tel: 15-62.32.79
                                  Fax: 15-62.48.73

Olgierd Roman Dziekonski Deputy Mayor of Warsaw
Warsaw City Council
Plac Bankowy 3/5
PL-00-950 Warsaw
Poland
Tel: 20.29.51
Fax: 20.11.78

Sten Engelstoft University of Copenhagen
Institute of Geography
Østervoldgade 10
DK-1350 Copenhagen K
Denmark
Tel: 33.13.21.05
Fax: 33.14.81.05

Péter Fazakas Megyeháza
9700 Szombathely
Berzsenyi tér. 1
Hungary
Tel: 94/11-211/179
Fax: 94/13-275

Maria Finzi Via R. Di Lauria 4
I-20149 Milan
Italy
Tel: 2-331.50.98
Fax:

Antje Flade Institut Wohnen und Umwelt GmbH
Annastraße 15
D-6100 Darmstadt
Federal Republic of Germany
Tel: 6151-290.40
Fax: 6151-290.497

Stephen Fox Commission of the European Communities
Directorate-General on Regional Policy
(DG XVI)
Rue de la Loi, 200
(CSTM 03/7)
B-1049 Brussels
Belgium
Tel: 2-235.59.17
Fax: 2-235.46.28

Marie Ganier-Raymond	Institut für Stadtforschung und Strukturpolitik Lützowstraße 93 D-1000 Berlin 30 Federal Republic of Germany Tel: 30-250.00.70 Fax: 30-262.90.02
José Garcia	European Committee for Housing Square Albert 1er, 32 B-1070 Anderlecht/Brussels Belgium Tel: 2-522.98.69 Fax: 2-524.18.16
Cristina P. de Jesus Garrett	Direcção-geral da Qualidade do Ambiente Rua de O Século, 51, 2º P-1200 Lisbon Portugal Tel: 1-346.32.41 Fax: 1-346.01.50
Wolfgang Gerke	Der Polizeipräsident in Berlin AG Gruppengewalt Eiswaldstraße 17 D-W-1000 Berlin 46 Federal Republic of Germany Tel: Fax:
Panayiotis Getimis	Pantion University of Social and Political Sciences Dept. of Urban and Regional Development 136, Syngrou Avenue Kalithea GR-17671 Athens Greece Tel: Fax: 1-92.36.90
Tony Gibson	Neighbourhood Initiatives Foundation Suite 23-25 Horsehay House, Horsehay Telford Shropshire TF4 3PY United Kingdom Tel: 81-449.06.20 / 952-50.36.28 Fax: 81-449.30.07

Sandro Giulianelli	Cabinet of Commissioner
Carlo Ripa Di Meana
Commission of the European Communities
Rue de la Loi, 200
(BERL 12/76)
B-1049 Brussels
Belgium
Tel: 2-235.9940/236.0026
Fax: 2-236.0750

Georges Glynos	Cabinet of Commissioner
Vasso Papandreou
Commission of the European Communities
Rue de la Loi, 200
(BERL 11/2A)
B-1049 Brussels
Belgium
Tel: 2-236.3353/235.7479
Fax: 2-236.0748

Rui Godinho	Municipality of Lisbon
Praça do Municipio
P-1194 Lisbon Cedex
Portugal
Tel: 1-342.70.40
Fax: 1-376.75.48

Margaret Grieco	Oxford University
Transport Studies Unit
11, Bevington Road
Oxford OX2 6NB
United Kingdom
Tel: 865-276.713 / 274.715
Fax: 865-515.194

Ekhart Hahn	Wissenschaftszentrum Berlin
Reichpietsufer 50
D-1000 Berlin 30
Federal Republic of Germany
Tel: 30-25.49.12.45
Fax: 30-25.49.16.84

David Harvey	University of Oxford
School of Geography
Mansfield Road
Oxford OX1 3TB
United Kingdom
Tel: 865-271.919
Fax: 865-271.929

Chris Jensen-Butler   University of Aarhus
Institute of Political Science
Universitetsparken
DK-8000 Aarhus C
Denmark
Tel: 86.13.01.11
Fax: 86.13.98.39

Richard V. Knight   University of Amsterdam
Economic Geographic Institute
Jodenbreestraat 23
Postbus 16539
NL-1011 RA Amsterdam
The Netherlands
Tel: 20-525.40.79
Fax
Fax: 20-525.24.91

Matthias Koch   Ressortleiter Personenverkehr/
Infrastruktur
Ingenieurgesellschaft Verkehr Berlin
Markgrafenstraße 24
D-O-1017 Berlin
Federal Republic of Germany
Tel:
Fax:

Paul Lawless   Sheffield City Polytechnic
School of Urban and Regional Studies
Pond Street
Sheffield S1 1WB
United Kingdom
Tel: 742-53.35.25
Fax: 742-53.35.53

Geneviève Lecamp   OECD
ILE Programme
2, rue André Pascal
F-75016 Paris
France
Tel: 45.24.92.94
Fax: 45.24.90.98

Bernard Le Marchand   UNICE/CLE
Avenue Victor Gilsoul, 76
B-1200 Brussels
Belgium
Tel: 2-771.58.71
Fax: 2-762.75.06

Claude Leroy	A.I.Q.V. "L'Homme et la Ville" 11, rue Tronchet F-75008 Paris France Tel: 1-42.66.20.70 Fax: 1-34.61.93.69
André Loeckx	Catholic University of Leuven Department of Architecture and Urban Design Kasteel Arenberg K. Mercierlaan 94 B-3001 Heverlee Belgium Tel: 16-22.09.31 Fax: 16-29.14.34
John Lomax	Bank of England Economics Division Threadneedle Street London EC 1 United Kingdom Tel: 71-601.56.85 Fax: 71-601.52.88
Peter Lumsden	Committee on Crime Dail Eireann Leinster House Dublin 2 Ireland Tel: 1-78.99.11 Fax: 1-78.55.34
Lindsay MacFarlane	OECD Urban Affairs Division 15, boulevard de l'Amiral-Bruix F-75116 Paris France Tel: 1-45.24.82.00 Fax: 1-45.24.78.76
Hilda Maelstaf	ELISE / AEIDL 34, rue Breydel B-1040 Brussels Belgium Tel: 2-230.52.34 Fax: 2-230.34.82

Thomas Maloutas	National Centre of Social Research 1, Sophocleous Str. GR-10559 Athens Greece Tel: 1-325.08.58 Fax: 1-321.64.71
Michel Marcus	Forum des Collectivités Territoriales Européennes pour la Sécurité Urbaine 126, rue de l'Université F-75007 Paris France Paris Tel: 1-40.63.58.48 Fax: 1-40.63.57.17
Lina Marsoni	Municipality of Milan Via Pirelli, 39 I-20123 Milan Italy Tel: 2-688.0238 Fax: 2-654.804
Alexander S. Matrosov	Deputy Premier Moscow City Government Housing and Municipal Engineering Committee B. Bronnaya Str. 14 Moscow 103104 U.S.S.R. Tel: 200.17.51 Fax: 200.22.65
Pierre-Yves Mauguen	Ministère de la Recherche et de la Technologie Centre de Prospective et d'Etudes 1 rue Descartes 75005 Paris France Tel: 1-46.34.32.69 Fax: 1-46.34.34.23
Voula Mega	European Foundation for the Improvement of Living and Working Conditions Loughlinstown House Shankill, Co. Dublin Ireland Tel: 1-28.26.888 Fax: 1-28.26.456

Jacqueline Miller	Université Libre de Bruxelles Institut de Sociologie Avenue Jeanne 44 B-1050 Brussels Belgium Tel: 2-650.31.83 Fax: 2-650.35.21
Michel Miller	ETUC Rue Montagne aux Herbes Potagères, 37 B-1000 Brussels Belgium Tel: 2-218.31.00 Fax: 2-218.35.66
Pascale Mistiaen	DEFIS A.S.B.L. 10, Avenue Clémenceau B-1079 Brussels Belgium Tel: 2-523.20.35 Fax: 2-523.20.31
Philippe Morin	RACINE 18, rue Friant F-75014 Paris France Tel: 1-40.44.80.20 Fax: 1-40.44.79.72
Eugène Muller	Chambre des Métiers 40, rue Glesener L-1631 Luxembourg Tel: 40.00.221 Fax: 49.23.80
Rainer Obst	Ingenieurgesellschaft Verkehr Berlin Markgrafenstraße 24 D-O-1017 Berlin Federal Republic of Germany Tel: Fax:
Wendy O'Conghaile	European Foundation for the Improvement of Living and Working Conditions Loughlinstown House Shankill, Co. Dublin Ireland Tel: 1-28.26.888 Fax: 1-28.26.456

John O'Connell   Dublin Travellers Education and
                                   Development Group
                                  Pavee Point
                                  46, North Great Charles Street
                                  Dublin 1
                                  Ireland
                                  Tel: 1-73.28.02
                                  Fax: 1-74.26.26

Francisco Orta Bueno   Union General de Trabajadores (UGT)
                                  Calle Puerto 28
                                  E-21001 Huelva
                                  Spain
                                  Tel: 55-24.47.87
                                  Fax: 55-24.85.34

Chara Paraskevopoulou   Hellenic Agency for Local Development
                                     and Local Government (E.E.T.A.A.)
                                  19, Omirou Str.
                                  GR-10672 Athens
                                  Greece
                                  Tel: 1-364.41.79
                                  Fax: 1-360.24.45

Josep Maria Pascual i Esteve   Comissionat per al Pla Estrategic
                                  Barcelona City Council
                                  Plaça Sant Jaume S/n, 3r. pis
                                  E-08002 Barcelona
                                  Spain
                                  Tel: 3-302.53.26
                                  Fax: 3-301.40.27 / 402.74.53

Jørn Pedersen   European Foundation for the Improvement
                                  of Living and Working Conditions
                                  Loughlinstown House
                                  Shankill, Co. Dublin
                                  Ireland
                                  Tel: 1-28.26.888
                                  Fax: 1-28.26.456

Laurie Pickup   Laurie Pickup & Associates
                                  43 Main Road
                                  Long Hanborough
                                  Oxford OX7 2BD
                                  United Kingdom
                                  Tel: 993-883.755
                                  Fax: 993-883.755

Carlo Pignocco

CISL - SICET
Viale Trastevere 221
I-00153 Rome
Italy
Tel: 6-58.18.524
Fax: 6-

Cornelia Poczka

Senatsverwaltung für Stadtentwicklung
und Umweltschutz
PressRef 1 - S
Lindenstraße 20-25
D-W-1000 Berlin 61
Federal Republic of Germany
Tel:
Fax:

Nuno Portas

University of Porto
Faculty of Architecture
R. Golgota 215
P-4100 Porto
Portugal
Tel: 2-30.74.42
Fax: 2-30.39.30

Cees Post

European Investment Bank
100, Boulevard Konrad Adenauer
L-2950 Luxembourg
Luxembourg
Tel: 43.79.32.23
Fax: 43.79.32.89

Philip Potter

Forschungs- und Entwicklungsverbund e.V.
Annostraße 27
D-5000 Köln 1
Federal Republic of Germany
Tel: 221-323.829
Fax: 221-315.292

Graziella Caiani Praturlon

Vice President, EUROPIL
Servizio Sociale Internazionale
Sezione Italiana
Via V. Veneto, 96
I-00187 Rome
Italy
Tel: 6-488.31.62
Fax: 6-481.76.05

Klaus-Peter Prüß   Senatsverwaltung für Stadtentwicklung
                                und Umweltschutz
                                I Abtl.
                                Lindenstraße 20-25
                                D-W-1000 Berlin 61
                                Federal Republic of Germany
                                Tel:
                                Fax:

Clive Purkiss   European Foundation for the Improvement
                                of Living and Working Conditions
                                Loughlinstown House
                                Shankill, Co. Dublin
                                Ireland
                                Tel: 1-28.26.888
                                Fax: 1-28.26.456

N. J. van Putten   Ministry of Internal Affairs
                                Kamer L255
                                Schedeldoekshaven 200
                                Postbus 20011
                                NL-2500 EA The Hague
                                The Netherlands
                                Tel: 70-36.39.153
                                Fax: 70-30.26.302

Mairín Quill   Committee on Crime
                                Dail Eireann
                                Leinster House
                                Dublin 2
                                Ireland
                                Tel: 1-78.99.11
                                Fax: 1-78.55.34

John Reid   University College Dublin
                                Department of Regional and Urban Planning
                                Richview, Clonskeagh Road
                                Dublin 14
                                Ireland
                                Tel: 1-73.01.33
                                Fax: 1-72.63.97

Enrique Retuerto   CEDEFOP
                                Bundesallee 22
                                D-1000 Berlin 15
                                Federal Republic of Germany
                                Tel: 30-88.41.20
                                Fax: 30-88.41.22.22

William Roe	CEI Consultants Limited 42, Frederick Street Edinburgh EH2 1EX United Kingdom Tel: 31-225.31.44 Fax: 31-226.22.59
Horst-Jürgen Rösgen	Senatsverwaltung für Verkehr und Betriebe, III C 3 An der Urania 4 D-W-1000 Berlin 30 Federal Republic of Germany Tel: Fax:
Julia V. Saratovskaya	Consultant Foreign Economic Relations Department Housing and Municipal Engineering Committee of Moscow B. Bronnaya, 14 Moscow 103104 U.S.S.R. Tel: 200.17.51 Fax: 200.22.65
Klaus Schlabbach	Town Planning Authority Darmstadt Bessungerstraße 125 D-6100 Darmstadt Federal Republic of Germany Tel: 6151-132.592 Fax: 6151-133.388
Ernst Schneider	WTU, Arbeitsförderungsgesellschaft für Wärme- und Umwelttechnik m.b.H. Kurze Straße 5-6 O-1106 Berlin Federal Republic of Germany Tel: 3.49.10.03 Fax: 4.82.73.74
René Schoonbroodt	Commission of the European Communties Directorate General on Environment, Nuclear Safety and Civil Protection (DG XI) rue de la Loi, 200 BREY 10/200 B-1049 Brussels Belgium Tel: 2-235.87.16 Fax: 2-236.27.21

Hermann Seiberth	Senatsverwaltung für Stadtentwicklung und Umweltschutz EurAk Lindenstraße 20-25 D-W-1000 Berlin 61 Federal Republic of Germany Tel: Fax:
Yelena Shomina	USSR Academy of Science Institute of Labour Studies Moscow Kolpachyny per 9a U.S.S.R. Tel: 095-451.52.25 Fax: 095-288.95.12
Alan Sinclair	The Wise Group 8, Elliot Place Glasgow G3 8EP United Kingdom Tel: 41-248.59.77 Fax: 41-774.05.66
Margaret Sweeney	SICA Innovation Consultants Limited 44, Fitzwilliam Square Dublin 2 Ireland Tel: 1-613.829 Fax: 1-763.564
Klára Szabó	Ministerium für Umwelt und Landesentwicklung H 1394 Budapest P.O.B 351 Budapest I.Fö utca 44/50 Hungary Tel: 1-201.1335, 201.4133/628 Fax: 1-201.3216
Maria Octavia Treistar	"FEMEIA" Magazine Pta. Preseilibere no. 1, sect. I Bucharest 71341 Romania Tel: 17.33.71 / 88.52.33 Fax:

Yannis Tsiomis Ecole d'Architecture Paris - La Villette
8, rue du Commandant Mouchotte
F-75014 Paris
France
Tel: 1-42.02.87.77
Fax: 1-42.02.85.30

Lia Vasconcelos Universidade Nova de Lisboa
Departamento de Ciencias e
   Engenharia do Ambiente
FCT
Quinta de Torre
P-2825 Monte Da Caparica
Portugal
Tel: 1-295.44.64, ext. 1001
Fax: 1-295.44.61

Eric Verborgh European Foundation for the Improvement
of Living and Working Conditions
Loughlinstown House
Shankill, Co. Dublin
Ireland
Tel: 1-28.26.888
Fax: 1-28.26.456

Andreas von Zadow Senatsverwaltung für Stadtentwicklung
und Umweltschutz
European Academy for the Urban Environment
Lindenstraße 20-25
D-W-1000 Berlin 61
Federal Republic of Germany
Tel: 30-2586.2549/2511.112
Fax: 30-2586.2000

Sandra Walklate University of Salford
Department of Sociology
Salford M5 4WT
United Kingdom
Tel: 61-745.50.00 ext. 3451
Fax: 61-745.59.99

Richard Welsh Brighton Polytechnic
Lewis Cohen Urban Studies Centre
68, Grand Parade
Brighton BN2 2JY
United Kingdom
Tel: 273-67.34.16
Fax: 273-67.91.79

Maria Wissen   Institut Luxembourgeois de
                          Recherches Sociales (ILRES)
                          6 rue du Marché aux Herbes
                          L-1728 Luxembourg
                          Luxembourg
                          Tel: 47.37.11 / 47.50.21
                          Fax: 46.26.20

Uwe Wullkopf   Institut Wohnen und Umwelt
                          Annastraße 15
                          D-6100 Darmstadt
                          Federal Republic of Germany
                          Tel: 6151-29.04.0
                          Fax: 6151-29.04.97

Organising Committee:

Foundation:	Jørn PEDERSEN
	Wendy O'CONGHAILE
	Voula MEGA
	Bríd NOLAN (Promotion)
	Ann McDONALD (Conference Officer)
Senate of Berlin:	Edith BRICKWELL
General Rapporteur:	Jacqueline MILLER
	Free University of Brussels

Conference Secretariat:

Foundation:	Hanne HANSEN
Senate of Berlin:	Gabrièle SCHUGK
	Hergen SCHWARZER

European Foundation for the Improvement of Living and Working Conditions

European Workshop
The Improvement of the Built Environment and Social Integration in Cities
Selected Papers and Conclusions

Luxembourg: Office for Official Publications of the European Communities, 1992

1992—322 pp.—21.0 × 29.7 cm

ISBN 92-826-3944-4

Price (excluding VAT) in Luxembourg: ECU 24

Venta y suscripciones • Salg og abonnement • Verkauf und Abonnement • Πωλήσεις και συνδρομές
Sales and subscriptions • Vente et abonnements • Vendita e abbonamenti
Verkoop en abonnementen • Venda e assinaturas

BELGIQUE / BELGIË

**Moniteur belge /
Belgisch Staatsblad**
Rue de Louvain 42 / Leuvenseweg 42
1000 Bruxelles / 1000 Brussel
Tél. (02) 512 00 26
Fax 511 01 84
CCP / Postrekening 000-2005502-27

Autres distributeurs /
Overige verkooppunten

**Librairie européenne/
Europese Boekhandel**
Avenue Albert Jonnart 50 /
Albert Jonnartlaan 50
1200 Bruxelles / 1200 Brussel
Tél. (02) 734 02 81
Fax 735 08 60

Jean De Lannoy
Avenue du Roi 202 /Koningslaan 202
1060 Bruxelles / 1060 Brussel
Tél. (02) 538 51 69
Télex 63220 UNBOOK B
Fax (02) 538 08 41

CREDOC
Rue de la Montagne 34 / Bergstraat 34
Bte 11 / Bus 11
1000 Bruxelles / 1000 Brussel

DANMARK

**J. H. Schultz Information A/S
EF-Publikationer**
Ottiliavej 18
2500 Valby
Tlf. 36 44 22 66
Fax 36 44 01 41
Girokonto 6 00 08 86

BR DEUTSCHLAND

Bundesanzeiger Verlag
Breite Straße
Postfach 10 80 06
5000 Köln 1
Tel. (02 21) 20 29-0
Telex ANZEIGER BONN 8 882 595
Fax 20 29 278

GREECE/ΕΛΛΑΔΑ

G.C. Eleftheroudakis SA
International Bookstore
Nikis Street 4
10563 Athens
Tel. (01) 322 63 23
Telex 219410 ELEF
Fax 323 98 21

ESPAÑA

Boletín Oficial del Estado
Trafalgar, 27
28010 Madrid
Tel. (91) 44 82 135

Mundi-Prensa Libros, S.A.
Castelló, 37
28001 Madrid
Tel. (91) 431 33 99 (Libros)
     431 32 22 (Suscripciones)
     435 36 37 (Dirección)
Télex 49370-MPLI-E
Fax (91) 575 39 98

Sucursal:

Librería Internacional AEDOS
Consejo de Ciento, 391
08009 Barcelona
Tel. (93) 301 86 15
Fax (93) 317 01 41

**Llibreria de la Generalitat
de Catalunya**
Rambla dels Estudis, 118 (Palau Moja)
08002 Barcelona
Tel. (93) 302 68 35
     302 64 62
Fax (93) 302 12 99

FRANCE

**Journal officiel
Service des publications
des Communautés européennes**
26, rue Desaix
75727 Paris Cedex 15
Tél. (1) 40 58 75 00
Fax (1) 40 58 75 74

IRELAND

Government Supplies Agency
4-5 Harcourt Road
Dublin 2
Tel. (1) 61 31 11
Fax (1) 78 06 45

ITALIA

Licosa Spa
Via Duca di Calabria, 1/1
Casella postale 552
50125 Firenze
Tel. (055) 64 54 15
Fax 64 12 57
Telex 570466 LICOSA I
CCP 343 509

GRAND-DUCHÉ DE LUXEMBOURG

Messageries Paul Kraus
11, rue Christophe Plantin
2339 Luxembourg
Tél. 499 88 88
Télex 2515
Fax 499 88 84 44
CCP 49242-63

NEDERLAND

SDU Overheidsinformatie
Externe Fondsen
Postbus 20014
2500 EA 's-Gravenhage
Tel. (070) 37 89 911
Fax (070) 34 75 778

PORTUGAL

Imprensa Nacional
Casa da Moeda, EP
Rua D. Francisco Manuel de Melo, 5
1092 Lisboa Codex
Tel. (01) 69 34 14

**Distribuidora de Livros
Bertrand, Ld.ª**
Grupo Bertrand, SA
Rua das Terras dos Vales, 4-A
Apartado 37
2700 Amadora Codex
Tel. (01) 49 59 050
Telex 15798 BERDIS
Fax 49 60 255

UNITED KINGDOM

HMSO Books (PC 16)
HMSO Publications Centre
51 Nine Elms Lane
London SW8 5DR
Tel. (071) 873 2000
Fax GP3 873 8463
Telex 29 71 138

ÖSTERREICH

**Manz'sche Verlags-
und Universitätsbuchhandlung**
Kohlmarkt 16
1014 Wien
Tel. (0222) 531 61-0
Telex 11 25 00 BOX A
Fax (0222) 531 61-39

SUOMI

Akateeminen Kirjakauppa
Keskuskatu 1
PO Box 128
00101 Helsinki
Tel. (0) 121 41
Fax (0) 121 44 41

NORGE

Narvesen information center
Bertrand Narvesens vei 2
PO Box 6125 Etterstad
0602 Oslo 6
Tel. (2) 57 33 00
Telex 79668 NIC N
Fax (2) 68 19 01

SVERIGE

BTJ
Box 200
22100 Lund
Tel. (046) 18 00 00
Fax (046) 18 01 25

SCHWEIZ / SUISSE / SVIZZERA

OSEC
Stampfenbachstraße 85
8035 Zürich
Tel. (01) 365 54 49
Fax (01) 365 54 11

CESKOSLOVENSKO

NIS
Havelkova 22
13000 Praha 3
Tel. (02) 235 84 46
Fax 42-2-264775

MAGYARORSZÁG

Euro-Info-Service
Budapest I. Kir.
Attila út 93
1012 Budapest
Tel. (1) 56 82 11
Telex (22) 4717 AGINF H-61
Fax (1) 17 59 031

POLSKA

Business Foundation
ul. Krucza 38/42
00-512 Warszawa
Tel. (22) 21 99 93, 628-28-82
International Fax&Phone
(0-39) 12-00-77

JUGOSLAVIJA

Privredni Vjesnik
Bulevar Lenjina 171/XIV
11070 Beograd
Tel. (11) 123 23 40

CYPRUS

**Cyprus Chamber of Commerce and
Industry**
Chamber Building
38 Grivas Dhigenis Ave
3 Deligiorgis Street
PO Box 1455
Nicosia
Tel. (2) 449500/462312
Fax (2) 458630

TÜRKIYE

**Pres Gazete Kitap Dergi
Pazarlama Dağitim Ticaret ve sanayi
AŞ**
Narlibahçe Sokak N. 15
Istanbul-Cağaloğlu
Tel. (1) 520 92 96 - 528 55 66
Fax 520 64 57
Telex 23822 DSVO-TR

CANADA

Renouf Publishing Co. Ltd
Mail orders — Head Office:
1294 Algoma Road
Ottawa, Ontario K1B 3W8
Tel. (613) 741 43 33
Fax (613) 741 54 39
Telex 0534783

Ottawa Store:
61 Sparks Street
Tel. (613) 238 89 85

Toronto Store:
211 Yonge Street
Tel. (416) 363 31 71

UNITED STATES OF AMERICA

UNIPUB
4611-F Assembly Drive
Lanham, MD 20706-4391
Tel. Toll Free (800) 274 4888
Fax (301) 459 0056

AUSTRALIA

Hunter Publications
58A Gipps Street
Collingwood
Victoria 3066

JAPAN

Kinokuniya Company Ltd
17-7 Shinjuku 3-Chome
Shinjuku-ku
Tokyo 160-91
Tel. (03) 3439-0121

Journal Department
PO Box 55 Chitose
Tokyo 156
Tel. (03) 3439-0124

AUTRES PAYS
OTHER COUNTRIES
ANDERE LÄNDER

**Office des publications officielles
des Communautés européennes**
2, rue Mercier
2985 Luxembourg
Tél. 49 92 81
Télex PUBOF LU 1324 b
Fax 48 85 73/48 68 17
CC bancaire BIL 8-109/6003/700